# CONCEPTS AND CHALLENGES

# THE DIVERSITY OF LIFE

Leonard Bernstein ◆ Martin Schachter ◆ Alan Winkler ◆ Stanley Wolfe

Stanley Wolfe
*Project Coordinator*

**GLOBE FEARON**
Pearson Learning Group

**The following people have contributed to the development of this product:**

*Art and Design:* Evelyn Bauer, Susan Brorein, Tracey Gerber, Bernadette Hruby, Carol Marie Kiernan, Mindy Klarman, Judy Mahoney, Karen Mancinelli, Elbaliz Mendez, April Okano, Dan Thomas, Jennifer Visco

*Editorial:* Stephanie P. Cahill, Gina Dalessio, Nija Dixon, Martha Feehan, Theresa McCarthy, Maurice Sabean, Marilyn Sarch, Maury Solomon, Jeffrey Wickersty, Shirley C. White, S. Adrienn Vegh-Soti

*Manufacturing:* Mark Cirillo, Tom Dunne

*Marketing:* Douglas Falk, Maureen Christensen

*Production:* Irene Belinsky, Linda Bierniak, Carlos Blas, Karen Edmonds, Cheryl Golding, Leslie Greenberg, Roxanne Knoll, Susan Levine, Cynthia Lynch, Jennifer Murphy, Lisa Svoronos, Susan Tamm

*Publishing Operations:* Carolyn Coyle, Thomas Daning, Richetta Lobban

*Technology:* Jessie Lin, Ellen Strain, Joanne Saito

*About the Cover:* There is a great variety of living things on Earth. The coral reef shown in the larger photograph is home to many diverse organisms, including plants, invertebrates, and vertebrates. The organisms in the smaller photograph are unicellular protists called diatoms.

ISBN: 0-13-024204-7

Printed in the United States of America

1 2 3 4 5 6 7 8 9  10 06 05 04 03

1-800-321-3106
www.pearsonlearning.com

# Acknowledgments

## Science Consultant

**Dr. Richard Lowell**
Ramapo College of
 New Jersey
Mahwah, NJ

## Laboratory Consultants

**Sean Devine**
*Science Teacher*
Ridge High School
Basking Ridge, NJ

**Vincent R. Dionisio**
*Science Teacher*
Clifton High School
Clifton, NJ

## Reading Consultant

**Sharon Cook**
*Consultant*
Leadership in Literacy

## Internet Consultant

**Janet M. Gaudino**
*Science Teacher*
Montgomery Middle School
Skillman, NJ

## ESL/ELL Consultant

**Elizabeth Jimenez**
*Consultant*
Pomona, CA

## Content Reviewers

**Dr. Daniel Bush** (Ch. 4)
*Professor*
USDA-ARS and Department of Plant Biology
University of Illinois at Urbana-Champaign
Urbana, IL

**Scott Denny** (pp. 44–45)
*Food Services Manager*
Denville, NJ

**Dr. Steven R. Hill** (Ch. 3)
*Associate Research Scientist*
Center for Biodiversity, Illinois Natural
 History Survey
Champaign, IL

**Tana M. Hoban-Higgins** (Ch. 5–6)
University of California, Davis
Davis, CA

**Helen McBride, Ph.D.** (Ch. 1 & 2)
*Postdoctoral Scholar*
California Institute of Technology
Pasadena, CA

**Terry Moran** (pp. 64–65)
Moran Research Service
Harvard, MA

**Hugh P. Taylor, Jr.** (pp. 116–117)
*Robert P. Sharp Professor of Geology*
Division of Geological and Planetary Sciences
MS 100-23
California Institute of Technology
Pasadena, CA

**Dr. Raymond C. Turner** (pp. 78–79, 142–143)
*Alumni Distinguished Professor Emeritus of Physics*
Department of Physics and Astronomy
Clemson University
Clemson, SC

## Teacher Reviewers

**Jennifer L. Salmon**
Belleville Middle School
Belleville, NJ

**Robert L. Fincham**
Keithley Middle School
Tacoma, WA

# Contents

## Scientific Skills and Investigations Handbooks

**Handbook A:** What are scientific skills? . . . . . . . . . . . . . . . . . . . . . . . . . 1

**Handbook B:** How do you conduct a scientific investigation? . . . . . . . . . 9

## Chapter *1* Classification                                                          **15**

1-1  What is classification? . . . . . . . . . . . . . . . . . . . . . . . . . . . . . . . . . 16

1-2  How are living things classified? . . . . . . . . . . . . . . . . . . . . . . . . . . 18

🔬  LAB ACTIVITY: Classifying Shells . . . . . . . . . . . . . . . . . . . . . . . . . . . 20

1-3  What are the kingdoms? . . . . . . . . . . . . . . . . . . . . . . . . . . . . . . . . 22

◆  THE Big IDEA Integrating Language Arts: How are organisms named? . . . . 24

1-4  What are viruses? . . . . . . . . . . . . . . . . . . . . . . . . . . . . . . . . . . . . . 26

*Chapter Summary and Challenges* . . . . . . . . . . . . . . . . . . . . . . . . . . . 28

## Chapter *2* Simple Organisms . . . . . . . . . . . . . . . . . . . . . . . .        **31**

2-1  What is the Kingdom Monera? . . . . . . . . . . . . . . . . . . . . . . . . . . . . 32

2-2  Why do scientists study bacteria? . . . . . . . . . . . . . . . . . . . . . . . . . 34

2-3  What is the Kingdom Protista? . . . . . . . . . . . . . . . . . . . . . . . . . . . . 36

🔬  LAB ACTIVITY: Examining Life in Pond Water . . . . . . . . . . . . . . . . . . . 38

2-4  What are algae and slime molds? . . . . . . . . . . . . . . . . . . . . . . . . . . 40

2-5  What is the Kingdom Fungi? . . . . . . . . . . . . . . . . . . . . . . . . . . . . . . 42

◆  THE Big IDEA Integrating Health: What simple organisms
exist in our daily lives? . . . . . . . . . . . . . . . . . . . . . . . . . . . . . . . . . . 44

2-6  How do yeasts and molds reproduce? . . . . . . . . . . . . . . . . . . . . . . 46

*Chapter Summary and Challenges* . . . . . . . . . . . . . . . . . . . . . . . . . . . 48

## Chapter *3* Types of Plants . . . . . . . . . . . . . . . . . . . . . . . . . .        **51**

3-1  How are plants classified? . . . . . . . . . . . . . . . . . . . . . . . . . . . . . . . 52

3-2  How do bryophytes reproduce? . . . . . . . . . . . . . . . . . . . . . . . . . . . 54

3-3  What are ferns? . . . . . . . . . . . . . . . . . . . . . . . . . . . . . . . . . . . . . . 56

🔬  LAB ACTIVITY: Examining the Structure
of a Fern Frond . . . . . . . . . . . . . . . . . . . . . . . . . . . . . . . . . . . . . . . . 58

3-4  What are gymnosperms? . . . . . . . . . . . . . . . . . . . . . . . . . . . . . . . . 60

3-5  What are angiosperms? . . . . . . . . . . . . . . . . . . . . . . . . . . . . . . . . . 62

◆  THE Big IDEA Integrating Social Studies: How do
plants affect the economy of the United States? . . . . . . . . . . . . . . . . . 64

*Chapter Summary and Challenges* . . . . . . . . . . . . . . . . . . . . . . . . . . . 66

## Chapter 4  Plant Structure and Function .................................. 69

4-1    What are roots? ................................................... 70

4-2    What are stems? .................................................. 72

4-3    What are leaves? ................................................. 74

4-4    What is photosynthesis? .......................................... 76

◈    THE Big IDEA  Integrating Physical Science: What are the physics of a tree? ........ 78

4-5    What are flowers? ................................................ 80

4-6    How do flowering plants reproduce? ............................... 82

4-7    What are seeds and fruits? ........................................ 84

🔬    LAB ACTIVITY: Identifying the Parts of a Flower ..................... 86

4-8    What are the parts of a seed? ..................................... 88

4-9    How do plants reproduce asexually? ............................... 90

4-10   What are tropisms? ............................................... 92

*Chapter Summary and Challenges* ....................................... 94

## Chapter 5  Animals Without Backbones ................................... 97

5-1    How are animals classified? ....................................... 98

5-2    What are sponges? ............................................... 100

5-3    What are cnidarians? ............................................. 102

5-4    What are worms? ................................................ 104

5-5    What are mollusks? .............................................. 106

5-6    What are echinoderms? ........................................... 108

5-7    What is regeneration? ............................................ 110

🔬    LAB ACTIVITY: Determining the Age of a Clam ...................... 112

5-8    What are arthropods? ............................................ 114

◈    THE Big IDEA  Integrating Environmental Science:
       Why should coral reefs be protected? .............................. 116

5-9    What are insects? ................................................ 118

5-10   How do insects develop? ......................................... 120

*Chapter Summary and Challenges* ....................................... 122

# Chapter 6   Animals With Backbones . . . . . . . . . . . . . . . . . . . **125**

6-1   What are chordates? . . . . . . . . . . . . . . . . . . . . . . . . . . 126

6-2   What are fish? . . . . . . . . . . . . . . . . . . . . . . . . . . . . . . . 128

6-3   What are amphibians? . . . . . . . . . . . . . . . . . . . . . . . . . 130

6-4   How do amphibians develop? . . . . . . . . . . . . . . . . . . . 132

6-5   What are reptiles? . . . . . . . . . . . . . . . . . . . . . . . . . . . . 134

6-6   What are birds? . . . . . . . . . . . . . . . . . . . . . . . . . . . . . . 136

    LAB ACTIVITY: Investigating an Owl Pellet . . . . . . . . . . 138

6-7   What are mammals? . . . . . . . . . . . . . . . . . . . . . . . . . . 140

    THE Big IDEA  Integrating Physical Science:
    How are the skeletons of vertebrates like levers? . . . . . 142

6-8   How do animal embryos develop? . . . . . . . . . . . . . . . 144

6-9   What are innate and learned behaviors? . . . . . . . . . . . 146

6-10   What are social behaviors? . . . . . . . . . . . . . . . . . . . . . 148

***Chapter Summary and Challenges*** . . . . . . . . . . . . . . . . . 150

# Appendices

**Appendix A:** Metric System . . . . . . . . . . . . . . . . . . . . . . . . . 153

**Appendix B:** Science Terms . . . . . . . . . . . . . . . . . . . . . . . . . 154

**Appendix C:** The Microscope . . . . . . . . . . . . . . . . . . . . . . . . 155

**Appendix D:** The Classification of Life . . . . . . . . . . . . . . . . . 157

**Glossary** . . . . . . . . . . . . . . . . . . . . . . . . . . . . . . . . . . . . . . . 158

**Index** . . . . . . . . . . . . . . . . . . . . . . . . . . . . . . . . . . . . . . . . . . 163

**Photo Credits** . . . . . . . . . . . . . . . . . . . . . . . . . . . . . . . . . . . 167

# Features

## Hands-On Activity

Handbook: Making Observations 2
Handbook: Organizing Living Things 3
Handbook: Calculating Area and Volume 6
Handbook: Reading a Thermometer 7
Handbook: Carrying Out an Experiment 12
1-1 Classifying Buttons 17
1-4 Modeling a Virus 27
2-6 Growing Mold 47
3-4 Observing Pine Cones 61
3-5 Classifying Monocots and Dicots 63
4-2 Transport in Plants 73
4-4 Separating Pigments 77
4-8 Growing Seeds 89
4-9 Growing Plants Asexually 91
5-3 Observing a Hydra 103
5-5 Modeling Squid Jet Propulsion 107
5-10 Observing Metamorphosis 121
6-2 Modeling a Swim Bladder 129
6-8 Observing a Bird Egg 145

## How Do They Know That?

5-9 Social Insects Form a Society 119

## ◈ Integrating the Sciences

2-3 Earth Science: White Cliffs of Dover 37
2-4 Earth Science: Algal Blooms 41
3-3 Earth Science: Prehistoric Ferns 57
4-1 Earth Science: Crop Rotation 71
4-3 Physical Science: The Chemistry of Changing Leaves 75
5-6 Physical Science: Hydraulic Systems in Sea Stars 109
6-4 Earth Science: Pollutants and Frog Development 133
6-6 Physical Science: The Mechanics of Bird Flight 137
6-10 Physical Science: Pheromones 149

## People in Science

2-1 Disease Detectives 33
4-6 Plant Geneticist 83
5-1 Taxonomist 99
6-1 Veterinarian 127

## Real-Life Science

2-5 Fungal Infections 43
4-5 Botanical Gardens 81
4-7 Seed Plants You Eat 85
5-2 Snorkeling 101
5-7 Regeneration in Sea Stars 111
6-5 Helpful Snakes 135

## Science and Technology

1-2 Using DNA to Classify Organisms 19
3-2 Use of Peat as a Fuel 55
5-8 Uses of Chitin 115
6-3 Computer Dissections 131

INVESTIGATE

| 2-5 | Observing the Structure of Mushrooms | 42 |
| 3-1 | Classifying Plants | 52 |
| 4-3 | Classifying Leaves | 74 |
| 4-10 | Observing Tropisms | 92 |
| 5-2 | Examining Sponges | 100 |
| 6-7 | Modeling Insulation | 140 |
| 6-9 | Observing Learning | 146 |

## Web InfoSearch

| 1-2 | John Ray | 19 |
| 2-2 | Pasteurization | 35 |
| 3-1 | Local Plant Life | 53 |
| 4-2 | Tree Rings | 73 |
| 4-9 | Grafting | 91 |
| 5-4 | Leeches | 105 |
| 5-7 | Regeneration of Human Tissue | 111 |
| 6-3 | Caecilians | 131 |
| 6-5 | Whiptail Lizards | 135 |
| 6-7 | Marine Mammals | 141 |

# What are scientific skills?

People are naturally curious. They want to understand the world around them. They want to understand what makes flowers grow and how their own bodies work. The field of science would probably not exist if it were not for human curiosity about the natural world.

People also want to be able to make good guesses about the future. They want to know when it will rain again and which nutrients in soil grow the best crops.

Scientists use many skills to explore the world and gather information about it. These skills are called science process skills. Another name for them is science inquiry skills.

Science process skills allow you to think like a scientist. They help you identify problems and answer questions. Sometimes they help you solve problems. More often, they provide some possible answers and lead to more questions. In this book, you will use a variety of science process skills to understand the facts and theories in life science. Science process skills are not only used in science. You compare prices when you shop and you observe what happens to foods when you cook them. You predict what the weather will be by looking at the sky. In fact, science process skills are really everyday life skills that have been adapted for problem solving in science.

**1 ▶ NAME:** What is the name for the skills scientists use to solve problems?

▲ **Figure 1** Scientists use science process skills to understand what makes trees grow, what attracts bees to flowers, and how the human digestive system works.

## Contents

1 Observing and Comparing
2 Classifying Data
3 Modeling and Simulating
4 Measuring
5 Analyzing Data and Communicating Results
6 Making Predictions

# 1 Observing and Comparing

**Making Observations**  An important part of solving any problem is observing, or using your senses to find out what is going on around you. The five senses are sight, hearing, touch, smell, and taste. When you look at the petals on a flower or touch the hard shell of a hermit crab, you are observing. When you observe, you pay close attention to everything that happens around you.

Scientists observe the world in ways that other scientists can repeat. This is a goal of scientific observation. It is expected that when a scientist has made an observation, other people will be able to make the same observation.

▶ **LIST:** What are the five senses?

**Comparing and Contrasting**  Part of observing is comparing and contrasting. When you compare data, you observe the characteristics of several things or events to see how they are alike. When you contrast data, you look for ways that similar things are different from one another.

▲ **Figure 2** Crocodiles and alligators are alike in many ways. They also have many differences.

▶ **COMPARE/CONTRAST:** How are a crocodile and an alligator similar? How are they different?

**Using Tools to Observe**  Sometimes an object is too small to see with your eyes alone. You need a special tool to help you make observations. One tool that life scientists use to observe things is a microscope. A microscope magnifies, or makes objects appear larger than they actually are.

▲ **Figure 3** Scientists use microscopes to observe very small objects.

▶ **INFER:** What are some things that scientists might need a microscope to see?

## Hands-On Activity

### MAKING OBSERVATIONS

*You and a partner will need 2 shoeboxes with lids, 2 rubber bands, and several small objects.*

1. Place several small objects into the shoebox. Do not let your partner see what you put into the shoebox.
2. Cover the shoebox with the lid. Put a rubber band around the shoebox to keep the lid on.
3. Exchange shoeboxes with your partner.
4. Gently shake, turn, and rattle the shoebox.
5. Try to describe what is in the shoebox without opening it. Write your descriptions on a sheet of paper.

**Practicing Your Skills**

6. IDENTIFY: What science process skill did you use?
7. IDENTIFY: Which of your senses was most important to you?
8. ANALYZE: Direct observation is seeing something with your eyes or hearing it with your ears. Indirect observation involves using a model or past experience to make a guess about something. Which kind of observation did you use?

# 2 Classifying Data

## Key Term

**data:** information you collect when you observe something

**Collecting and Classifying Data** The information you collect when you observe something is called **data**. The data from an experiment or from observations you have made are first recorded, or written down. Then, they are classified.

When you classify data, you group things together based on how they are alike. This information often comes from making comparisons as you observe. You may classify by size, shape, color, use, or any other important feature. Classifying data helps you recognize and understand the relationships between things. Classification makes studying large groups of things easier. For example, life scientists use classification to organize the different types of living things.

▶ 5 **EXPLAIN:** How can you classify data?

## Hands-On Activity

### ORGANIZING LIVING THINGS

*You will need 15 index cards with photographs of living things taped to them.*

1. Look at the pictures on the index cards. Classify the photographs into two categories, *Plants* and *Animals*.

2. Look at the pictures you classified as *Plants*. Choose a general characteristic, such as if they have flowers or not. Divide the plants into two groups based on that specific characteristic.

3. Repeat Step 2 for the pictures you classified as *Animals*.

4. Divide these four groups into smaller groups.

### Practicing Your Skills

5. **ANALYZE:** How did you classify the pictures?

6. **EXPLAIN:** Why is a classification system useful?

# 3 Modeling and Simulating

## Key Terms

**model:** tool scientists use to represent an object or process

**simulation:** computer model that usually shows a process

**Modeling** Sometimes things are too small to see with your eyes alone. Other times, an object is too large to see. You may need a model to help you examine the object. A **model** is a good way to show what a very small or a very large object looks like. A model can have more details than what may be seen with just your eyes. It can be used to represent a process or an object that is hard to explain with words. A model can be a three-dimensional picture, a drawing, a computer image, or a diagram.

▶ 6 **DEFINE:** What is a model?

**Simulating** A **simulation** is a kind of model that shows a process. It is often done using a computer. You can use a simulation to predict the outcome of an experiment. Scientists use simulations to study everything from the insides of a frog to the development of an embryo.

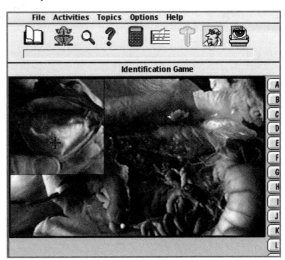

▲ **Figure 4** Some schools use a computer simulation program instead of dissecting a preserved frog.

▶ 7 **DEFINE:** What is a simulation?

# 4 Measuring

## Key Terms

**unit:** amount used to measure something

**meter:** basic unit of length or distance

**mass:** amount of matter in something

**gram:** basic unit of mass

**volume:** amount of space an object takes up

**liter:** basic unit of liquid volume

**meniscus:** curve at the surface of a liquid in a thin tube

**temperature:** measure of the amount of heat energy something contains

**Two Systems of Measurement** When you measure, you compare an unknown value with a known value using standard units. A **unit** is an amount used to measure something. The metric system is an international system of measurement. Examples of metric units are the gram, the kilometer, and the liter. In the United States, the English system and the metric system are both used. Examples of units in the English system are the pound, the foot, and the gallon.

There is also a more modern form of the metric system called SI. The letters *SI* stand for the French words *Système International.* Many of the units in the SI are the same as those in the metric system.

The metric and SI systems are both based on units of 10. This makes them easy to use. Each unit in these systems is ten times greater than the one before it. To show a change in the size of a unit, you add a prefix to the unit. The prefix tells you whether the unit is larger or smaller. For example, a centimeter is ten times bigger than a millimeter.

| PREFIXES AND THEIR MEANINGS | |
|---|---|
| kilo- | one thousand (1,000) |
| hecto- | one hundred (100) |
| deca- | ten (10) |
| deci- | one-tenth (1/10) |
| centi- | one-hundredth (1/100) |
| milli- | one-thousandth (1/1,000) |

◄ Figure 5

**8** ▶ IDENTIFY: What are two measurement systems?

**Units of Length** Length is the distance from one point to another. In the metric system, the basic unit of length or distance is the **meter.** A meter is about the length from a doorknob to the floor. Longer distances, such as the distances between cities, are measured in kilometers. A kilometer is 1,000 meters. Centimeters and millimeters measure shorter distances. A centimeter is 1/100 of a meter. A millimeter is 1/1,000 of a meter. Figure 6 compares common units of length. It also shows the abbreviation for each unit.

| SI/METRIC UNITS OF LENGTH | |
|---|---|
| 1,000 millimeters (mm) | 1 meter (m) |
| 100 centimeters (cm) | 1 meter |
| 10 decimeters (dm) | 1 meter |
| 10 millimeters | 1 centimeter |
| 1,000 meters | 1 kilometer (km) |

▲ Figure 6

Length can be measured with a meter stick. A meter stick is 1 m long and is divided into 100 equal lengths by numbered lines. The distance between each of these lines is equal to 1 cm. Each centimeter is divided into ten equal parts. Each one of these parts is equal to 1 mm.

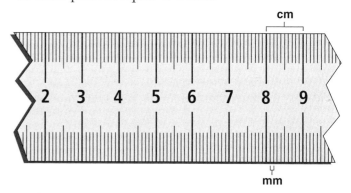

▲ Figure 7 A meter stick is divided into centimeters and millimeters.

**9** ▶ CALCULATE: How many centimeters are there in 3 m?

**Measuring Area** Do you know how people find the area of the floor of a room? They measure the length and the width of the room. Then, they multiply the two numbers. You can find the area of any rectangle by multiplying its length by its width. Area is expressed in square units, such as square meters (m²) or square centimeters (cm²).

$$\text{Area} = \text{length} \times \text{width}$$

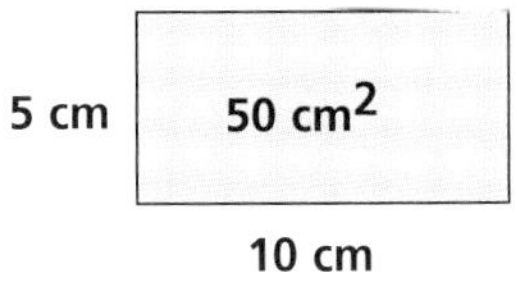

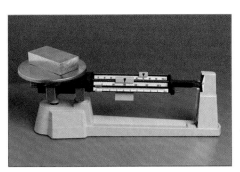

◀ **Figure 8** The area of a rectangle equals length times width.

**10** ▶ **CALCULATE:** What is the area of a rectangle 2 cm × 3 cm?

**Mass and Weight** The amount of matter in something is its **mass.** The basic metric unit of mass is called a **gram (g).** A paper clip has about 1 g of mass. Mass is measured with an instrument called a balance. A balance works like a seesaw. It compares an unknown mass with a known mass.

One kind of balance that is commonly used to measure mass is a triple-beam balance. A triple-beam balance has a pan. The object being measured is placed on the pan. The balance also has three beams. Weights, called riders, are moved along each beam until the object on the pan is balanced. Each rider gives a reading in grams. The mass of the object is equal to the total readings of all three riders.

◀ **Figure 9** A triple-beam balance

Mass and weight are related; however, they are not the same. The weight of an object is a measure of Earth's pull of gravity between Earth and that object. Gravity is the force that pulls objects toward the center of Earth. The strength of the pull of gravity between two objects depends on the distance between the objects and how much mass they each contain. So, the weight changes as its distance from the center of Earth changes.

**11** ▶ **IDENTIFY:** What instrument is used to measure mass?

**Volume** The amount of space an object takes up is its **volume.** You can measure the volume of liquids and solids. Liquid volume is usually measured in **liters.** Soft drinks in the United States often come in 2-liter bottles.

A graduated cylinder is used to measure liquid volume. Graduated cylinders are calibrated, or marked off, at regular intervals. Look at Figure 10. It shows a graduated cylinder. On this graduated cylinder, each small line is equal to 0.05 mL. The longer lines mark off every 0.25 mL up to 5.00 mL. However, every graduated cylinder is not calibrated in this manner. They come in different sizes up to 2,000 mL, with different calibrations.

Always read the measurement at eye level. If you are using a glass graduated cylinder, you will need to read the mark on the graduated cylinder closest to the bottom of the meniscus. A **meniscus** is the curve at the surface of a liquid in a thin tube. A plastic graduated cylinder does not show a meniscus.

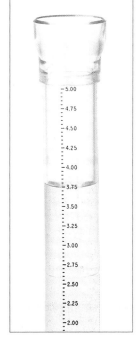

▲ **Figure 10** This glass graduated cylinder shows a meniscus.

The volume of solid objects is often measured in cubic centimeters. One cubic centimeter is the same as 1 milliliter (mL).

Look at Figure 11. Each side of the cube is 1 cm long. The volume of the cube is 1 cubic centimeter ($cm^3$). Now, look at the drawing of the box in Figure 12. Its length is 3 cm. Its width is 2 cm. Its height is 2 cm. The volume of the box can be found by multiplying length by width by height. In this case, volume equals $3 \times 2 \times 2$. Therefore, the volume of the box in Figure 12 is 12 $cm^3$.

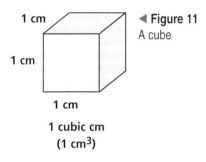

◀ **Figure 11**
A cube

1 cubic cm
(1 $cm^3$)

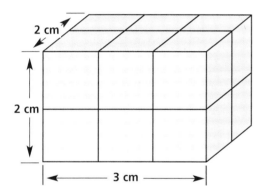

▲ **Figure 12** The volume of a box equals length by width by height.

$$V = l \times w \times h$$

If you have a box that is 10 cm on each side, its volume would be 1,000 $cm^3$. A liter is the same as 1,000 $cm^3$. One liter of liquid will fill the box exactly.

**12▶ CALCULATE:** How many milliliters of water would fill a 12-$cm^3$ box?

## Hands-On Activity

### CALCULATING AREA AND VOLUME

*You will need 3 boxes of different sizes, paper, and a metric ruler.*

1. Measure the length, width, and height of each box in centimeters. Record each measurement in your notes.

2. Calculate the volume of each box. Record each volume in your notes.

3. Find the surface area of each box. Record each area in your notes.

**Practicing Your Skills**

4. **ANALYZE:** Which of the three boxes has the largest volume?

5. **CALCULATE:** How many milliliters of liquid would fill each box?

6. **ANALYZE:** What is the surface area of the largest box?

**Temperature** **Temperature** is a measure of the amount of heat energy something contains. An instrument that measures temperature is called a thermometer.

Most thermometers are glass tubes. At the bottom of the tube is a wider part, called the bulb. The bulb is filled with liquid. Liquids that are often used include mercury, colored alcohol, or colored water. When heat is added, the liquid expands, or gets larger. It rises in the glass tube. When heat is taken away, the liquid contracts, or gets smaller. The liquid falls in the tube. On the side of the tube is a series of marks. You read the temperature by looking at the mark on the tube where the liquid stops.

Temperature can be measured on three different scales. These scales are the Fahrenheit (F) scale, the Celsius (C) scale, and the Kelvin (K) scale. The Fahrenheit scale is part of the English system of measurement. The Celsius scale is usually used in science. Almost all scientists, even in the United States, use the Celsius scale. Each unit on the Celsius scale is a degree Celsius (°C). The degree Celsius is the metric unit of temperature. Water freezes at 0°C. It boils at 100°C.

Scientists working with very low temperatures use the Kelvin scale. The Kelvin scale is part of the SI measurement system. It begins at absolute zero, or 0K. This number indicates, in theory at least, a total lack of heat.

| COMPARING TEMPERATURE SCALES | | | |
|---|---|---|---|
| | Kelvin | Fahrenheit | Celsius |
| Boiling point of water | 373K | 212°F | 100°C |
| Human body temperature | 310K | 98.6°F | 37°C |
| Freezing point of water | 273K | 32°F | 0°C |
| Absolute zero | 0K | −459.67°F | −273.15°C |

▲ Figure 13

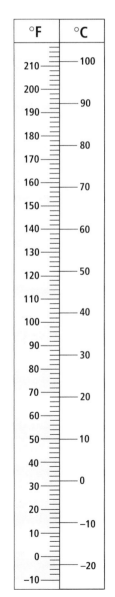

°F °C
210 — 100
200 —
190 — 90
180 —
170 — 80
160 — 70
150 —
140 — 60
130 —
120 — 50
110 —
100 — 40
90 —
80 — 30
70 — 20
60 —
50 — 10
40 —
30 — 0
20 —
10 — −10
0 —
−10 — −20

◄ Figure 14 The Fahrenheit and Celsius scales

**13▶** NAME: What are the three scales used to measure temperature?

## Hands-On Activity
### READING A THERMOMETER

*You will need safety goggles, a lab apron, 2 beakers, a heat source, ice water, a wax pencil, a ruler, and a standard Celsius thermometer.*

1. Boil some water in a beaker.
   ⚠CAUTION: Be very careful when working with heat. Place your thermometer in the beaker. Do not let the thermometer touch the sides or bottom of the beaker. Wait until the mercury rises as far as it will go. Record the temperature.

2. Fill a beaker with ice water. Place the unmarked thermometer into this beaker. Wait until the mercury goes as low as it will go. Record the temperature.

▲ STEP 1 Record the temperature of the boiling water.

**Practicing Your Skills**

3. IDENTIFY: What is the temperature at which the mercury rose as high as it would go?

4. IDENTIFY: What is the temperature at which the mercury went as low as it would go?

# 5 Analyzing Data and Communicating Results

## Key Term

**communication:** sharing information

**Analyzing Data** When you organize information, you put it in a logical order. In scientific experiments, it is important to organize your data. Data collected during an experiment are not very useful unless they are organized and easy to read. It is also important to organize your data if you plan to share the results of your experiment.

Scientists often organize information visually by using data tables, charts, graphs, and diagrams. By using tables, charts, graphs, and diagrams, scientists can display a lot of information in a small space. They also make it easier to compare and interpret data.

Tables are made up of rows and columns. Columns run up and down. Rows run from left to right. Tables usually show numerical data. Information in the table can be arranged in time order. It can also be set up to show patterns or trends. A table showing the number of endangered species born over a period of time, for example, can reveal a pattern of extinction rates. Figure 15 shows a table of elements in living things.

| ELEMENTS FOUND IN LIVING THINGS ||
|---|---|
| Element | Percentage |
| Oxygen | 64.5 |
| Carbon | 18 |
| Hydrogen | 10 |
| Sulfur, phosphorus, and others | 4.5 |
| Nitrogen | 3 |

▲ Figure 15

Graphs, such as bar graphs, line graphs, and circle graphs, often use special coloring, shading, or patterns to represent information. Keys indicate what the special markings represent. Line graphs have horizontal ($x$) and vertical ($y$) axes to indicate such things as time and quantities.

**14** ▶ EXPLAIN: How do tables and graphs help you analyze data?

**Sharing Results** When you talk to a friend, you are communicating, or sharing information. If you write a letter or a report, you are also communicating but in a different way. Scientists communicate all the time. They communicate to share results, information, and opinions. They write books and magazine or newspaper articles. They may also create Web sites about their work. This is called written **communication.**

Graphs are a visual way to communicate. The circle graph in Figure 16 is showing the same information as Figure 15. The circle graph presents the information in a different way.

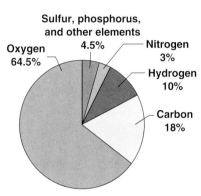

▲ **Figure 16** Circle graphs are a good way to show parts of a whole.

**15** ▶ LIST: What are some ways to communicate the results of an experiment?

# 6 Making Predictions

## Key Terms

**infer:** to form a conclusion

**predict:** to state ahead of time what you think is going to happen

**Thinking of Possibilities** When you **infer** something, you form a conclusion. This is called making an inference. Your conclusion will usually be based on observations or past experience. You may use logic to form your statement. Your statement might be supported by evidence and perhaps can be tested by an experiment. An inference is not a fact. It is only one possible explanation.

When you **predict,** you state ahead of time what you think will happen. Predictions about future events are based on inferences, evidence, or past experience. The two science process skills of inferring and predicting are very closely related.

**16** ▶ CONTRAST: What is the difference between inferring and predicting?

# How do you conduct a scientific investigation?

By now, you should have a good understanding of the science process skills. These skills are used to solve many science problems. There is also a basic procedure, or plan, that scientists usually follow when conducting investigations. Some people call this procedure the scientific method.

The scientific method is a series of steps that can serve as a guide to solving problems or answering questions. It uses many of the science process skills you know, such as observing and predicting.

Not all experiments use all of the steps in the scientific method. Some experiments follow all of them, but in a different order. In fact, there is no one right scientific method. Each problem is different. Some problems may require steps that another problem would not. However, most investigations will follow the same basic procedure.

**1 DESCRIBE:** What is the scientific method?

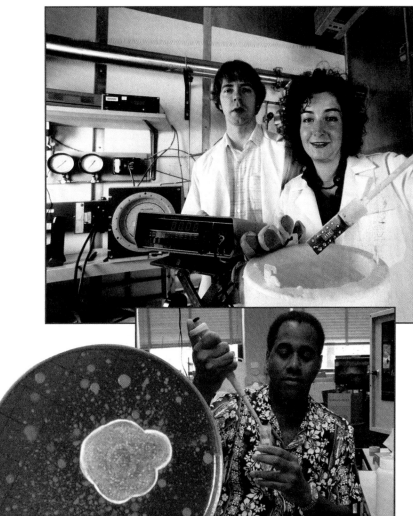

▲ **Figure 1** Scientists use the scientific method to guide experiments.

## Contents

1 Identifying a Problem and Doing Research

2 Forming a Hypothesis

3 Designing and Carrying Out an Experiment

4 Recording and Analyzing Data

5 Stating a Conclusion

6 Writing a Report

# 1 Identifying a Problem and Doing Research

**Starting an Investigation** Scientists often state a problem as a question. This is the first step in a scientific investigation. Most experiments begin by asking a scientific question. That is, they ask a question that can be answered by gathering evidence. This question is the reason for the scientific investigation. It also helps determine how the investigation will proceed.

Have you ever done background research for a science project? When you do this kind of research, you are looking for data that others have already obtained on the same subject. You can gather research by reading books, magazines, and newspapers, and by using the Internet to find out what other scientists have done. Doing research is the first step of gathering evidence for a scientific investigation.

 **IDENTIFY:** What is the first step of a scientific investigation?

## BUILDING SCIENCE SKILLS

***Researching Background Information*** Suppose you notice that there is moss growing in your backyard. You also notice that the moss in the shady area of your backyard seems to grow faster and look healthier than the moss that grows in sunlight. You wonder if sunlight affects moss growth.

To determine if sunlight affects moss growth, look for information on moss in encyclopedias, in botany books, or on the Internet. Put your findings in a report.

▲ **Figure 2** Moss grows best in shady areas.

# 2 Forming a Hypothesis

## Key Terms

**hypothesis:** suggested answer to a question or problem

**theory:** set of hypotheses that have been supported by testing over and over again

**Focusing the Investigation** Scientists usually state clearly what they expect to find out in an investigation. This is called stating a hypothesis. A **hypothesis** is a suggested answer to a question or a solution to a problem. Stating a hypothesis helps to keep you focused on the problem and helps you decide what to test.

To form their hypotheses, scientists must think of possible explanations for a set of observations or they must suggest possible answers to a scientific question. One of those explanations becomes the hypothesis. In science, a hypothesis must include something that can be tested.

A hypothesis is more than just a guess. It must consider observations, past experiences, and previous knowledge. It is an inference turned into a statement that can be tested. A set of hypotheses that have been supported by testing over and over again by many scientists is called a **theory.** An example is the theory that explains how living things have evolved, or changed, over time.

A hypothesis can take the form of an "if…then" statement. A well-worded hypothesis is a guide for how to set up and perform an experiment.

**DESCRIBE:** How does a scientist form a hypothesis?

## BUILDING SCIENCE SKILLS

***Developing a Hypothesis*** If you are testing how sunlight affects moss growth, you might write down this hypothesis:

*Moss that grows in the shade is healthier than moss that grows in sunlight.*

However, what do you mean by healthier? Is the moss greener? Does it grow faster? You need to make your hypothesis specific. Revise the hypothesis above to make it more specific.

# 3 Designing and Carrying Out an Experiment

## Key Terms

**variable:** anything that can affect the outcome of an experiment

**constant:** something that does not change

**controlled experiment:** experiment in which all the conditions except one are kept constant

**Testing the Hypothesis** Scientists need to plan how to test their hypotheses. This means they must design an experiment. The plan must be a step-by-step procedure. It should include a record of any observations made or measurements taken.

All experiments must take variables into account. A **variable** is anything that can affect the outcome of an experiment. Room temperature, amount of sunlight, and water vapor in the air are just some of the many variables that could affect the outcome of an experiment.

**4▶ DEFINE:** What is a variable?

**Controlling the Experiment** One of the variables in an experiment should be what you are testing. This is what you will change during the experiment. All other variables need to remain the same. In this experiment, you will vary the amount of sunlight.

A **constant** is something that does not change. If there are no constants in your experiment, you will not be sure why you got the results you did. An experiment in which all the conditions except one are kept constant is called a **controlled experiment.**

Some experiments have two setups. In one setup, called the control, nothing is changed. In the other setup, the variable being tested is changed. Later, the control group can be compared with the other group to provide useful data.

**5▶ EXPLAIN:** Explain how a controlled experiment is set up.

**Designing the Procedure** Suppose you now want to design an experiment to determine if sunlight affects moss growth. You have your hypothesis. You decide your procedure is to grow moss. Your procedure will be to grow one moss plant in sunlight and the other in shade. You will then check your plants after a few days to see if your hypothesis was correct.

Suppose you water the moss that is growing in the sunlight but forget to water the moss in the shade? The moss in the sunlight might grow faster than the moss in the shade. Is the difference caused by the sunlight or by the water? You would have no way of knowing if your experiment had more than one variable.

In designing your experiment, you need to identify the variables. The amount of water you give the mosses, temperature, and the type of soil are all variables that could affect the outcome of your experiment. Everything about growing the mosses needs to be the same except the amount of sunlight each receives.

Finally, you should decide on the data you will collect. How will you measure the "health" of the moss? In this case, you might want to record the thickness of the moss, its color, and whether it reproduces.

The hands-on activity on page 12 is an example of an experiment you might have designed.

**6▶ LIST:** How do constants and variables affect an experiment?

## Hands-On Activity

### CARRYING OUT AN EXPERIMENT

*You will need 4 clumps of fresh moss, 4 medium-sized paper cups, soil, a hand lens, a metric ruler, water, and safety goggles.*

1. Fill the four paper cups with the soil and plant a clump of moss in each cup. Label cups 1 and 2 *Sunlight*. Label cups 3 and 4 *Shade*.

2. Examine each moss plant with a hand lens. Measure the heights of each sample. Record your observations in your notes.

3. Place cups 1 and 2 in an area where the moss plants will receive sunlight for most of the day. Place cups 3 and 4 where the moss plants will be in shade for most of the day.

4. Water the moss plants each day. Be sure to give the same amount of water to each plant.

5. After a week, examine the moss plants with a hand lens. Describe the moss plants in each cup.

▲ **STEP 1** Plant a clump of moss in each cup.

### Practicing Your Skills

6. **COMPARE:** Compare the color of the moss plants grown in direct sunlight with the color of the moss plants grown in indirect sunlight.

7. **MEASURE:** Measure the heights of each sample. Is there a relationship between height and sunlight?

# 4 Recording and Analyzing Data

**Dealing With Data** During an experiment, you must keep careful notes about what you observe. For example, you might need to note down the time of day that you made your observations. Was there any change of temperature or color? This is important information that might affect your conclusion.

At the end of an experiment, you will need to study the data to find any patterns. Much of the data you will deal with is written text, such as a report or a summary of an experiment. However, scientific information is often a set of numbers or facts presented in other, more visual ways. These visual presentations can make the information easier to understand. Tables, charts, and graphs can help you understand a collection of facts on a topic.

After your data have been organized, you need to ask what the data show. Do they support your hypothesis? Do they show something wrong in your experiment? Do you need to gather more data by performing another experiment?

**7 ▶ LIST:** What are some ways to display data?

### BUILDING SCIENCE SKILLS

*Analyzing Data* You made the following notes during your experiment. How would you display this information?

Day 1 Each moss is green. Each moss is about 2 cm in height.

Day 2 Watered the moss.

Day 3 Watered the moss. It was rainy outside, so the moss labeled "Sunlight" did not receive sun today.

Day 4 Watered the moss.

Day 5 The moss labeled "Shade" appears to be greener than the moss labeled "Sunlight." The moss labeled "Shade" is 3 cm high. The moss labeled sunlight is 1.5 cm high.

▲ **Figure 3** Possible notes

# 5 Stating a Conclusion

**Drawing Conclusions**   A conclusion is a statement that sums up what you have learned from an experiment. When you draw a conclusion, you need to decide whether the data you collected supported your hypothesis. You may need to repeat an experiment several times before you can draw any conclusions from it. Conclusions often lead you to ask new questions and plan new experiments to answer them. Sometimes a scientist's conclusion is to find that his or her hypothesis was incorrect. This will then lead to a new hypothesis.

**8 ▸ EXPLAIN:** Why might it be necessary to repeat an experiment?

## BUILDING SCIENCE SKILLS

***Stating a Conclusion***   Review your hypothesis statement regarding the effect of sunlight on moss plants. Then, review the data you obtained during your experiment.

- Was your hypothesis correct? Use your observations to support your answer.

- Which moss plants grew best? What type of light is best for the growth of moss plants?

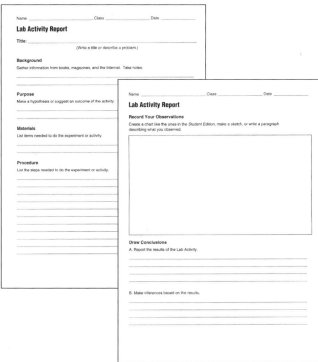

▲ **Figure 4**  Throughout this program, you may use forms like these to organize your lab reports.

# 6 Writing a Report

**Communicating Results**   Scientists keep careful written records of their observations and findings. These records are used to create a lab report. Lab reports are a form of written communication. They explain what happened in the experiment. A good lab report should be written so that anyone reading it can duplicate the experiment. It should contain the following information:

- A title
- A purpose
- Background information
- Your hypothesis
- Materials used
- Your step-by-step procedure
- Your observations
- Your recorded data
- Your analysis of the data
- Your conclusions

Your conclusions should relate back to the questions you asked in the "purpose" section of your report. Also, the report should point out any experimental errors that might have caused unexpected results. For example, did you follow the steps in the correct order? Did an unexpected variable interfere with your results? Was your equipment clean and in good working order? This explanation of possible errors should also be part of your conclusions.

**9 ▸ EXPLAIN:** Why is it important to explain possible errors in your lab report?

## BUILDING SCIENCE SKILLS

***Writing a Lab Report***   Write a lab report to communicate to other scientists your discoveries about the effect of sunlight on moss plants. Your lab report should include a title, your hypothesis statement, a list of materials you used, the procedure and your observations, and your conclusions. Try to include one table of data in your report.

# LAB SAFETY

Working in a science laboratory can be both exciting and meaningful. However, you must always be aware of safety precautions when carrying out experiments. There are a few basic rules that should be followed in any science laboratory:

- Read all instructions carefully before the start of an experiment. Follow all instructions exactly and in the correct order.

- Check your equipment to make sure it is clean and working properly.

- Never taste, smell, or touch any substance in the lab that you are not told to do so. Never eat or drink anything in the lab. Do not chew gum.

- Never work alone. Tell a teacher at once if an accident occurs.

Experiments that use chemicals or heat can be dangerous. The following list of rules and symbols will help you avoid accidents. There are also rules about what to do if an accident does occur. Here are some rules to remember when working in a lab:

1. Do not use glass that is chipped or metal objects with broken edges. Do not try to clean up broken glassware yourself. Notify your teacher if a piece of glassware is broken.

2. Do not use electrical cords with loose plugs or frayed ends. Do not let electrical cords cross in front of working areas. Do not use electrical equipment near water.

3. Be very careful when using sharp objects such as scissors, knives, or tweezers. Always cut in a direction away from your body.

4. Be careful when you are using a heat source. Use proper equipment, such as tongs or a ringstand, when handling hot objects.

5. Confine loose clothing and hair when working with an open flame. Be sure you know the location of the nearest fire extinguisher. Never reach across an open flame.

6. Be careful when working with poisonous or toxic substances. Never mix chemicals without directions from your teacher. Remove any long jewelry that might hang down and end up in chemicals. Avoid touching your eyes or mouth when working with chemicals.

7. Use extreme care when working with acids and bases. Never mix acids and bases without direction from your teacher. Never smell anything directly. Use caution when handling chemicals that produce fumes.

8. Wear safety goggles, especially when working with an open flame, chemicals, and any liquids.

9. Wear lab aprons when working with substances of any sort, especially chemicals.

10. Use caution when handling or collecting plants. Some plants can be harmful if they are touched or eaten.

11. Use caution when handling live animals. Some animals can injure you or spread disease. Handle all live animals as humanely as possible.

12. Dispose of all equipment and materials properly. Keep your work area clean at all times.

13. Always wash your hands thoroughly with soap and water after handling chemicals or live organisms.

14. Follow the  **CAUTION** and safety symbols you see used throughout this book when doing labs or other activities.

# Chapter 1 Classification

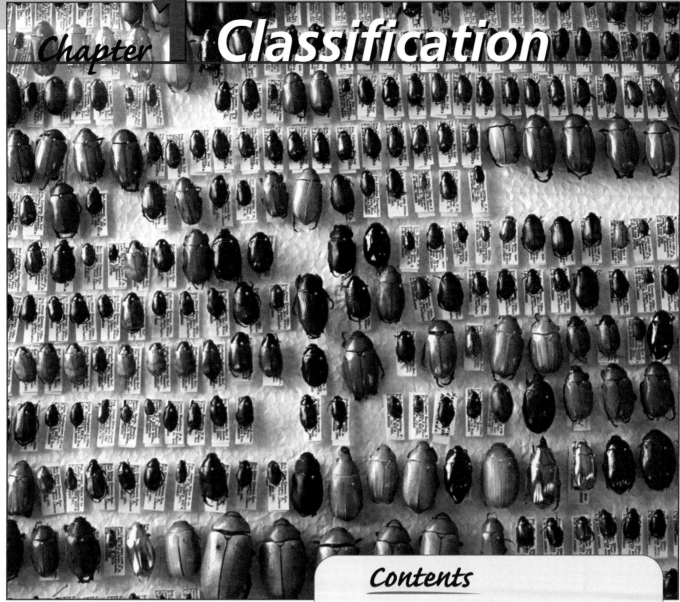

▲ **Figure 1-1** This beetle collection has been classified by a person who studies insects, called an entomologist.

Scientists have identified at least 2.5 million different kinds of organisms so far. Every year, many more new species are discovered. It is important for scientists to keep information about the different species organized. To do this, many scientists use a classification system based on five kingdoms.

►How would you classify living things?

## Contents

**1-1** What is classification?

**1-2** How are living things classified?

■ **Lab Activity:** Classifying Shells

**1-3** What are the kingdoms?

■ **The Big Idea:** How are organisms named?

**1-4** What are viruses?

# 1-1 What is classification?

## Objective

Explain why it is necessary to classify things.

## Key Terms

**classification** (klas-uh-fih-KAY-shuhn)**:** grouping things according to similarities

**taxonomy** (tak-SAHN-uh-mee)**:** science of classifying living things

**Classification** You are in a library, looking for a mystery novel. You look at the signs above each group of books. Each sign tells you what types of books are in each area. In no time at all, you find your book and are on your way. In a library, you are able to find books quickly because they are classified, or grouped, by subject. Grouping things according to similarities, or how they are alike, is called **classification.**

▶ **CLASSIFY:** Name one other way you could classify books.

▲ **Figure 1-2** Like books in a library, insects can be classified according to similarities.

**Taxonomy** About 2.5 million different kinds of organisms have been discovered so far. Each year the list of living things grows longer. How do scientists keep track of so many organisms? Scientists use a system of classification. The science of classifying living things is called **taxonomy.** Scientists who classify living things are taxonomists.

Why do scientists classify living things? Classification is a way of organizing information about different kinds of living things. Classification also makes it easier for scientists to identify a newly discovered organism.

▶ **NAME:** What is the science of classifying living things called?

**Classifying Living Things** Organisms are classified based on how they are alike. Taxonomists do not group organisms together simply because they look alike. Taxonomists use many characteristics to classify organisms. For example, taxonomists study the cells of an organism and the organelles that make up the cell. They study the way the organism grows and develops before it is born. They also study the blood of animals. Sometimes they study an organism's DNA. Taxonomists also study how an organism gets its energy.

▶ **STATE:** What are two ways scientists classify organisms?

**Early Classification Systems** One of the first known systems used to classify living things was developed more than 2,000 years ago by the Greek philosopher Aristotle (AR-ihs-taht-ul). Aristotle classified organisms as either plants or animals. Animals were classified into smaller groups based upon where they lived. Aristotle's classification system had three groups of animals: land, water, and air.

One of Aristotle's students, Theophrastus (thee-uh-FRAS-tuhs) classified plants according to their sizes and kind of stem. Small plants with soft stems were called herbs. Medium-sized plants with many woody stems were called shrubs. Large plants with one woody stem were called trees.

In the eighteenth century, a Swedish botanist named Carolus Linnaeus (li-NEE-uhs) developed a new way to classify organisms. Linnaeus classified organisms according to their physical characteristics. Organisms that looked alike were grouped together. Linnaeus is known as the father of modern taxonomy.

▲ **Figure 1-3** In Aristotle's classification system, walruses could have been classified as water animals.

 **LIST:** What are the three groups of animals in Aristotle's classification system?

## ✔ CHECKING CONCEPTS

1. When you classify, you put things into _____ according to similarities.

2. The science of classifying living things is _____.

3. Taxonomists study the way organisms grow and develop before they are _____.

4. About _____ million different kinds of organisms have been discovered so far.

## 💡 THINKING CRITICALLY

5. **INFER:** Why is taxonomy an ongoing science?

6. **APPLY:** Food is classified in a supermarket. Books are classified in a library. Name two other classification systems that are used in daily life.

7. **ANALYZE:** Why do you think taxonomists do not use appearance alone to classify organisms?

## BUILDING SCIENCE SKILLS

***Comparing*** When you compare things, you look at how the things are alike and how they are different. Libraries classify books using either the Dewey Decimal System or the Library of Congress classification system. Find out how these two classification systems compare. What are some similarities and differences between the two systems?

## *Hands-On Activity*
## CLASSIFYING BUTTONS

*You will need a sheet of paper, a pencil, and an assortment of buttons.*

1. Carefully examine the buttons.
2. On a sheet of paper, list as many characteristics of the buttons as you can.
3. Classify the buttons according to one of their characteristics.
4. Repeat Step 3 two more times. Each time, use a different characteristic.

▲ **Figure 1-4** Classify an assortment of buttons.

**Practicing Your Skills**
5. **EXPLAIN:** What characteristics did you use to classify the buttons?
6. **ANALYZE:** Which classification system had the most groups?
7. **ANALYZE:** Which classification system had the fewest groups?

# 1-2 How are living things classified?

## Objective
Explain the different levels of classification.

## Key Terms
**kingdom:** classification group made up of related phyla

**phylum** (FY-luhm), *pl.* **phyla:** classification group made up of related classes

**genus:** classification group made up of related species

**species:** group of organisms that look alike and can reproduce among themselves

**Classification Levels** Organisms that are classified in the same group are alike in some ways. The more alike organisms are, the more classification groups they share.

Altogether, there are seven major classification levels. The number of different kinds of organisms in each level decreases as you move from the kingdom level to each of the next smaller levels. From largest to smallest, the classification groups are kingdom, phylum, class, order, family, genus, and species.

**1** SEQUENCE: List the seven classification levels from largest to smallest.

**Comparing the Levels** The largest classification group is a **kingdom.** Organisms in the same kingdom have similar cell structure and functions. In Figure 1-5, all of the organisms in Kingdom Animalia are multicellular and get energy from food. Each kingdom is divided into levels called phyla. The organisms in a phylum have similar body plans or structures. Each phylum is divided into still smaller levels. These levels are called classes. The organisms in a class have more details of structure and function in common. Classes are further divided into orders. Orders are divided into families. Families are divided into genuses.

A **species** is the smallest classification group. A species is a group of organisms that have similar characteristics and can reproduce among

themselves. For example, all dogs belong to the same species. A **genus** is made up of two or more species that are very much alike. For example, dogs and wolves belong to different species, but they belong to the same genus.

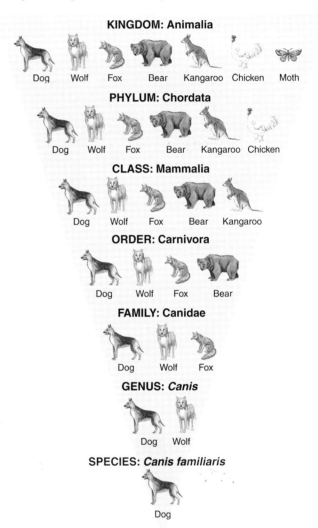

**KINGDOM: Animalia**
Dog  Wolf  Fox  Bear  Kangaroo  Chicken  Moth

**PHYLUM: Chordata**
Dog  Wolf  Fox  Bear  Kangaroo  Chicken

**CLASS: Mammalia**
Dog  Wolf  Fox  Bear  Kangaroo

**ORDER: Carnivora**
Dog  Wolf  Fox  Bear

**FAMILY: Canidae**
Dog  Wolf  Fox

**GENUS: *Canis***
Dog  Wolf

**SPECIES: *Canis familiaris***
Dog

▲ **Figure 1-5** Dogs share some classification groups with other animals.

All organisms are classified using this system. For example, humans are members of Kingdom Animalia. They belong to the Phylum Chordata. They are members of the Class Mammalia. The order humans belong to is Primate and the family is Hominid. Humans are members of genus *Homo* and species *Homo sapiens*.

**2** RELATE: Name an animal that belongs to the same phylum as humans.

**Naming Organisms** In Carolus Linnaeus's classification system, each kind of organism is identified by a two-part scientific name. A scientific name is made up of the genus and species names of an organism. For example, the scientific name for humans is *Homo sapiens*. When writing scientific names, always capitalize the genus name.

 **NAME:** What are the two parts of a scientific name?

## ✓ CHECKING CONCEPTS

1. The largest classification group is the _____.

2. The classification group that is made up of related species is the _____.

3. A group of organisms that look alike and can reproduce among themselves is a _____.

4. The organisms in a phyla have similar body _____.

##  THINKING CRITICALLY

*Use Figure 1-5 to answer the following questions.*

5. **INTERPRET:** How many classification groups do dogs and bears have in common?

6. **APPLY:** What is the scientific name for a pet dog?

7. **ANALYZE:** Which two animals are the most closely related?

### Web InfoSearch

**John Ray** In the seventeenth century, an English botanist named John Ray identified and classified more than 18,600 different kinds of plants. Many of his ideas are used in modern plant taxonomy.

**SEARCH:** Use the Internet to find out more about taxonomy. Start your search at www.conceptsandchallenges.com. Some key search words are **John Ray** and **taxonomy.** Write your findings in a report.

## *Science and Technology*

### USING DNA TO CLASSIFY ORGANISMS

In addition to looking at an organism's physical traits, scientists are now using DNA to classify organisms. By testing an organism's DNA, scientists also can identify related organisms. In the late 1990s, scientists studied the DNA of whales and hippopotamuses. Both species have similar mutations in their DNA that are not found in other animals. This means that whales and hippopotamuses may have had a common ancestor.

DNA studies can also help scientists identify new species. In 2000, scientists studied DNA samples from living right whales in the Atlantic and Pacific Oceans and from museum specimens as much as 100 years old. They

▲ **Figure 1-6** Right whales of the North Pacific

found that the right whales of the North Pacific show definite DNA differences from the two species of right whales that live in the Atlantic Ocean. These differences are large enough to classify the North Pacific right whales as a separate species.

**Thinking Critically** Why do you think scientists use DNA to classify organisms?

# LAB ACTIVITY
## Classifying Shells

### Materials

25-30 Shells of various types

Paper

Pen

### BACKGROUND

Scientists need a system to keep track of the millions of living things discovered. A classification system groups things according to similarities. Such a system helps scientists organize information as well as identify newly discovered organisms.

### PURPOSE

In this activity, you will classify shells based on similar characteristics.

### PROCEDURE

1. Copy the chart in Figure 1-7 onto a sheet of paper.

2. Take several minutes to examine each of your seashells. Pay close attention to any similarities and differences among the shells.

3. With a partner, discuss how the shells should be classified. Some ways to classify shells are by color, by texture, and by shape.

4. Determine a classification system with at least three levels of classification. Divide the shells accordingly. Label each level. Then, draw and describe the shells that fit into each level.

▲ **STEP 3** Discuss how the shells should be classified.

▲ **STEP 4** Divide the shells.

5. Pick one of the levels of shells. Classify the shells in that level into three smaller groups.

6. Count the number of shells in each smaller level and complete the chart. Compare your chart with the charts of your classmates.

▲ **STEP 5** Classify the shells into three smaller groups.

## Classifying Shells

| Group Name | Group Features | Number of Shells |
|------------|----------------|------------------|
|            |                |                  |
|            |                |                  |
|            |                |                  |
|            |                |                  |

▲ **Figure 1-7** Copy this chart onto a sheet of paper.

## CONCLUSIONS

1. **EXPLAIN:** What characteristics helped you determine each level?

2. **ANALYZE:** How did the number of shells in each level change as the levels became more specific?

3. **COMPARE:** How did your classification system compare with those of your classmates?

4. **DISCUSS:** What is the importance of a classification system?

5. **APPLY:** Have your partner describe a new shell. Decide into which classification group it should be placed.

# 1-3 What are the kingdoms?

## Objective
Name and describe the kingdoms of living organisms.

## Key Terms
**fungus** (FUHN-guhs), *pl.* **fungi**: plantlike organism that lacks chlorophyll

**moneran** (muh-NEER-uhn): single-celled organism that does not have a true nucleus

**protist** (PROHT-ihst): simple organism that has cells with nuclei

**Naming the Kingdoms** At one time, all organisms were classified as either plants or animals. With the invention of the microscope, new organisms were discovered. These microscopic organisms were placed into a third kingdom. As more and more powerful microscopes were developed and used, scientists discovered that microscopic organisms are not all alike. Some microscopic organisms do not have nuclei or lack various cell organelles. These organisms were placed into a kingdom of their own. Studies also showed that a **fungus** and a plant were not as closely related as previously thought. Fungi are plantlike organisms that do not have chloroplasts in their cells. Scientists placed fungi in a kingdom of their own.

The five-kingdom classification system that is widely used today was developed by Robert Whittaker, an American ecologist and botanist. In 1969, he presented his ideas for classifying organisms. In his system, organisms are classified according to whether their cells contain a nuclear membrane or true nucleus, whether they are one-celled or many-celled, and how they obtain food. Today, most scientists accept the five-kingdom classification system.

▲ Figure 1-8
Robert Whittaker

▶ **HYPOTHESIZE:** Could the five-kingdom classification system change over time?

**Kingdom Monera** The **monerans** are single-celled organisms. Unlike members of the other four kingdoms, a moneran does not have a real nucleus. Instead monerans have genetic material that is coiled and located in one region. Monerans also lack many of the organelles found in other kinds of cells. Bacteria are examples of monerans.

Some scientists would like to break up the moneran kingdom into two separate kingdoms: Archaebacteria and Eubacteria. Archaebacteria live in extreme environments. These include hot springs, very salty or acidic conditions, and the bottom of the ocean. Eubacteria live in more normal environments. They can be found in the soil, in water, and even on your body. Both types of bacteria are unicellular. However, they have different types of cell walls and cell membranes. As new information becomes available, more scientists may use a classification system with two different bacterial kingdoms.

▶ **IDENTIFY:** What is an example of a moneran?

**Kingdom Protista** Most **protists** are unicellular organisms, such as parameciums. Others, such as algae, form colonies and are multicellular. Unlike monerans, the cells of protists have a nucleus surrounded by a membrane. The cells of protists also have a variety of organelles. The protist kingdom includes both plantlike and animal-like organisms. Some protists can make their own food, whereas others cannot. An amoeba is an example of a protist that cannot make its own food. A euglena is a protist that has a chloroplast and can make its own food.

▶ **CONTRAST:** How are protists different from monerans?

**Kingdom Fungi** Most fungi are made up of many cells. Mushrooms are multicellular fungi. Some fungi, such as yeast, are unicellular. Like plants, the cells of most fungi have a cell wall. However, fungi do not have chlorophyll. Fungi do not make their own food. They absorb food from their environment. Most fungi feed on dead organisms.

▶ **ANALYZE:** Why is "nature's recycler" a good nickname for fungi?

| THE FIVE-KINGDOM CLASSIFICATION SYSTEM | | | | |
|---|---|---|---|---|
| **Monera** | **Protista** | **Fungi** | **Plantae** | **Animalia** |
| | | | | |
| Monerans are simple, unicellular organisms. | Protists are simple, unicellular or multicellular organisms. | Fungi are unicellular or multicellular plantlike organisms. | Plants are multicellular organisms. | Animals are multicellular organisms. |
| A moneran cell does not have a true nuclues. | A protist cell does have a true nucleus. | Fungi get the food they need from dead organisms. | Plants use chlorophyll to make their own food. | Animals get their food by eating other organisms. |
| Bacteria are monerans. | Amoebas and diatoms are protists. | Yeasts and mushrooms are fungi. | Trees and flowers are plants. | Birds, reptiles, fish, and mammals are animals. |

▲ **Figure 1-9** This table shows the characteristics of organisms in each kingdom.

**Kingdom Plantae**   Plants are multicellular organisms. Plant cells have a cell wall made up of cellulose. Plant cells also have chloroplasts. Plants use chlorophyll contained in chloroplasts to make their own food. Members of the plant kingdom usually do not move on their own. Trees, grasses, and flowering plants are all members of the plant kingdom.

**5** ▶ INFER: Why do you think the movement of plants is limited?

**Kingdom Animalia**   Animals are made up of many cells. Most animals have organs that form organ systems. Animal cells do not have a cell wall or chlorophyll. Animals obtain food by eating plants and other animals. Unlike most members of other kingdoms, animals are able to move great distances on their own. Mammals, insects, and birds are all examples of animals.

**6** ▶ APPLY: Why can't animals make their own food?

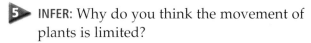

## ✔ CHECKING CONCEPTS

1. At one time, all organisms were classified as either plants or _____.
2. Robert Whittaker developed the _____-kingdom classification system.
3. The cell of a _____ does not have a real nucleus.
4. Amoebas are members of the _____ kingdom.
5. Some scientists use a classification system with two _____ kingdoms.
6. The yeasts belong to the _____ kingdom.

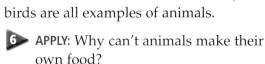

## THINKING CRITICALLY

7. ANALYZE: Why are protists and monerans placed in separate kingdoms?
8. ANALYZE: Why are fungi and plants placed in separate kingdoms?
9. PREDICT: How might new technologies affect the current classification system?

## INTERPRETING VISUALS

*Use Figure 1-9 to answer the following questions.*

10. INTERPRET: What kingdom do trees belong to?
11. ANALYZE: How many kingdoms contain unicellular organisms?
12. INFER: What types of organisms belong to the animal kingdom?

# THE Big IDEA

## How are organisms named?

In the Middle Ages, Latin and Greek were the languages used in universities and literature. They were also used in government and law. Scientists wrote in Latin and Greek.

Many terms in science come from Latin and Greek words. The names of the five kingdoms are examples of terms that come from Latin and Greek words. Plantae, for example, comes from the Latin *planta*, or "plant." Monera comes from the Greek *moneres*, which means "single." The word *genus* is a Latin term that means "type."

A prefix is a word part that is added to the beginning of a root word. A suffix is a word part that is added to the end of a root word. These additions change the meaning of a word. In science, many prefixes and suffixes come from the Latin language.

The table on page 25 lists some common Latin word parts used in science. You can use this table to identify some of the organisms in Figure 1-10. Then, follow the directions in the science log to learn more about "the big idea."◆

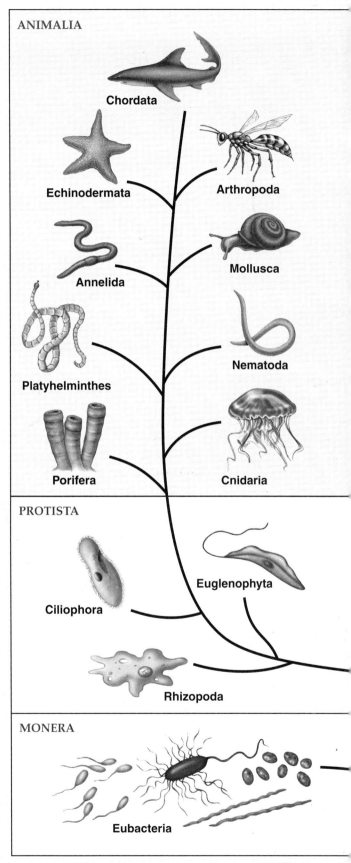

ANIMALIA

Chordata

Echinodermata

Arthropoda

Annelida

Mollusca

Platyhelminthes

Nematoda

Porifera

Cnidaria

PROTISTA

Ciliophora

Euglenophyta

Rhizopoda

MONERA

Eubacteria

▲ **Figure 1-10** Many of the Latin word parts used in science describe an organism's characteristics.

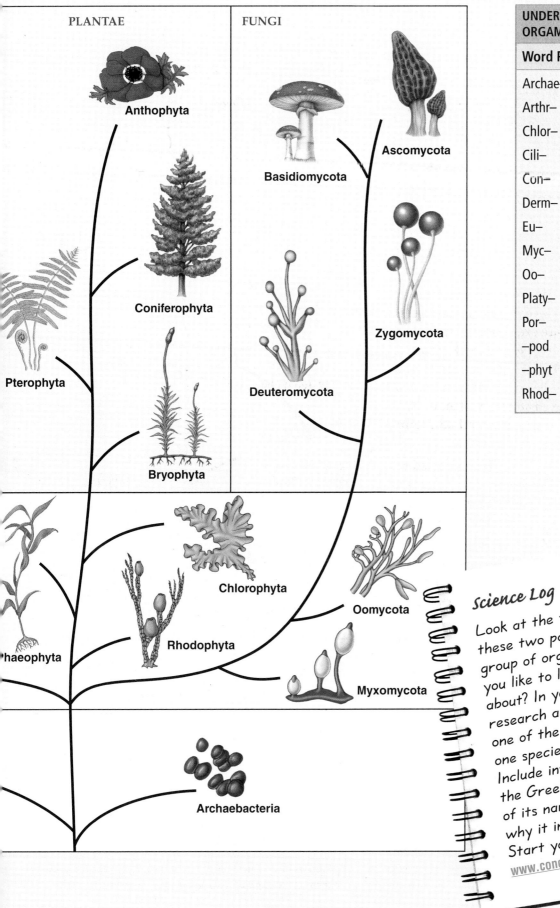

PLANTAE

Anthophyta

Coniferophyta

Pterophyta

Bryophyta

FUNGI

Basidiomycota

Ascomycota

Zygomycota

Deuteromycota

Chlorophyta

Oomycota

Rhodophyta

Myxomycota

Phaeophyta

Archaebacteria

| UNDERSTANDING ORGAMISM NAMES | |
| --- | --- |
| **Word Part** | **Meaning** |
| Archae– | Ancient |
| Arthr– | Joint |
| Chlor– | Green |
| Cili– | Small hair |
| Con– | Cone |
| Derm– | Skin |
| Eu– | True |
| Myc– | Fungus |
| Oo– | Water |
| Platy– | Flat |
| Por– | Pore |
| –pod | Foot |
| –phyt | Plant |
| Rhod– | Red |

# 1-4 What are viruses?

## Objective

Describe the structure of a virus.

## Key Terms

**virus** (VY-ruhs): nonliving particle made up of a piece of nucleic acid covered with a protein

**capsid** (KAP-sihd): protein covering of a virus

**bacteriophage** (bak-TIHR-ee-uh-fayj): virus that infects bacteria

**Viruses** A **virus** is a nonliving particle. It is very different from a living cell. A virus does not have any organelles. Viruses do not grow, take in food, or make waste. A virus is just a piece of nucleic acid covered with an outer coat of protein called a **capsid.** The capsid makes up most of the virus and gives it its shape. Some viruses are round. Others look like long rods, like the one in Figure 1-11. This virus attacks and destroys bacteria. A virus that infects bacterial cells is called a **bacteriophage.** Viruses depend on living cells in order to reproduce.

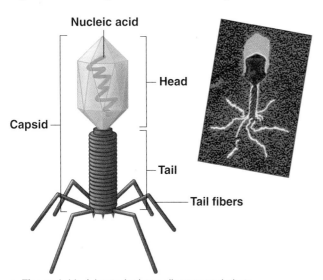

**Nucleic acid**

**Head**

**Capsid**

**Tail**

**Tail fibers**

▲ **Figure 1-11** A bacteriophage diagram and photo

▶ DEFINE: What is a capsid?

**Reproduction in Viruses** Even though they are not living, viruses are like living cells in one important way. They are able to reproduce more viruses. However, viruses can reproduce more viruses only inside a living cell.

Scientists first learned about reproduction in viruses by studying bacteriophages. Figure 1-12 shows a bacteriophage reproducing. When a bacteriophage attacks a bacterial cell, it uses special proteins in its tail fibers to attach itself to the surface of the cell. The virus then gives off enzymes, a type of chemical. The enzymes make a hole in the cell wall of the bacterium. The genetic material of the virus is injected into the cell through this hole. Once inside, the virus takes control of the cell. The genetic material from the virus directs the cell to make new virus parts. The parts form new viruses. The cell membrane bursts, releasing the new viruses. The new viruses attack other cells.

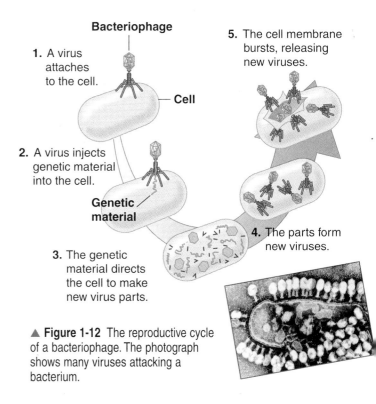

**Bacteriophage**

**1.** A virus attaches to the cell.

**Cell**

**2.** A virus injects genetic material into the cell.

**Genetic material**

**3.** The genetic material directs the cell to make new virus parts.

**5.** The cell membrane bursts, releasing new viruses.

**4.** The parts form new viruses.

▲ **Figure 1-12** The reproductive cycle of a bacteriophage. The photograph shows many viruses attacking a bacterium.

A virus can enter a cell and remain inactive, or dormant. However, when activated, the virus can cause disease. Have you ever had a cold sore? A cold sore is caused by a virus that may remain dormant in your cells for years.

When viruses leave the cell, the cell is often destroyed. This is what causes some infections in people with a cold or flu virus. Other kinds of viruses reproduce differently. For example, when the HIV virus takes over a cell, it can force the cell to release new viruses gradually by budding, without causing the cell to burst.

 **SEQUENCE:** What happens once a virus enters a living cell?

**Classifying Viruses** Because viruses do not have all the characteristics of living things, they are not classified in the five kingdom system. Scientists used to classify viruses based on which type of organism they infected. For example, there were plant viruses, animal viruses, and viruses that infect bacteria. Today scientists classify these viruses based on their shape and structure. There are three basic characteristics used to classify viruses. One is the structure of their capsid. Another characteristic is the type of nucleic acid they contain. Viruses can be DNA viruses or RNA viruses. The last characteristic is the way in which the virus reproduces.

Sometimes the common name of a virus is based on the disease that it causes. For example, the virus that causes the plant disease, tobacco mosaic disease, is called the tobacco mosaic virus. The common name for the virus that causes rabies is the rabies virus.

 **EXPLAIN:** How do scientists classify viruses?

 **CHECKING CONCEPTS**

1. A virus is a piece of _____ covered with a protein coat.
2. Scientists classify viruses based on their shape and _____.
3. A virus that infects a bacterial cell is called a _____.
4. Viruses can reproduce more viruses only inside ___ ___ cells.
5. Scientists first learned about reproduction in viruses by studying _____.

**THINKING CRITICALLY**

6. **CONTRAST:** How does a virus differ from a living cell?
7. **HYPOTHESIZE:** Why is it difficult to classify viruses?
8. **SEQUENCE:** List the steps of viral reproduction.

**HEALTH AND SAFETY TIP**

Viruses can be contagious. This means they can be spread from one organism to another. The common cold is caused by a virus. One way to keep from spreading it is to wash your hands often.

 *Hands-On Activity*

**MODELING A VIRUS**

*You will need a 5-inch dowel screw, 1 acorn nut that fits the screw, pliers, 3 pieces of metal wire, and a pipe cleaner.*

1. Screw the acorn nut onto the top of the screw.
2. Wrap the pipe cleaner around the middle of the screw.
3. Twist the 3 pieces of metal wire around the opposite end of the screw. Use the pliers to bend the ends of the wires down.

**Practicing Your Skills**

4. **IDENTIFY:** What type of virus does the model represent?
5. **IDENTIFY:** What kinds of organisms can be infected by the virus represented by the model?
6. **APPLY:** In which part of your model would the substance that enters living cells be contained?

▲ **STEP 3** Twist metal wire around the end of the screw.

## Chapter Summary

### Lesson 1-1

- Grouping things according to how they are alike is called **classification.**
- **Taxonomy** is the science of classifying living things.
- Classification is a way of organizing information about living things.
- Taxonomists use many features to classify living things.

### Lesson 1-2

- Organisms are classified into a series of groups or levels.
- The seven classification levels from largest to smallest are **kingdom, phylum,** class, order, family, **genus,** and **species.**
- A species is a group of organisms that look alike and can reproduce among themselves.
- The two parts of a scientific name include the genus and species names of an organism.

### Lesson 1-3

- Most scientists follow the five-kingdom classification system.
- As new information becomes available, the five-kingdom classification system may change.
- Organisms can be classified as either **monerans, protists, fungi,** plants, or animals.

### Lesson 1-4

- **Viruses** are made up of a strand of nucleic acid covered by a protein coat.
- **Capsids** give viruses their shape.
- Viruses can reproduce only inside a living cell.
- Once inside a living cell, the virus's genetic material takes control of the cell.
- Viruses are classified according to their shape and structure.

## Key Term Challenges

bacteriophage (p. 26)
capsid (p. 26)
classification (p. 16)
fungus (p. 22)
genus (p. 18)
kingdom (p. 18)
moneran (p. 22)
phylum (p. 18)
protist (p. 22)
species (p. 18)
taxonomy (p. 16)
virus (p. 26)

**MATCHING** Write the Key Term from above that best matches each description.

1. plantlike organisms that lack chlorophyll
2. virus that infects bacteria
3. way of grouping things together based on how they are similar
4. unicellular organisms that have a nucleus
5. protein covering of a virus
6. science of classifying things
7. classification group made up of related phyla
8. unicellular organism that does not have a real nucleus

**IDENTIFYING WORD RELATIONSHIPS** Explain how the words in each pair are related. Write your answers in complete sentences.

9. genus, species
10. classification, taxonomy
11. capsid, virus
12. kingdom, phylum

# Content Challenges TEST PREP

**MULTIPLE CHOICE** **Write the letter of the term or phrase that best completes each sentence.**

1. Grouping things according to how they are alike is
   a. taxonomy.
   b. classification.
   c. photosynthesis.
   d. organization.

2. Scientists first learned about viral reproduction by studying
   a. fungi.
   b. algae.
   c. bacteriophages.
   d. bacteria.

3. The largest classification group is the
   a. order.
   b. class.
   c. phylum.
   d. kingdom.

4. Today, most scientists accept a classification system with
   a. two kingdoms.
   b. three kingdoms.
   c. five kingdoms.
   d. seven kingdoms.

5. Organisms that look alike and can reproduce among themselves make up a
   a. species.
   b. genus.
   c. family.
   d. kingdom.

6. The kingdom made up of mostly single-celled organisms that have real nuclei is the
   a. plant kingdom.
   b. animal kingdom.
   c. fungi kingdom.
   d. protist kingdom.

7. The smallest classification group or level is a
   a. genus.
   b. species.
   c. class.
   d. kingdom.

8. Two groups of viruses are DNA viruses and
   a. capsid viruses.
   b. protist viruses.
   c. RNA viruses.
   d. yeast viruses.

9. Bacteria are
   a. monerans.
   b. protists.
   c. fungi.
   d. animals.

10. The two parts of a scientific name include the
    a. family and order names.
    b. genus and species names.
    c. kingdom and phylum names.
    d. class and order names.

**TRUE/FALSE** **Write *true* if the statement is true. If the statement is false, change the underlined term to make the statement true.**

11. Some scientists would like to make two kingdoms for <u>fungi</u>.

12. Taxonomy is the <u>study</u> of living things.

13. There are <u>ten</u> major classification groups for living things.

14. Dogs and wolves belong to the same <u>genus</u>.

15. Scientists who classify living things are <u>botanists</u>.

16. The protein covering of a virus is called a <u>capsid</u>.

# Concept Challenges TEST PREP

WRITTEN RESPONSE  Answer each of the following questions in complete sentences.

1. **ANALYZE:** If you were to discover a new species, how would you determine its classification?

2. **EXPLAIN:** Why is taxonomy a complex subject?

3. **HYPOTHESIZE:** Why is it difficult to treat an infection caused by a virus?

4. **LIST:** What do scientists use to classify an organism?

5. **ANALYZE:** Fungi were once called the nongreen plants. Why do you think fungi were described in this way?

INTERPRETING A DIAGRAM  Use Figure 1-13 to answer the following questions.

6. **IDENTIFY:** What is shown in the diagram?

7. **IDENTIFY:** What is the structure labeled *A* called?

8. **IDENTIFY:** What is the structure labeled *B* called?

9. **OBSERVE:** What is happening in Step 2?

10. **OBSERVE:** What is happening in Step 5?

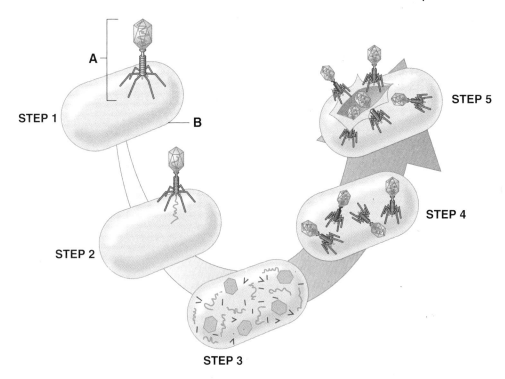

▲ **Figure 1-13** Virus reproduction

# Chapter 2 Simple Organisms

▲ **Figure 2-1** Diatoms come in many interesting shapes and patterns.

Diatoms are microscopic organisms that live in water. These organisms are capable of making their own food through photosynthesis. Diatoms have shells made of silica, a component of glass. When diatoms die, their shells fall to the bottom of the ocean and form layers of material called diatomaceous earth, or DE. This material is a rough powder because of the silica shells. DE is mined for use in many products, such as cleaning products, filters, and even toothpaste!

▶ Why do you think DE would be used in toothpaste?

## Contents

2-1    What is the Kingdom Monera?

2-2    Why do scientists study bacteria?

2-3    What is the Kingdom Protista?

■    **Lab Activity:** Examining Life in Pond Water

2-4    What are algae and slime molds?

2-5    What is the Kingdom Fungi?

■    **The Big Idea:** What simple organisms exist in our daily lives?

2-6    How do yeasts and molds reproduce?

# 2-1 What is the Kingdom Monera?

## Objectives
Describe a bacterium. Classify bacteria by shape.

## Key Terms
**coccus** (KAHK-uhs), *pl.* **cocci:** spherical-shaped bacterium

**spirillum** (spy-RIHL-uhm), *pl.* **spirilla:** spiral-shaped bacterium

**bacillus** (buh-SIHL-uhs), *pl.* **bacilli:** rod-shaped bacterium

**flagellum** (fluh-JEHL-uhm), *pl.* **flagella:** whiplike structure on a cell

**endospore:** inactive bacterium surrounded by a thick wall

**Kingdom Monera** Bacteria are simple, one-celled organisms. They are only visible under a microscope. A bacterial cell is made up of cytoplasm, a cell membrane, and a cell wall. It does not have a nucleus. The genetic material of a bacterial cell is in a ring located in the cytoplasm. Bacteria usually reproduce asexually, by means of binary fission. The Kingdom Monera includes all bacteria.

**1** ▶ COMPARE: How is a bacterial cell different from an animal cell?

**Grouping Bacteria** Bacteria are grouped according to their shapes. Some bacteria are round and look like tiny beads. Bacteria with a round, or spherical, shape are called **cocci** (KAHK-sy). Cocci often grow in pairs, chains, or large clusters that look like a bunch of grapes. Other types of bacteria are curved or shaped like a spiral. Many of these bacteria are called **spirilla.** The most common kind of bacteria are shaped like rods. These bacteria are called **bacilli.** Bacilli may grow in pairs or in chains.

**2** ▶ IDENTIFY: What are the three shapes of bacteria?

**Movement in Bacteria** Some bacilli and spirilla have a whiplike structure called a **flagellum.** By moving their flagellum, these bacteria can move through liquids. Cocci cannot move on their own because they do not have flagella.

**3** ▶ DESCRIBE: How do bacilli move?

**Needs of Bacteria** Many bacteria need water and the proper temperature to be active. Most bacteria thrive in darkness. Some bacteria need oxygen. Others can live without oxygen.

Some bacteria get their food by living inside plants or animals. Most bacteria feed on the remains of dead plants and animals. The bacteria break down and absorb nutrients found in the body of the dead plant or animal. Other bacteria can use sunlight to make their own food.

Certain bacteria can live through periods of extreme heat or cold. When their environments are not ideal, these bacteria form protective walls around themselves. A bacterium with a protective wall is called an **endospore.** When the

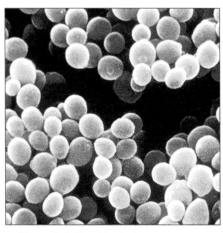

▲ **Figure 2-2** Cocci bacteria

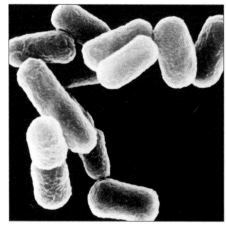

▲ **Figure 2-3** Bacilli bacteria

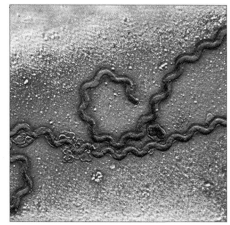

▲ **Figure 2-4** Spirilla bacteria

environment becomes favorable, the endospore breaks open. The bacterium becomes active again.

 **IDENTIFY:** What is an endospore?

**Unusual Bacteria** Blue-green bacteria, also known as cyanobacteria, are unusual bacteria. Like plants, blue-green bacteria contain the green pigment chlorophyll that is needed for photosynthesis. They use sunlight to make their own food.

Some bacteria live in very extreme environments, such as hot springs or very salty waters. They are called archaebacteria. Archaebacteria have been found near underwater structures called deep-sea vents. These bacteria make their own food through a process similar to photosynthesis. Archaebacteria live off the chemicals released by the vents rather than from energy found in sunlight. Archaebacteria are thought to be the most primitive type of bacteria. Some scientists place archaebacteria in their own kingdom.

 **EXPLAIN:** Why can blue-green bacteria make their own food?

## ✔ CHECKING CONCEPTS

1. Bacteria are simple, _____ organisms.
2. A bacterial cell does not contain a _____.
3. Whiplike structures that help a bacterium move in liquids are called _____.
4. A bacterium with a protective wall is called an _____.
5. The most primitive bacteria are called _____.

## 💡 THINKING CRITICALLY

6. **INFER:** One kind of bacteria feeds on the remains of dead plants. Are these likely to be blue-green bacteria?
7. **PREDICT:** The Dead Sea is one of the saltiest bodies of water on Earth. What type of bacteria do you think would be found here?

## BUILDING LANGUAGE ARTS SKILLS

***Using Word Parts*** Look up the prefixes "*diplo-*," "*staphylo-*," and "*strepto-*" in the dictionary. Then, use the prefixes to define the following terms: *diplobacillus, streptococcus,* and *staphylococcus.*

 *People in Science*
## DISEASE DETECTIVES

Many diseases are caused by bacteria. Scientists who study bacteria are called bacteriologists. Many bacteriologists work on controlling the spread of diseases such as tuberculosis and meningitis. They also try to prevent health problems like asthma. To do this, they must first determine the particular bacterium that causes the disease. They also must study how people catch or develop these illnesses.

Louise McFarland worked as a "disease detective" for the Louisiana Office of Public Health for forty years. As a public health scientist, she studied ways to prevent the spread of illnesses in her state. She collected information on outbreaks of disease and met with other scientists. McFarland was particularly interested in controlling infectious diseases in day care settings. McFarland also helped state officials cope with outbreaks of hepatitis, a disease of the liver, and malaria, a disease spread by mosquitoes.

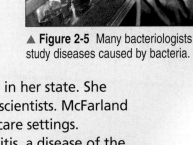
▲ **Figure 2-5** Many bacteriologists study diseases caused by bacteria.

**Thinking Critically** Why is it important to know how diseases are spread?

# 2-2 Why do scientists study bacteria?

## Objective

Explain how some bacteria are useful and others are harmful.

## Key Terms

**bacteriology** (bak-tihr-ee-AHL-uh-jee)**:** study of bacteria

**decomposition:** breakdown of dead material by simple organisms

**Bacteriology** In the mid-1800s, the French scientist Louis Pasteur showed the importance of bacteria. Pasteur proved that bacteria cause many diseases. He started the new science of **bacteriology**, or the study of bacteria. Pasteur is often called the father of bacteriology.

**1** IDENTIFY: Who discovered the importance of bacteria?

**Bacteria and Foods** Many food products are made with the help of bacteria. For example, the action of certain bacteria gives flavor to butter. Other types of bacteria are used to make buttermilk, yogurt, cheese, and sauerkraut. Bacteria play an important part in the digestion of the food you eat. Your digestive tract contains billions of bacteria that help digest nutrients. Some digestive bacteria even help in the formation of important vitamins.

◀ **Figure 2-6** Bacteria are used to create different kinds of cheese.

**2** LIST: Name three foods made by using bacteria.

**Bacteria and Soil** Plants need nitrogen to make proteins. Most of the air is nitrogen. However, plants and animals cannot use nitrogen directly from the air. Plants can only use nitrogen that has been combined with other elements. Bacteria in soil and in the roots of some plants change nitrogen into compounds plants can use. These bacteria are called nitrogen-fixing bacteria. The "fixed" nitrogen is taken in and used by plants. Animals get the nitrogen they need by eating plants.

▲ **Figure 2-7** Some bacteria in the roots of plants are nitrogen-fixing bacteria.

Bacteria are also important to the soil for another reason. Bacteria break down dead materials such as leaves and animal wastes. Bacteria then turn this material into useable organic compounds. This process is called **decomposition.** Decomposition is important because it puts important nutrients back into the soil.

▲ **Figure 2-8** Bacteria break down, or decompose, dead materials.

**3** EXPLAIN: Why do living things need nitrogen?

**Bacterial Diseases** Some types of bacteria can be harmful. Blight is a plant disease sometimes caused by bacteria. Blight makes the flowers, young leaves, and stems of a plant die quickly. Rot is another plant disease often caused by bacteria. Rot destroys the cell walls of plant tissues. Millions of dollars are lost each year from crop damage caused by these bacterial diseases.

Bacteria can also cause diseases in animals, including humans. Strep throat, tuberculosis, anthrax, and some kinds of pneumonia are just a few examples of diseases caused by bacteria. Lyme disease is also caused by bacteria. The bacterium *Borella burgdorferi* is transmitted to humans by the deer tick. If you are bitten by a tick, you may get the disease. The symptoms of Lyme disease include swollen and painful joints.

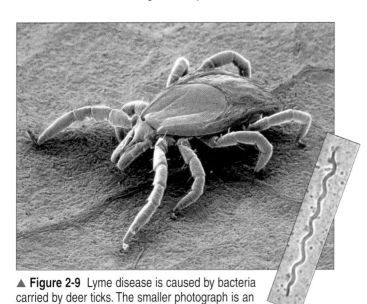

▲ **Figure 2-9** Lyme disease is caused by bacteria carried by deer ticks. The smaller photograph is an SEM picture of the bacterium *Borella burgdorferi*.

▶4 **DESCRIBE:** What effect does rot have on a plant?

**Bacteria and Food Decay** Bacteria can cause foods to spoil or decay. Some bacteria produce poisons while they are acting on food. Cooking foods thoroughly at high temperatures kills harmful bacteria. Canning, pickling, and freezing food are other ways of preventing or slowing down the action of harmful bacteria.

Sometimes heating and canning are not enough. Eating foods that contain bacterial poisons can make you very sick. The bacteria that causes the disease botulism can withstand the canning process by forming endospores. After the canned food has cooled, the bacteria can become active again. One sign of this harmful bacterium is bulging or exploded cans.

▶5 **INFER:** Why are many foods refrigerated?

## ☑ CHECKING CONCEPTS

1. The study of bacteria is called _____.
2. Bacteria in the digestive tract can help digest ____ _____.
3. Bacteria that can change nitrogen from the air into compounds that plants can use are called _____.
4. The plant disease that causes flowers, young leaves, and stems to die quickly is called _____.
5. Some bacteria produce _____ while acting on foods.

## 💡 THINKING CRITICALLY

6. **INFER:** What should you do if you have a sealed can of food that is bulging?
7. **EXPLAIN:** Foods that are canned are cooked at high temperatures and pressures, and then placed in airtight containers. What effect do these actions have on the food?
8. **APPLY:** Identify three ways that bacteria affect your life.

## Web InfoSearch

**Pasteurization** Pasteurization is a process used to slow down the spoiling of milk and other dairy products. Pasteurized milk that is kept refrigerated is safe to drink for many days.

**SEARCH:** Use the Internet to find out more about the process of pasteurization. List and describe each step of the process in a report or flow chart. Begin your search at www.conceptsandchallenges.com. Some key words are **pasteurization** and **dairy science**.

# 2-3 What is the Kingdom Protista?

## Objective
Identify some common protists and how they move.

## Key Terms
**protozoan** (proht-uh-ZOH-uhn): one-celled, animal-like protist

**pseudopod** (SOO-doh-pahd): fingerlike extension of cytoplasm

**cilium** (SIHL-ee-uhm), *pl.* **cilia**: tiny, hairlike structures

**Kingdom Protista** Kingdom Protista, or the protist kingdom, is made up of very simple organisms. Most protists are unicellular. A few kinds are multicellular. A protist cell has a nucleus surrounded by a membrane. The protist kingdom is divided into three large groups. The three groups are the protozoans, the algae, and the slime molds. These groups are made up of many different phyla of organisms.

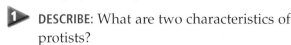 **DESCRIBE:** What are two characteristics of protists?

**Animal-like Protists** **Protozoans** are one-celled, or unicellular, organisms. They often are called the animal-like protists because they cannot make their own food. They need to get food by eating other organisms. Most protozoans can move about on their own. Amoebas, paramecia, and trypanosomes are all examples of animal-like protists.

**2 LIST:** Name three animal-like protists.

**Amoeba** An amoeba is a protozoan. Most amoeba live in fresh water. They have fingerlike projections of cytoplasm called **pseudopods.** The cell membrane of an amoeba is very flexible, so the pseudopods can stretch and shrink. An amoeba uses its pseudopods to move through water and to trap and take in food. When the amoeba approaches a food particle, its pseudopods surround the particle and form a food vacuole around it.

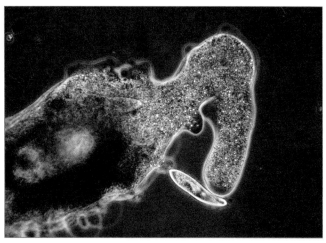
▲ **Figure 2-10** This amoeba is about to eat a paramecium.

**3 EXPLAIN:** How are pseudopods beneficial to the amoeba?

**Paramecium** A paramecium is a slipper-shaped protozoan. Like an amoeba, a paramecium lives in fresh water. It is part of a phylum of protozoa that use **cilia** for movement. Cilia are tiny, hairlike structures that move. They are found around the edge of the paramecium. The cilia move back and forth like tiny oars. The beating of cilia moves a paramecium through water.

The cilia also help the paramecium get food. When the paramecium finds food, the moving cilia create a current in the water. This current moves the food particles down into a mouthlike structure called an oral groove.

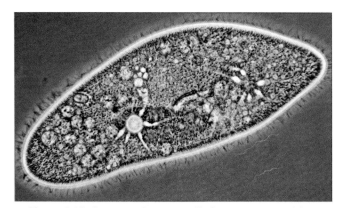
▲ **Figure 2-11** A paramecium uses cilia for movement and for capturing food.

**4 IDENTIFY:** What structures does a paramecium use to move?

**Trypanosomes** A trypanosome is a disease-causing protozoan. In humans, it causes a disease called African sleeping sickness. Trypanosomes also cause diseases in horses and cattle. Trypanosomes are part of a group of protozoa with flagella. The common name for this group is the flagellates. Some flagellates have one flagellum. Others have two or more flagella.

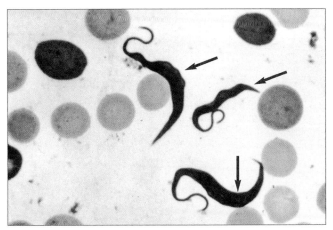

▲ **Figure 2-12** Trypanosomes (shown with arrows) are protozoans that cause African sleeping sickness.

 **NAME:** How do flagellates move?

 **CHECKING CONCEPTS**

1. Protozoans, algae, and slime molds are all classified in the _____ kingdom.
2. Amoebas move by extending their _____.
3. A paramecium moves by beating the _____ that extend from its surface.
4. Protozoa with flagella are called _____.
5. Sleeping sickness is caused by a _____.

**THINKING CRITICALLY**

6. **ANALYZE:** Why is it important that protozoans have structures that help them move?
7. **COMPARE:** How are flagella and cilia alike?

**BUILDING SCIENCE SKILLS**

*Modeling* Make a model of one of the three protozoans described in this lesson. Make sure your model shows the structures that the organism uses for movement and capturing food. Present your model to the class.

## Integrating Earth Science

**TOPICS:** sediments

### WHITE CLIFFS OF DOVER

The Strait of Dover is a narrow body of water that connects the English Channel with the North Sea. Both English and French shores of the strait are formed mainly by chalk cliffs. The most famous of these cliffs may be the White Cliffs of Dover in southeast England.

▲ **Figure 2-13** The White Cliffs of Dover, in the larger picture, are made from the shells of the foraminifera, shown in the smaller picture.

The chalk cliffs were formed during the Cretaceous Period, about 100 million years ago. At that time, Earth's climate was warmer and sea levels were much higher. Warm seas covered most of Europe, providing an ideal place for protozoans to live. Protozoa that still flourish there are called foraminifera. Some of these protists have tiny shells made of calcium carbonate ($CaCO_3$). When these protists die, their shells sink to the ocean bottom as fine sediment. Gradually, this sediment builds up to become hundreds of meters thick. The thick sediment eventually is compressed to form solid white rock cliffs.

**Thinking Critically** Why do you think the cliffs of Dover are white?

# LAB ACTIVITY
## Examining Life in Pond Water

### Materials
Safety goggles
Lab apron
1 Microscope
1 Slide
1 Cover slip
Pond water
1 Eye dropper
Methyl cellulose
1 Toothpick

### BACKGROUND

A sample of water taken from a stream, pond, or lake may contain hundreds of living organisms. Many of the organisms belong to the Kingdom Protista. Most protists are too small to see with your eyes alone. You can use a microscope to observe these organisms.

### PURPOSE

In this activity you will observe the structure and behavior of several organisms found in pond water by using a microscope.

### PROCEDURE

1. Put on goggles. Using an eye dropper or pipette, place 1 to 2 drops of pond water onto a clean slide. ⚠ CAUTION: Be careful when handling the slide.

2. Add a drop of methyl cellulose to the sample. Use a toothpick to carefully mix the methyl cellulose with the pond water. This substance forms a thick mixture with water and slows down the movement of organisms swimming in it.

3. Gently place a cover slip on top of your slide. Try not to get any air bubbles under the cover slip.

4. Place the slide onto the stage of your microscope. Secure the slide with the stage clips. Make sure to use the lowest power objective lens.

5. Focus the microscope using the coarse and fine adjustment knobs. Do you see any living things? How do you know they are alive? Copy the chart in Figure 2-14 onto a sheet of paper. Record your observations in this chart.

6. Try to identify each of the organisms in your sample. Base your decision on shape, structure, and movement. Record whether they are plantlike or animal-like protists in your chart. Use your science book or other references if you need to.

▲ **STEP 1** Place a drop of pond water on a slide.

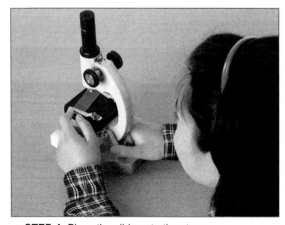

▲ **STEP 4** Place the slide onto the stage.

7. Move the high power objective lens into place. ⚠ CAUTION: Be sure the objective does not touch the slide. Focus the microscope using the fine adjustment knob only. For a review of microscope use, see Appendix C.

8. Observe the pond water sample under high power. What can you see now that you could not see before? Record your observations in your chart.

9. Draw several of the organisms in your pond water sample. Make sure your drawing shows the correct shape, structure, and color of each organism.

▲ STEP 8 Observe the pond water under high power.

| Magnification | General Observations | Plantlike Organisms | Animal-like Organisms |
|---|---|---|---|
| Low power | | | |
| High power | | | |

▲ Figure 2-14 Copy this chart onto a sheet of paper.

## CONCLUSIONS

1. **OBSERVE:** How many different types of organisms did you observe?

2. **COMPARE:** How were the organisms you observed alike? How were they different?

3. **CLASSIFY:** List the types of organisms you observed. Provide reasons for placing organisms in certain groups.

4. **CALCULATE:** Include the power of magnification next to each of your drawings. To calculate the power of magnification, multiply the magnification of the eyepiece by the magnification of the objective lens the organism was viewed under. The formula is eyepiece × objective = total power of magnification.

# 2-4 What are algae and slime molds?

## Objective

Identify and describe different kinds of algae.

## Key Term

**plankton** (PLANK-tuhn): microscopic organisms that float on or near the water's surface

**Algae** Algae are classified in the protist kingdom. Some algae are unicellular. Others are multicellular. All algae contain chlorophyll. Because they have chlorophyll, algae can make their own food through photosynthesis. For this reason, algae are sometimes called plantlike protists.

▶ 1 **COMPARE:** How are algae and plants alike?

**Unicellular Algae** Some kinds of algae are made up of only one cell. Most unicellular algae live in a watery environment. They float on the surface of the water. Some of these unicellular algae are part of plankton. **Plankton** is any collection of microscopic organisms that float on or near the surface of the oceans. Diatoms are a type of unicellular algae that make up a large percent of the world's plankton. Diatoms have an unusual geometric shape.

Although all algae have chlorophyll, not all kinds of algae are green. Fire algae are unicellular algae that are red in color. Golden-brown algae can have a color ranging from yellowish-green to golden-brown. These differences in color are due to the pigments, or colorings, in the algae.

▶ 2 **IDENTIFY:** What is plankton?

**Euglena** The euglena is a unicellular alga. It is both plantlike and animal-like. The euglena is so unique that it has its own phylum within the protist kingdom. Like all algae, the euglena contains chlorophyll. It uses the chlorophyll to carry out photosynthesis. A structure in the euglena called the eyespot can detect light. The euglena uses its eyespot to find light in the water. The euglena then moves to the light by beating the flagellum that extends from its body. When light is not available, the euglena can also take in food.

The euglena also has a flexible outer covering. This allows it to change shape.

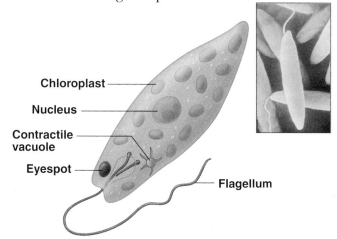

Chloroplast — Nucleus — Contractile vacuole — Eyespot — Flagellum

▲ **Figure 2-15** The euglena, shown in the photograph, contains chloroplasts used during photosynthesis.

▶ 3 **EXPLAIN:** How is the euglena animal-like?

**Multicellular Algae** Some kinds of algae are made up of many cells. These are the multicellular algae. Pigments in multicellular algae may give them a green, red, or brown coloring. Many green algae live in fresh water.

Red and brown algae live in the ocean. Brown algae often are called seaweed or kelp. Brown algae grow to be the largest of all algae. If you have visited a beach, you may have seen brown algae washed up along the shoreline.

▲ **Figure 2-16** Kelp can grow to heights of more than 100 meters.

▶ 4 **INFER:** Why are some types of algae a color other than green?

**Slime Molds** The protist kingdom also contains several funguslike organisms. These protists are multicellular. Two examples of funguslike protists are the slime molds and the water molds. Slime molds can be found living in moist soil or on rotting logs. Some slime molds are bright yellow or red in color. Water molds can be found in lakes and ponds. They can also be found on diseased aquarium fish. Many water molds are parasites, or live off other organisms.

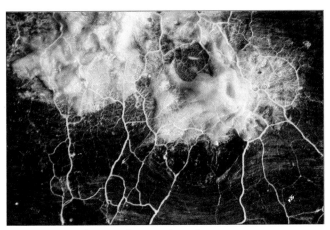

▲ **Figure 2-17** Slime molds grow in moist areas.

 **CONTRAST:** How are slime molds and water molds different?

☑ **CHECKING CONCEPTS**

1. Algae make their own food through _____.
2. Plants and algae both contain the green pigment _____.
3. A euglena uses its _____ to detect light.
4. The largest kind of algae is _____.

**THINKING CRITICALLY**

5. **COMPARE:** How is a euglena similar to a trypanosome?
6. **HYPOTHESIZE:** Where would you go to collect a water sample that contained both algae and protozoans? Explain.

**DESIGNING AN EXPERIMENT**

*Design an experiment to solve the following problem. Include a hypothesis, variables, a procedure, and the type of data to be collected.*

**PROBLEM:** Autotrophs are organisms that can make their own food during photosynthesis. Heterotrophs must take in food. How can you prove that the euglena can be considered both an autotroph and a heterotroph?

---

## Integrating Earth Science

**TOPIC: pollution**

### ALGAL BLOOMS

Algae make their own food by photosynthesis. For photosynthesis to occur, chlorophyll, sunlight, and carbon dioxide must be present. Algae also need water and other nutrients, such as nitrogen, to carry out their life processes. When all of these elements are present, algae can reproduce quickly and in large numbers. A sudden large growth of algae is called an algal bloom.

▲ **Figure 2-18** Algal blooms can be caused by green algae such as the spirogyra shown in the circle.

Algal blooms often occur when wastes such as fertilizers and detergents are dumped into ponds or lakes. These products contain the nutrients that allow the algae to reproduce quickly. Algal blooms can be very harmful to the organisms that live in the lake or pond. Bacteria use oxygen in the water to help them break down dead algae. If the bacteria use too much oxygen, other organisms in the water do not have enough oxygen to survive. As a result, these organisms die.

**Thinking Critically** How do you think unwanted algal blooms could be prevented?

# 2-5 What is the Kingdom Fungi?

## Observing the Structure of Mushrooms
### HANDS-ON ACTIVITY

STEP 3

1. Examine the structure of three to six different kinds of mushrooms, such as white button, shiitake, and portobello.
2. Record your observations in your notebook.
3. Use a hand lens to examine the underside of the top cap of each mushroom.
4. Describe the appearance. Draw and label each mushroom in your notebook.

**THINK ABOUT IT:** How are mushrooms similar to plants? How are they different from plants?

## Objective

Describe the different kinds of fungi.

## Key Terms

**stalk:** stemlike part of a mushroom

**cap:** umbrella-shaped top of a mushroom

**hypha** (HY-fuh), *pl.* **hyphae** (HY-fee): threadlike structure that makes up the body of molds and mushrooms

**gills:** structures in a mushroom that produce spores

**spore:** reproductive structure in fungi

**fermentation:** process by which a cell releases energy from food without using oxygen

**Kingdom Fungi** Fungi are like plants in some ways. The cells of fungi have cell walls. Many fungi also are multicellular, or many-celled, organisms. Like most plants, fungi grow well in soil. For these reasons, scientists once classified fungi in the plant kingdom.

Later, scientists discovered that fungi and plants are not really very much alike. The cells of fungi do not have chloroplasts or chlorophyll. Therefore, fungi cannot make their own food as plants do. Fungi usually get the food they need from dead and decaying organisms. They grow well in dark, warm, and wet places. Today, scientists classify fungi in a kingdom of their own. The fungi kingdom includes yeasts, molds, and mushrooms.

▷ **DESCRIBE:** Where do fungi usually grow?

**Mushrooms** You probably know a mushroom when you see one because of its shape. The stemlike part of a mushroom is called the **stalk.** At the top of the stalk is an umbrella-shaped top, or **cap.** The body of a mushroom is made up of threadlike structures called **hyphae.** The underside of the cap is lined with **gills.** The gills are made of many hyphae tightly packed together. The gills produce spores. **Spores** are the reproductive structures of mushrooms. They are light in weight and easily carried by wind and water, or on the bodies of insects.

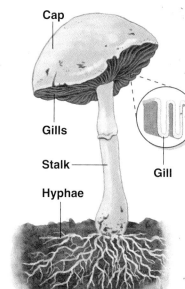

Cap

Gills

Stalk

Hyphae

Gill

▲ **Figure 2-19** A mushroom

▷ **INFER:** What is the job of the stalk of a mushroom?

**Molds** Molds are a common kind of fungi. They grow on bread, fruits, vegetables, and even leather. Most molds look like a mass of threads. These threads are the hyphae. The hyphae in molds are not as closely packed together as in mushrooms. If you look closely at a bread mold, you will see hyphae growing along the surface of the bread. The hyphae in bread mold are not divided into separate cells. Instead, each strand has many nuclei.

 **COMPARE:** How are molds different from mushrooms?

**Yeasts** Yeasts are colorless, unicellular fungi. Yeast cells are surrounded by a cell membrane and a cell wall. The cell contains cytoplasm and a nucleus. Yeasts grow well where sugar is present. They use the sugar for food. Yeasts are used to make bread rise. As yeast cells break down sugar, bubbles of carbon dioxide gas form. This causes the dough to rise. This process is called fermentation. **Fermentation** is a type of cellular respiration that takes place without oxygen.

 **DESCRIBE:** What structures are found in a yeast cell?

## ✔ CHECKING CONCEPTS

1. What are three kinds of fungi?
2. Why is it that fungi cannot make their own food?
3. Which fungi are colorless and unicellular?
4. Where are the gills of a mushroom located?

5. What are the reproductive structures of a mushroom?
6. Where are spores produced in mushrooms?

 ## THINKING CRITICALLY

7. **INFER:** A mushroom may develop hundreds of kilometers away from the parent mushroom. How might this happen?
8. **HYPOTHESIZE:** Mushrooms produce a large number of spores. Why is the ground not covered with mushrooms?

## HEALTH AND SAFETY TIP

Never eat mushrooms that you find growing outdoors. Many mushrooms are poisonous and can be deadly if consumed. The Amanita mushroom can destroy the human liver in one week. Poisonous mushrooms and edible mushrooms look very similar. Use library references to find out the names of three kinds of poisonous mushrooms. Then, draw a picture of each type. Identify any unique trait for each poisonous mushroom you choose.

 *Real-Life Science*

## FUNGAL INFECTIONS

Some fungi can cause infections and diseases in people, animals, and plants. Chemical preparations called fungicides are used to prevent or cure diseases caused by fungi. Athlete's foot is a common infection caused by fungi. Fungal diseases are a concern for humans not only because they attack us, but because they attack our food crops as well.

Many types of fungi are plant pathogens, which means they attack and destroy plants. Wheat can suffer from a fungal infection called wheat rust. Corn plants can become infected with a fungus that causes corn smut. This fungus attacks the corn kernels, causing them to expand and burst. Other fungi destroy important food crops such as peaches, onions, squash, and tomatoes. These fungal infections can spread very quickly and cause substantial damage to crops. Scientists are researching ways to prevent or slow down these infections.

▲ Figure 2-20 Corn smut

**Thinking Critically** What are some ways to reduce possible fungal infections without using fungicides?

# THE Big IDEA

## What simple organisms exist in our daily lives?

From the time we are very young, we learn about safety in the kitchen, such as being careful with knives or staying away from hot ovens. Harmful microorganisms pose a different danger in the kitchen. You can become very sick if you eat food that harbors certain types of bacteria or protozoans.

Whereas some bacteria and fungi play a helpful role in producing or flavoring foods like cheese and yogurt, others can cause foods to spoil or decay. Some bacteria produce toxins while they are acting on food. They can be present in raw eggs, meat, and shellfish. Eating them can cause digestive problems. Some people can get very sick or die.

Protozoans have also been known to cause disease in humans. Parasitic protozoans can be spread to humans through contaminated water or foods. Many times these harmful protozoans are found on vegetables or fruits that have been fertilized with manure or washed with contaminated water.

Most illnesses caused by microorganisms in foods can be prevented. The key is to kill or slow the action of the bacteria. You can do this by following basic rules for food safety.

Look at the text and photos that appear on this page and the next. They point out helpful and harmful simple organisms. Follow the directions in the science log to learn more about "the big idea." ◆

### Mold in Cheese

Bacteria and molds are used to ripen cheeses. *Penicillium roqueforti* is a mold like the one shown here. It causes the blue veins in Roquefort cheese. Bacteria are responsible for the holes in Swiss cheese. The bacteria give off gases that produce the holes.

### Bacteria in Yogurt

Two types of bacteria are needed to convert milk into yogurt. One is called *Streptococcus thermophilus*. The other is *Lactobacillus bulgaricus* (shown below). Evidence suggests that live bacteria in yogurt aid digestion. Researchers are still studying other possible health benefits.

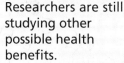
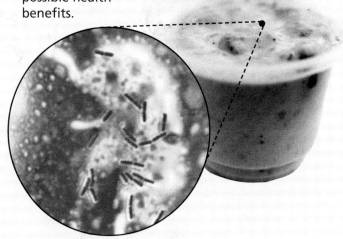

## Basic Rules for Food Safety

1. Wash foods thoroughly.
2. Keep cold foods cold and hot foods hot.
3. Cook foods to the proper temperature.
4. Clean hands and surfaces with hot soapy water.
5. Keep raw meat, eggs, and seafood away from foods that are ready to eat.

## Red Algae in Ice Cream

Many desserts such as ice cream and frozen yogurt contain an ingredient called carageenan. Carageenan is a sticky substance that coats the cells of some types of red algae like the *Euchema* algae shown below. Carageenan gives ice cream a smooth, creamy texture.

## Protozoa in Water

The protozoan *Giardia lamblia*, shown here is found in some streams, lakes, and reservoirs. Drinking water contaminated with this organism can lead to intestinal problems. Water treatment facilities destroy harmful organisms, providing safe drinking water. It can be dangerous to drink water that hasn't been treated.

### WRITING ACTIVITY

### science Log

If you owned a restaurant or food store, how would you make sure your customers were safe from harmful microorganisms? Research safety precautions used in the food industry. Write a plan for your business that maintains high safety standards. Start your search at www.conceptsandchallenges.com.

# 2-6 How do yeasts and molds reproduce?

## Objective

Compare and contrast reproduction of yeasts and molds.

## Key Terms

**budding:** kind of asexual reproduction in which a new organism forms from a bud on a parent

**spore case:** structure that contains spores

**sporulation** (spawr-yoo-LAY-shuhn)**:** kind of asexual reproduction in which a new organism forms from spores released from a parent

**Budding**   One kind of asexual reproduction is **budding**. In budding, a new cell is formed from a tiny bud on a parent cell. Most yeasts reproduce by budding. During budding, the cell wall of the parent cell pushes outwards. This is the beginning of the bud. The cell nucleus moves toward the bud. The nucleus divides. One nucleus moves into the bud. The other nucleus stays in the parent cell. The bud remains attached to the parent cell and grows larger. In time, a cell wall forms between the parent cell and the bud. The bud breaks away from the parent cell and develops into a mature yeast cell.

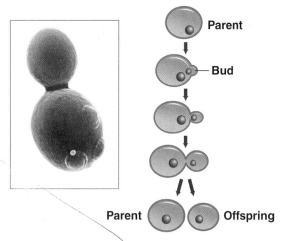

▲ Figure 2-21 Budding in yeast

**1** ▶ CLASSIFY: By what kind of asexual reproduction do yeast cells reproduce?

**Sporulation**   Have you ever seen mold growing on bread? It looks like tangled cotton. Many parts of it are black or gray. Under the low power of a microscope, bread mold looks like many tiny threads. On the top of some of the threads you will see a ball. This is the **spore case.** Each spore case holds thousands of spores.

When a spore case breaks, thousands of microscopic spores are released. Each spore can eventually grow into a new mold offspring if it lands in a warm and moist environment. This kind of reproduction is called **sporulation.** Sporulation is another kind of asexual reproduction. It produces many more offspring than budding does.

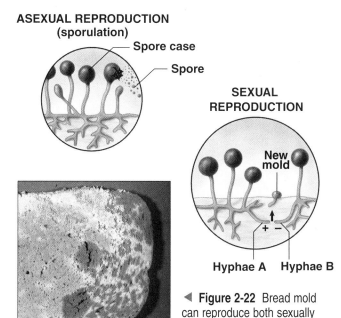

◀ Figure 2-22 Bread mold can reproduce both sexually and asexually.

**2** ▶ CLASSIFY: What kind of reproduction is sporulation?

**Sexual Reproduction in Fungi**   Fungi do not always reproduce asexually. Sometimes molds and mushrooms can reproduce sexually. This type of reproduction occurs when the hyphae of two different molds come into contact with each other as shown in Figure 2-22.

Mushrooms can also reproduce sexually. When the underground hyphae of one mushroom comes into contact with the hyphae of another mushroom, the nucleus of one hypha can combine with the nucleus of another hypha. This produces a new cell with genetic information from both mushrooms. This cell can eventually grow into a new mushroom.

 **COMPARE:** Compare the two types of reproduction in fungi.

**Mold and Penicillin** In 1928, a scientist named Alexander Fleming accidentally discovered a mold that could destroy many different kinds of bacteria. Fleming had set aside a dish containing bacteria and forgot to throw it away. A mold called penicillium grew in the dish. Surprisingly, no bacteria were found growing near the mold. Penicillium reproduces asexually by producing spores. As the mold grows, it produces a chemical that kills bacteria. This is why there were no bacteria growing near the mold. The chemical produced by penicillium is used to make the antibiotic penicillin. Penicillin is one of the most common medicines used today.

 **EXPLAIN:** Why do you think Fleming's discovery was important?

 **CHECKING CONCEPTS**

1. What are two ways that fungi can reproduce?
2. What fungus reproduces by budding?
3. How many spores are inside a spore case?
4. What is budding?
5. Which type of reproduction is sporulation?

**THINKING CRITICALLY**

6. **COMPARE:** How is the reproduction of mushrooms similar to that of mold?
7. **HYPOTHESIZE:** Why do you think molds are not growing all over everything around you?
8. **EXPLAIN:** How do mushrooms reproduce?
9. **INFER:** Why do you think sporulation produces more offspring than budding?

**INTERPRETING VISUALS**

Use Figure 2-22 to answer the following question.
10. **INFER:** Why does sporulation produce more offspring than sexual reproduction?

 *Hands-On Activity*

**GROWING MOLD**

*You will need three plastic containers with covers, damp paper towels, a hand lens, a slice of bread made without preservatives, an orange rind, and a slice of potato.*

1. Line the bottom of each container with damp paper towels. Place the bread in one container, the orange in another container, and the potato slice in the third container.
2. Store the containers in a dark place for a few days.
3. Use the hand lens to observe the changes in each food sample. Draw a diagram to show the structures you see.

▲ **STEP 1** Place the orange in the container.

**Practicing Your Skills**

4. **IDENTIFY:** On which food samples did mold grow?
5. **OBSERVE:** Are the molds all the same color? Describe the color of each mold.
6. **INFER:** What do the differences in color tell you about the molds?
7. **INFER:** What conditions were needed to grow molds?
8. **HYPOTHESIZE:** How could the food samples have been protected from mold growth?

# Chapter 2 Challenges

## Chapter Summary

### Lesson 2-1
- All bacteria are classified in the Kingdom Monera.
- Bacterial cells have cytoplasm, a cell membrane, and a cell wall. They do not have a nucleus.
- An **endospore** is a bacterium covered by a protective outer wall.

### Lesson 2-2
- **Bacteriology** is the study of bacteria.
- Examples of ways bacteria are helpful include making many foods, decomposing dead matter, and adding nitrogen to the soil. Examples of ways bacteria are harmful include causing diseases and causing food to spoil.

### Lesson 2-3
- The protist kingdom includes very simple organisms such as **protozoans**, algae, and slime molds.
- Protozoans are animal-like protists that move freely. Algae are plantlike protists that can make their own food. Slime molds are funguslike protists.

### Lesson 2-4
- All algae contain chlorophyll and make their own food by photosynthesis.
- Some kinds of algae are unicellular. The euglena is a unicellular alga that is both plantlike and animal-like. Some algae are multicellular. Red and brown algae are multicellular algae.

### Lesson 2-5
- The fungi kingdom includes organisms with cell walls that live in warm, moist conditions. Fungi can be unicellular or multicellular. Fungi cannot make their own food, cannot move freely, and have large cells with many nuclei.
- Yeast are one-celled fungi. Molds are common fungi that are made up of many threads, or **hyphae.** Mushrooms have a **stalk, cap,** and **gills.**

### Lesson 2-6
- Yeast can reproduce asexually by **budding**.
- Molds and mushrooms can reproduce both asexually and sexually. Molds and mushrooms have **spore cases** that contain thousands of spores. **Sporulation** is a kind of asexual reproduction.

## Key Term Challenges

bacillus (p. 32)
bacteriology (p. 34)
budding (p. 46)
cap (p. 42)
cilium (p. 36)
coccus (p. 32)
decomposition (p. 34)
endospore (p. 32)
fermentation (p. 42)
flagellum (p. 32)
gills (p. 42)
hypha (p. 42)
plankton (p. 40)
protozoan (p. 36)
pseudopod (p. 36)
spirillum (p. 32)
spore (p. 42)
spore case (p. 46)
sporulation (p. 46)
stalk (p. 42)

**MATCHING  Write the Key Term from above that best matches each description.**

1. curved or spiral-shaped bacterium
2. one-celled, animal-like protist
3. threadlike structure that makes up the body of molds and mushrooms
4. inactive bacterium surrounded by a thick wall
5. fingerlike projection of cytoplasm, used for movement and food-getting
6. spherical bacterium
7. microscopic organisms that float on or near the ocean's surface

**IDENTIFYING WORD RELATIONSHIPS  Explain how the words in each pair are related. Write your answers in complete sentences.**

8. spore cases, sporulation
9. bacteriology, bacillus
10. cilia, flagella
11. cap, gills
12. asexual reproduction, budding
13. chlorophyll, algae
14. pseudopod, protozoan

# Content Challenges TEST PREP

**MULTIPLE CHOICE** Write the letter of the term or phrase that best completes each statement.

1. Fire algae are
   a. white.
   b. red.
   c. green.
   d. brown.

2. The fungi kingdom includes yeasts, molds, and
   a. slime molds.
   b. algae.
   c. mushrooms.
   d. protists.

3. Blight is caused by
   a. bacteria.
   b. fungi.
   c. trypanosomes.
   d. protists.

4. A paramecium moves by means of
   a. pseudopods.
   b. flagella.
   c. eyespots.
   d. cilia.

5. Yeasts can reproduce asexually by
   a. budding.
   b. sporulation.
   c. photosynthesis.
   d. pasteurization.

6. Bacteria with a round shape are called
   a. cocci.
   b. spirilla.
   c. bacilli.
   d. flagella.

7. African sleeping sickness is caused by
   a. a paramecium.
   b. a slime mold.
   c. an amoeba.
   d. a trypanosome.

8. The reproductive cells of fungi are called
   a. rhizoids.
   b. gills.
   c. spores.
   d. threads.

9. The algae that grow to be the largest are the
   a. red algae.
   b. brown algae.
   c. green algae.
   d. golden-brown algae.

10. Nitrogen is changed into compounds that plants can use by
    a. fungi.
    b. bacteria.
    c. algae.
    d. protists.

**TRUE/FALSE** Write *true* if the statement is true. If the statement is false, change the underlined term to make the statement true.

11. Most amoeba live in <u>salt</u> water.

12. The stemlike part of a mushroom is called the <u>cap</u>.

13. All algae contain <u>chlorophyll</u>.

14. <u>Green</u> algae often are called seaweed.

15. Bacteria are grouped according to their <u>colors</u>.

16. Most protists are <u>many-celled</u> organisms.

17. A bread mold reproduces by <u>budding</u>.

18. The paramecium is a slipper-shaped <u>bacteria</u>.

19. The Kingdom <u>Fungi</u> includes all bacteria.

20. Sporulation produces <u>fewer</u> offspring than budding does.

21. The most common bacteria have a <u>spiral</u> shape.

22. <u>Protozoans</u> often are called plantlike protists.

# Concept Challenges TEST PREP

**WRITTEN RESPONSE** Answer each of the following questions in complete sentences.

1. **EXPLAIN:** How do canning, pickling, and freezing foods prevent the growth of bacteria?

2. **ANALYZE:** Why do you think algae were originally classified as plants?

3. **COMPARE:** How are fungi similar to plants? How are they different?

4. **HYPOTHESIZE:** If you wanted to find fungi where you live, where would you look? Explain your answer.

5. **INFER:** All living things depend on energy from the Sun. How can archaebacteria live deep in the ocean where there is no sunlight?

**INTERPRETING A DIAGRAM** Use Figure 2-23 to answer the following questions.

6. What is the part labeled *A* called?

7. What are the parts labeled *B* called?

8. What is the function of the parts labeled *B*?

9. What is the part labeled *C* called?

10. What is the body of the mushroom made up of?

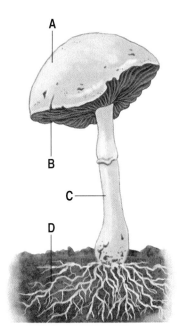

▲ **Figure 2-23** A mushroom

# Chapter 3 Types of Plants

**▲ Figure 3-1** Tropical rain forests are home to tens of thousands of different plant species.

Tropical rain forests are found in warm regions near the equator. A tropical rain forest is filled with plant life of all shapes and sizes. Large amounts of rainfall, moderate temperatures, and year-round sunlight lead to the high growth rate in a rain forest. The trees in a rain forest can grow to great heights. Many other plants such as vines, mosses, and orchids grow on the trees themselves.

▶ Strangely, the floor of a tropical rain forest has only a small amount of plant life. Why do you think most of the plants in a rain forest live near the treetops?

## Contents

**3-1** How are plants classified?

**3-2** How do bryophytes reproduce?

**3-3** What are ferns?

■ **Lab Activity:** Examining the Structure of a Fern Frond

**3-4** What are gymnosperms?

**3-5** What are angiosperms?

■ **The Big Idea:** How do plants affect the economy of the United States?

# 3-1 How are plants classified?

## INVESTIGATE

### Classifying Plants
#### HANDS-ON ACTIVITY

1. Examine the leaves, stems, and flowers of several different plants.

2. Record your observations of each plant. Include characteristics such as size, shape, texture, and color.

3. Based on your observations, classify the plants into different categories. Make sure you give evidence or reasons for putting plants in certain categories.

4. Make a classification chart based on your conclusions.

**THINK ABOUT IT:** How did the similarities and differences of the plant parts help you classify the plants?

## Objective

Identify the characteristics of plants.

## Key Terms

**tracheophytes** (TRAY-kee-uh-fyts): group of plants that have transport tubes

**vascular plant:** plant that contains transport tubes

**bryophytes** (BRY-oh-fyts): group of plants that do not have transport tubes

**nonvascular plant:** plant that does not have transport tubes

**Characteristics of Plants** Some organisms, such as algae, look like plants. How do scientists classify organisms as plants? Plants are multicellular. These cells also have cell walls and contain chloroplasts.

Plants use chlorophyll in the chloroplasts to absorb the energy in sunlight. Plants use the Sun's energy to combine carbon dioxide and water to make food in the form of sugar. The food-making process is called photosynthesis. Photosynthesis provides plants with the food they need for growth and development.

$$\text{Water + Carbon dioxide} \xrightarrow{\text{Light energy}} \text{Sugar + Oxygen}$$

▲ **Figure 3-2** In photosynthesis, plants use light energy to make food.

Plant cells are organized into tissues and organs. Tissues are groups of cells that look alike and work together. Tissues are often named for the job they do. Organs are a group of tissues that work together to do a special job. Some organs in plants are the roots, stem, and leaves. In flowering plants, the flower is also an organ.

▶ **STATE:** What are three plant characteristics?

**Plant Divisions** Botanists have classified more than 250,000 organisms in the plant kingdom. They have divided the plant kingdom into two large groups. The groups are based on how water and dissolved nutrients are moved throughout the plant. The two groups are the tracheophytes and the bryophytes.

| Tracheophytes | Bryophytes |
|---|---|
| • Vascular, grow larger, have well-developed root system<br>• Examples are ferns, pine trees, roses | • Nonvascular, small, live in damp areas<br>• Examples are mosses, liverworts, hornworts |

▲ **Figure 3-3** Characteristics of tracheophytes and bryophytes

▶  **IDENTIFY:** What are the two large groups of the plant kingdom?

**Tracheophytes** Most of the plants you are familiar with are probably tracheophytes. Ferns, pine trees, rose bushes, and cherry trees are all examples of tracheophytes. **Tracheophytes** are a group of plants that have transport tissue. This means that water and nutrients move through special tubelike cells to all parts of the plant. These tubelike cells make up the transport tissue of the plant. Tracheophytes are considered **vascular plants** because they have this transport tissue.

Plant tissue in tracheophytes is organized into roots, stems, and leaves. The roots of a tracheophyte anchor the plant in the soil. The vascular tissue takes in water and dissolved nutrients from the soil. Stems help to support a plant. The vascular tissue found in stems transfers water and nutrients throughout the plant. The presence of this tissue also gives strength to the plant, allowing some tracheophytes to grow very tall.

▲ **Figure 3-4** A cherry tree is a tracheophyte.

▶3 **DESCRIBE:** What are two jobs of vascular tissue?

**Bryophytes** If you have seen moss growing on the side of a tree, then you have seen a **bryophyte.** Bryophytes are a group of plants that do not have transport tissue. In bryophytes, water and nutrients seep from one cell to another. Because bryophytes do not have transport tissue, they are called **nonvascular plants.** Bryophytes do not have true roots, stems, or leaves. They have rootlike and leaflike structures. Bryophytes are small plants. They usually grow to be only a few centimeters in height.

Bryophytes are land plants. However, they need water to reproduce. For this reason, botanists believe that bryophytes may have evolved from a water plant.

▲ **Figure 3-5** The moss on these trees is a bryophyte.

▶4 **INFER:** Why do you think that bryophytes cannot grow to great heights?

## ✔ CHECKING CONCEPTS

1. The two large plant groups are the tracheophytes and the _____ .
2. Tubelike cells make up the _____ tissue of tracheophytes.
3. Among tracheophytes, plant tissues are organized into roots, stems, and _____.
4. Bryophytes need _____ to reproduce.

## THINKING CRITICALLY

5. **CONTRAST:** How do bryophytes differ from tracheophytes?
6. **HYPOTHESIZE:** Why do you think tracheophytes are successful land plants?

### Web InfoSearch

**Local Plant Life** The types of plants that are able to grow in a specific area depend on many factors, such as soil, climate, and altitude.

**SEARCH:** Use the Internet to research plants in your area. Make a poster showing examples of local plant life. Begin your search at www.conceptsandchallenges.com. Some key words are **plants** and **flora.**

# 3-2 How do bryophytes reproduce?

## Objective
Describe how bryophytes reproduce.

## Key Terms
**spore:** reproductive cell in some plants

**rhizoid** (RY-zoid)**:** fine, hairlike structure that acts as a root

**Bryophytes** The most primitive plants on Earth are the bryophytes. Mosses are classified in the phylum Bryophyta (BRY-oh-fy-tuh). Mosses can be found growing on the sides of trees or on the forest floor. Two other kinds of plants classified as bryophytes are shown in Figures 3-6 and 3-7. They are liverwort and hornwort. Even though they live on land, bryophytes can live only where there is a good supply of water. Because they are nonvascular plants, they do not have transport tubes to carry water throughout the plant. They also need water for reproduction. Bryophytes are spore plants, which means that they produce spores instead of seeds. A **spore** is a reproductive cell in some plants.

▲ **Figure 3-6** Liverwort

▲ **Figure 3-7** Hornwort

 **EXPLAIN:** Why do mosses have to grow in moist areas?

**Structure of Bryophytes** Bryophytes are small plants that differ from most other plants. Unlike most plants, bryophytes do not have true roots,

stems, or leaves. Instead of roots, they have fine hairlike structures called **rhizoids.** Rhizoids anchor the plant in the soil. They also take in water and dissolved minerals.

 **IDENTIFY:** What are two characteristics of bryophytes?

**Mosses** If you look closely at a moss plant, you will see thin stalks with tiny leaflike parts. The leaflike parts and green stems make food for the plants. Rhizoids anchor the mosses. You also may see taller stalks. At the top of these stalks, there are spore cases. The spore cases are filled with spores.

▲ **Figure 3-8** Moss grows in moist areas.

 **NAME:** What structure of a moss holds the spores?

**Life Cycle of Bryophytes** Bryophytes have a life cycle that consists of two phases. The plant looks very different during each of the two phases. The first phase is the gamete-producing phase. During this phase, sperm and egg cells are produced. The gamete-producing phase of the plant is the larger green part of the plant shown in Figure 3-9.

Once fertilization occurs, the fertilized egg grows into a new plant. This is called the spore-producing phase. In Figure 3-9, the spore-producing plant has a tall, thin stalk and a round spore case at the top. During this phase, the plant forms spores and then releases them into the air. The spores can develop into another gamete-producing plant. Then, the cycle starts all over again.

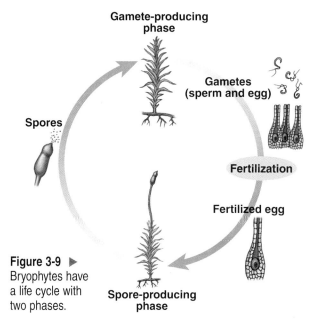

Gamete-producing phase

Gametes (sperm and egg)

Spores

Fertilization

Fertilized egg

Spore-producing phase

**Figure 3-9** ▶ Bryophytes have a life cycle with two phases.

 **DESCRIBE:** Describe the two phases in the bryophyte life cycle.

**Pioneer Plants** Bryophytes are sometimes called pioneer plants. Pioneer plants are the first plants to grow in bare or rocky places. Their rhizoids help break down rocks to form soil. As the plants die and decay, they add nutrients to the soil. As the soil layer builds up, other plants may grow.

**5 DEFINE:** What are pioneer plants?

## ✔ CHECKING CONCEPTS

1. What are the reproductive cells of bryophytes called?
2. Name three kinds of bryophytes.
3. What are the rootlike structures of bryophytes called?
4. In what structure are the spores of mosses produced?

## 💡 THINKING CRITICALLY

5. **INFER:** In what ways are bryophytes less suited to life on land than other plants?
6. **COMPARE:** In what ways are rhizoids like roots?

## BUILDING LANGUAGE ARTS SKILLS

**Building Vocabulary** *Bryophyte* is made up of the word parts *bryo* and *phyt*. Look up the word parts in a dictionary or Appendix D. Find two other life science words that contain the word part *phyt*. Define the two words. To what kind of living things do the word parts relate?

# *Science and Technology*

## USE OF PEAT AS A FUEL

Sphagnum (SFAG-nuhm) moss can grow under very wet conditions. The plants that die decompose very slowly, forming a bog of wet, spongy soil. The partly decayed plant matter that builds up over thousands of years is called peat. Today, peat bogs cover about 4 million square kilometers of North America, northern Europe, and Asia.

▲ **Figure 3-10** Peat moss grows in bogs around the world. Here the peat is being harvested.

Peat is an important energy source for many countries. About 1,400 square kilometers are harvested each year. This peat moss is converted into about 70 million cubic meters of "energy peat." The peat is burned, producing an energy source. This energy is then used for heating homes and for cooking.

Peat is a renewable resource. Peat bogs can be restored to thriving wetlands within 5 to 20 years after the peat is harvested. New peat forms at a rate of 1 to 2 millimeters a year.

**Thinking Critically** Do you think it is more important to use the peat as fuel or to protect the bogs for wildlife? Explain.

# 3-3 What are ferns?

## Objective
Name and describe the structure of a fern.

## Key Terms
**frond:** leaf of a fern

**rhizome** (RY-zohm)**:** horizontal underground stem

**Ferns** Ferns are one of the oldest groups of tracheophytes. They have a system of transport tubes that carry water and nutrients throughout the plant. Ferns are spore plants. They are considered seedless tracheophytes. They grow in great numbers in warm, moist areas, but they also live in cooler, drier areas. Most ferns can be recognized by their featherlike leaves. Ferns vary greatly in size and shape. Most ferns are about a half meter tall. Some ferns are only 3 centimeters tall. Other ferns, however, are giants. For example, fern trees of the South Pacific can grow to be more than 10 meters tall.

▲ **Figure 3-11** Ferns are spore plants.

**1** DESCRIBE: What are two characteristics of ferns?

**Structure of a Fern** Ferns have true roots, stems, and leaves. The leaves are called **fronds.** The fronds are the part of the fern that can be seen above ground. In many ferns, the fronds are divided into smaller leaf-like parts called leaflets. Fern stems usually grow underground. The underground stems are called **rhizomes.** They

grow parallel to the surface. Roots grow downward from the rhizome, while the fronds grow upward.

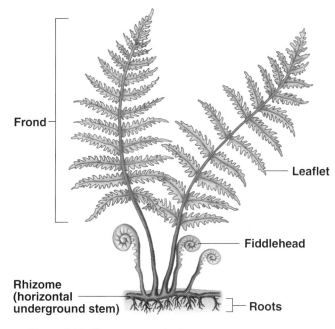

▲ **Figure 3-12** The structure of a fern

Ferns reproduce by spores. If you look at the underside of some kinds of fern fronds, you will see tiny brown spots. These are spore cases. Each case is filled with hundreds of spores. Ferns also have structures called fiddleheads. These structures resemble the end of a violin. They are young fronds that are tightly coiled.

▲ **Figure 3-13** Spores can be found on the underside of a frond.

**2** IDENTIFY: What is the underground stem of a fern called?

**Fern Life Cycle** Like bryophytes, ferns have a two-phase life cycle. Ferns look different in each of the two phases. In ferns, the spore-producing plant is the larger plant. The ferns you usually see are in the spore-producing phase. Most of a fern's life is spent in the spore-producing phase. The gamete-producing plant is small and heart-shaped. The gamete-producing phase does not last very long.

 **IDENTIFY:** Which is the shorter phase in the life cycle of a fern?

## ✓ CHECKING CONCEPTS

1. The featherlike leaves of ferns are the _____.

2. The rhizome of a fern is an underground _____.

3. Ferns have true roots, _____, and leaves.

4. In most ferns, spore cases form on the underside of the _____.

5. The _____ is a tightly coiled young frond.

6. The _____ phase is the longer of the two phases in ferns.

## THINKING CRITICALLY

7. **MODEL:** Draw a diagram of a fern. Label the frond, rhizome, and blades.

8. **INFER:** What part of a fern makes food for the fern? How do you know?

9. **MODEL:** Draw a diagram that shows the life cycle of a fern. Include the phases, gametes, and ferns.

## DESIGNING AN EXPERIMENT

*Design an experiment to solve the following problem. Make sure you include materials to be used, a procedure, variables, and possible data to be collected.*

Megan wants to grow her own ferns at home. She has several spores but does not know what to do with them. She needs to find out what conditions are best for growing ferns.

---

## ◈ *Integrating Earth Science*

**TOPIC: geologic time**

### PREHISTORIC FERNS

About 300 million years ago, giant tree ferns were the most common kind of land plant. This time in Earth's history is often called the Carboniferous Period. During this time, fern forests covered much of Earth. Most of the giant tree ferns died out about 225 million years ago.

▲ **Figure 3-14** Ferns were one of the dominant plants during the Carboniferous Period.

The giant tree ferns usually grew in swamps. As the ferns died, their remains fell into the water and stayed there. They were covered by mud, water, and other sediments. The remains of these and other plants eventually became buried under thick layers of earth. Heat, pressure, and the actions of certain bacteria slowly caused chemical changes to take place. After millions of years, most of the compounds in the plants changed so that only carbon was left. This condensed form of carbon became coal. Coal is a fossil fuel. It has been used as a fuel since the 1800s. Coal is burned to produce electricity. This electricity is then transferred to homes, businesses, and schools.

**Thinking Critically** Why do you think coal is referred to as a "fossil fuel"?

# LAB ACTIVITY
# Examining the Structure of a Fern Frond

## BACKGROUND

Ferns are spore plants that grow in fields, forests, and wetlands. The stem of a fern, or rhizome, is underground. The leaves of a fern are called fronds. Each frond is made up of leaflets. On the underside of the leaflets, spore cases develop. If the environmental conditions are right, each spore can grow into a new fern plant.

## PURPOSE

In this activity, you will examine the structure of a fern frond.

## PROCEDURE

1. Obtain one fern frond.

2. Observe the fern frond. Sketch the entire frond on a sheet of paper. Label the main stalk and the leaflets.

3. Copy the chart in Figure 3-15 onto your own paper. Using a hand lens, examine the upper and lower sides of the frond. Draw what you see on your paper.

4. Using a hand lens, observe the spore cases on the underside of the frond. Draw what you see.

5. Estimate the number of spore cases on one fern frond. Record your estimate in your chart.

6. Using tweezers, scrape a few of the spore cases off the frond onto a clean white sheet of paper. Gently crush the spore cases by rolling a pencil over the cases.

7. Using a hand lens, examine the spores. Estimate the number of spores in one spore case. Record your estimate.

**Materials**

Fern frond
White paper
Hand lens
Paper cup
Planting soil
Tweezers
Clear plastic wrap

▲ **STEP 2** Sketch the entire frond on a sheet of paper.

▲ **STEP 4** Using a hand lens, observe the spore cases on the underside of the frond.

8. Use your estimates from steps 5 and 7 to determine an estimated number of spores on an entire fern frond. Record this estimate in your chart.

9. Fill a small paper cup three-quarters of the way with moist soil. Now sprinkle several of the spores from the opened spore cases onto the soil. Cover the cup with clear plastic wrap. Place your cup in a warm area with indirect light.

10. After 2 weeks have passed, observe your paper cup. Do you see any growth?

▲ **STEP 6**
Scrape a few of the spore cases off the frond.

| Item | Estimated Number |
|---|---|
| Spore cases on entire frond | |
| Spores in one spore case | |
| Spores on entire frond | |

▲ **Figure 3-15** Copy this chart onto a sheet of paper.

## CONCLUSIONS

1. **OBSERVE:** Does the fern frond have veins or tubes to transport water?

2. **INFER:** Is the fern a vascular or nonvascular plant?

3. **INFER:** Is the fern frond the spore-producing phase or the gamete-producing phase of the plant? How can you tell?

4. **CALCULATE:** Suppose a fern plant has 10 fronds on it. Use your estimate from step 8 to determine the approximate number of spores on the entire fern.

5. **OBSERVE:** Did your fern produce a new plant? What stage was this new plant in?

6. **HYPOTHESIZE:** If a fern plant produces so many spores, why isn't Earth covered in ferns?

# 3-4 What are gymnosperms?

## Objectives

Name and describe three kinds of gymnosperms.

## Key Terms

**gymnosperm** (JIHM-noh-spuhrm): type of land plant that has uncovered seeds

**seed:** structure that contains a tiny living plant and food for its growth; a reproductive cell

**conifer** (KAHN-uh-fuhr): tree that produces cones and has needlelike leaves

**Gymnosperms** Millions of years after the appearance of ferns, a group of woody land plants arose. These plants were gymnosperms. The **gymnosperms** are a large group of vascular land plants that have uncovered, exposed seeds. A **seed** is a reproductive structure of a plant. The seeds of many vascular plants are enclosed in a fruit. The seeds of gymnosperms, however, are not. Gymnosperms have true roots, stems, and leaves. They have stiff, woody stems. They have a system of tubes for carrying water and dissolved materials.

▲ **Figure 3-16** Gymnosperms such as spruce and pine trees have leaves on year-round.

▶ **DEFINE:** What is a gymnosperm?

**Conifers** The most common and best known of the gymnosperms are the **conifers.** Conifers are plants that produce cones. The seeds are in the cones. Many conifers have special leaves

called needles. The needles of most conifers stay green throughout the year. For this reason, many conifers are called "evergreens." Pines, cedars, spruces, and hemlocks are examples of evergreen conifers.

Conifers grow in many different climates and soil types. Many conifers grow in the forests of northern Europe and North America. The giant redwood trees, or sequoias (si-KWOI-uhz), of California also are conifers. Some of these trees are more than 100 meters tall and 9 meters in diameter.

▲ **Figure 3-17** Pine cones contain seeds.

▶ **INFER:** Why are some conifers also called evergreens?

**Importance of Conifers** The conifers are an important group of plants. They are widely used as a source of lumber and fuel. They also are used in the production of paper, turpentine, charcoal, and tar. In some northern areas, spruces and firs are planted along the edges of fields. This wall of trees slows down the wind, keeping soil from blowing away.

▶ **LIST:** What are three uses of gymnosperms?

**Ginkgos and Cycads** Two other kinds of gymnosperms are ginkgoes (GIN-kohs) and cycads (SY-kadz). Ginkgoes have fan-shaped leaves. Unlike the evergreens, ginkgoes shed their leaves in the fall. Ginkgoes often are grown along city streets because they grow well even in polluted air.

Cycads grow mainly in tropical areas. Most look like small palm trees. They have large, feathery, fernlike leaves. Many plant species, such as cycads, have separate male and female plants. Female cycads produce seeds. The male plant produces pollen. Cycads often have very large cones.

▲ **Figure 3-18** Cycads grow in warm, tropical regions.

 **NAME:** What are two other groups of gymnosperms?

## ✓ CHECKING CONCEPTS

1. The most common gymnosperms are _____.

2. A pine tree is an example of a _____.

3. Conifers produce _____ in cones.

4. Conifers have special leaves called _____.

5. Gymnosperms have transport tubes so they are called _____ plants.

6. In autumn, _____ shed their leaves.

## 💡 THINKING CRITICALLY

7. **MODEL:** A giant redwood tree has a diameter of 9 m. Use the scale 1 mm equals 50 cm. Draw a circle to represent the 9 m diameter of the redwood tree's trunk. Draw a second circle inside the first showing the trunk of an oak tree that is 2 m in diameter.

8. **INFER:** What characteristics of a giant sequoia allow it to grow so tall?

## HEALTH AND SAFETY TIP

*Dietary Supplements* Many plants are used as dietary supplements. A Chinese root called ginseng has been used to build up the body's resistance to disease. *Ginkgo biloba* has been used to increase memory. The benefits of herbal supplements are highly controversial. Because herbs are not yet required to undergo safety tests, it is difficult to be sure any are completely safe. Never take any dietary supplements without talking to a doctor first.

## *Hands-On Activity*

### OBSERVING PINE CONES

*You will need several different conifer cones, a hand lens, a field guide to trees, and a metric ruler.*

1. Gather cones from three different conifers.

2. Use the field guide to help you identify which kind of tree each cone comes from. Label the cones.

3. Use a hand lens to look at the cones. Each scale of the cone can hold a seed. Count the number of scales in one cone. Record the number of seeds possible in that cone.

4. Remove a few seeds from one cone. Examine the seeds and draw a diagram of one.

▲ **STEP 3** Count the number of scales in each cone.

### Practicing Your Skills

5. **COMPARE AND CONTRAST:** How are the cones from the same tree alike? How are they different?

6. **HYPOTHESIZE:** Why do you not find a seed behind every scale?

7. **INFER:** Why are there seeds in some cones but not others?

# 3-5 What are angiosperms?

## Objective

Identify monocots and dicots as two kinds of angiosperms.

## Key Terms

**angiosperm** (AN-jee-oh-spuhrm): type of vascular flowering plant

**cotyledon** (kaht-uh-LEED-uhn): leaflike structure inside a seed that contains food for the developing plant

**monocot:** flowering plant with one cotyledon, or seed leaf, in its seeds

**dicot:** flowering plant with two cotyledons, or seed leaves, in its seeds

**Angiosperms** The **angiosperms** are the flowering plants. Scientists estimate that angiosperms first appeared about 150 million years ago. They gradually replaced the gymnosperms as the major land plants. Today, scientists have classified about 250,000 kinds of angiosperms. They are the largest plant group.

▶ **IDENTIFY:** What are angiosperms?

**Characteristics of Angiosperms** Most of the plants you see every day are angiosperms. Angiosperms are tracheophytes. Like gymnosperms, angiosperms have true roots, stems, and leaves. They also have a highly developed vascular system of transport tubes.

All angiosperms have flowers. No other plant group has flowers. In some angiosperms, the flowers are not very noticeable. You probably have never seen the flowers of grasses, oak trees, or corn. They have very small flowers. Other angiosperms, such as tulips, sunflowers, and lilies, have large, colorful flowers.

▶ **NAME:** What is the main characteristic of angiosperms?

**Seeds and Fruits** Like gymnosperms, angiosperms are seed plants. The flowers of angiosperms produce seeds and fruits. The seeds of angiosperms are inside the fruit, which covers and protects them. The next time you eat a piece of fruit look for the seeds. You will see one seed or many seeds. Peaches have one seed, whereas apples have many. Most angiosperms produce a lot of seeds.

▶ **NAME:** What do the flowers of angiosperms produce?

**Monocots and Dicots** Angiosperms are classified into two groups based on their seed structure. Within the seeds of angiosperms are leaflike structures that contain food for the developing plant. These structures are called **cotyledons.** The seeds of one group of angiosperms contain a single cotyledon. Plants of this group are **monocots.** Corn and wheat are examples of monocots. In the second group, the seeds have two cotyledons. These plants are **dicots.** Greenbeans and roses are examples of dicots.

▶ **IDENTIFY:** What is a cotyledon?

▲ **Figure 3-19** These sunflowers produce thousands of seeds.

**Identifying Monocots and Dicots** You can tell if a plant is a monocot or a dicot by looking at its seeds, flowers, and leaves. Monocots have flowers with petals arranged in groups of three. Petals are the colorful parts of the flower. The veins in the leaves of monocots are parallel. Dicots have flowers with petals arranged in groups of four or five. The veins in the leaves of dicots are branched.

| Monocot | Dicot |
|---|---|
| **Seed** | |
| Single cotyledon | Two cotyledons |
| **Leaf** | |
| Parallel veins | Branched veins |
| **Flower** | |
| Petals in groups of 3 | Petals in groups of 4 or 5 |

▲ **Figure 3-20** Characteristics of monocots and dicots

**5** ▶ **CONTRAST:** In what way are monocot flowers and dicot flowers different?

✓ **CHECKING CONCEPTS**

1. Monocots have leaves with _____ veins.
2. The seeds of angiosperms are enclosed in _____ .
3. Angiosperms are also called the _____ plants.
4. Fruits are produced by the plant parts called _____ .
5. The number of cotyledons in a dicot seed is _____ .

💡 **THINKING CRITICALLY**

6. **HYPOTHESIZE:** What may have caused the angiosperms to become more common than the gymnosperms?
7. **MODEL:** Draw a model of a monocot plant and a dicot plant. Label the number of petals and the pattern of leaf veins in each.

**BUILDING LANGUAGE ARTS SKILLS**

***Using Prefixes*** Monocots are also called monocotyledons. Dicots are called dicotyledons. What do the prefixes *mono-* and *di-* tell you about the difference between the words monocot and dicot? Use the meaning of the prefixes *mono-* and *di-* to define the words *monorail, monosyllable,* and *disaccharide.*

## *Hands-On Activity*

### CLASSIFYING MONOCOTS AND DICOTS

*You will need five different leaves, flowers, and seeds.*

1. Observe the seeds. Record your observations in a table.
2. Observe the flowers. Count the number of petals on each flower. Record your observations in your table.
3. Draw the vein patterns in each leaf.

**Practicing Your Skills**

4. **ANALYZE: a.** Which parts came from monocots?
   **b.** Which came from dicots?

▲ **Figure 3-21** In Step 3, you will draw the veins of each leaf.

# THE Big IDEA

## How do plants affect the economy of the United States?

Economics is a branch of social studies. It looks at how goods and services are made, distributed, and used. The United States has the largest economy in the world. There are several ways to measure the economy. One way is to add up the value of everything produced in the United States. That figure is called the gross domestic product, or GDP. The GDP for the United States is about $10 trillion. Two percent of that comes from agriculture, or farming. That is almost $200 billion.

About 100 different plants are grown as major food crops. Trees are used for building materials and for making paper. Some plants are used to make medicines. The oils for perfume come from flowers and other plant parts. Plants are also used to make rubber, cloth, paints, plastics, and film. Plants are bought and sold for landscaping and decorating.

The economy of a state or region may depend a lot on certain plants. In Idaho, for example, potatoes are a very important crop. They make up about 15% of Idaho's economy. Plant crops also provide jobs. More than 100,000 people work in Florida's citrus fruit industry.

Look at the map that appears on this page and the next. It points out plants that are important in certain states or regions. Follow the directions in the Science Log to learn more about "the big idea." ◆

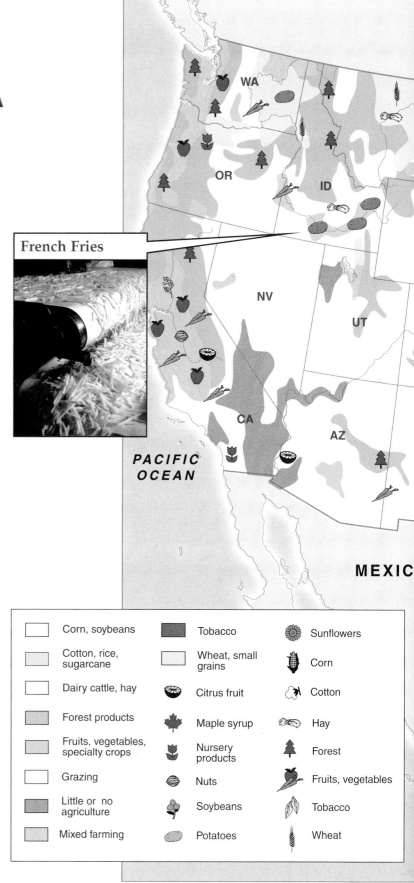

French Fries

**Map legend:**

| | | | |
|---|---|---|---|
| Corn, soybeans | Tobacco | Sunflowers | |
| Cotton, rice, sugarcane | Wheat, small grains | Corn | |
| Dairy cattle, hay | Citrus fruit | Cotton | |
| Forest products | Maple syrup | Hay | |
| Fruits, vegetables, specialty crops | Nursery products | Forest | |
| Grazing | Nuts | Fruits, vegetables | |
| Little or no agriculture | Soybeans | Tobacco | |
| Mixed farming | Potatoes | Wheat | |

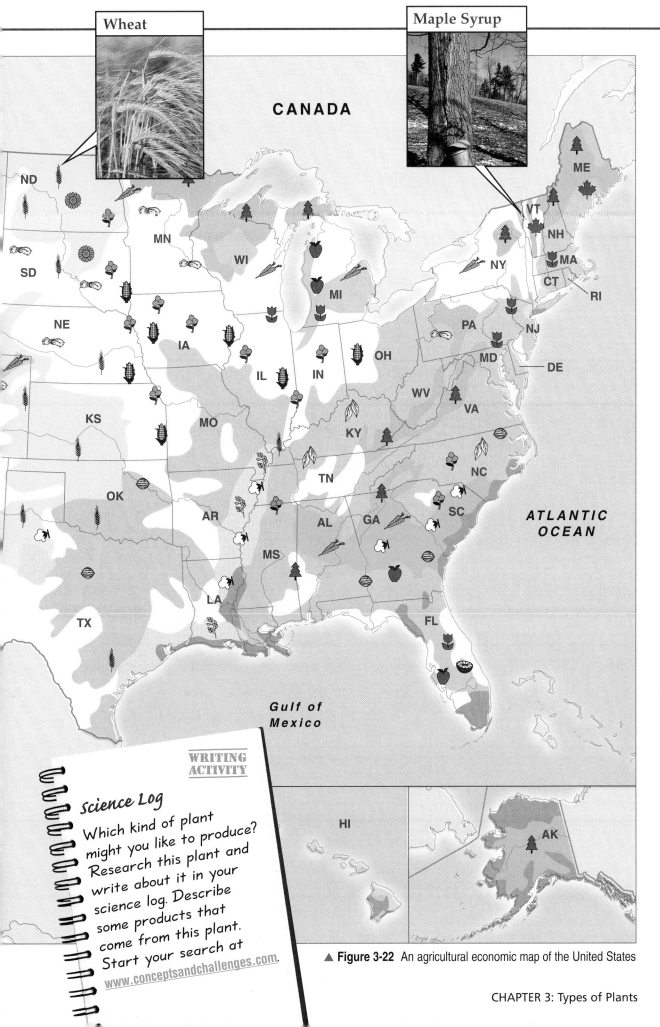

**Wheat**

**Maple Syrup**

CANADA

ND

MN

WI

MI

SD

NE

IA

IL

IN

OH

KS

MO

KY

WV

VA

OK

AR

TN

NC

SC

ATLANTIC OCEAN

MS

AL

GA

TX

LA

FL

*Gulf of Mexico*

ME

VT

NH

NY

MA

CT

RI

PA

NJ

MD

DE

**WRITING ACTIVITY**

*Science Log*

Which kind of plant might you like to produce? Research this plant and write about it in your science log. Describe some products that come from this plant. Start your search at www.conceptsandchallenges.com.

HI

AK

▲ **Figure 3-22** An agricultural economic map of the United States

# Chapter 3 Challenges

## Chapter Summary

### Lesson 3-1

- The plant kingdom is divided into two large groups: **bryophytes** and **tracheophytes.**
- Bryophytes are small plants that lack transport tissues. Bryophytes do not have true roots, stems, or leaves.
- Tracheophytes have tubelike cells used to transport materials to all plant parts. They are **vascular plants.** Tracheophytes have true roots, stems, and leaves.

### Lesson 3-2

- The phylum Bryophyta includes mosses, liverworts, and hornworts.
- Bryophytes are **spore** plants. Bryophytes have a life cycle that includes two phases.
- Pioneer plants are the first plants to grow in bare or rocky places.

### Lesson 3-3

- Ferns are seedless tracheophytes that have spores.
- Ferns have true roots, stems, and leaves. The leaves of a fern are called **fronds.**

### Lesson 3-4

- **Gymnosperms** are woody land plants that have true roots, stems, and leaves, and uncovered seeds. Gymnosperms are vascular plants.
- **Conifers** are a group of gymnosperms that produce **seeds** in cones and have needles. Seeds are reproductive cells.
- Conifers are used as a source for many different products such as lumber and fuel.
- Cycads and ginkgos are two other groups of gymnosperms.

### Lesson 3-5

- **Angiosperms** are the flowering plants. Angiosperms have true leaves, roots, and stems. They are vascular plants. The flowers of angiosperms produce seeds inside fruits.
- Angiosperms are classified as **monocots** and **dicots** based upon the number of **cotyledons** in their seeds.
- Monocots and dicots can be identified by examining their seeds, leaf vein patterns, and the number of petals that make up the flowers.

## Key Term Challenges

angiosperm (p. 62)
bryophytes (p. 52)
conifer (p. 60)
cotyledon (p. 62)
dicot (p. 62)
frond (p. 56)
gymnosperm (p. 60)
monocot (p. 62)
nonvascular plant (p. 52)
rhizoid (p. 54)
rhizome (p. 56)
seed (p. 60)
spore (p. 54)
tracheophytes (p. 52)
vascular plant (p. 52)

**MATCHING  Write the Key Term from above that best matches each description.**

1. fine, hairlike structure that acts as a root

2. tree with cones and needlelike leaves

3. flowering plant

4. group of flowering plants with parallel leaf veins

5. reproductive cell of bryophytes and ferns

6. seed plant with two cotyledons

7. group of plants without transport tissues

**IDENTIFYING WORD RELATIONSHIPS  Explain how the words in each pair are related. Write your answers in complete sentences.**

8. seed, angiosperm

9. bryophyte, spore

10. conifers, gymnosperms

11. stem, rhizome

12. cotyledons, monocots

13. root, rhizoid

14 frond, leaf

15. conifer, evergreen

## Content Challenges TEST PREP

**MULTIPLE CHOICE** **Write the letter of the term or phrase that best completes each sentence.**

1. A group of gymnosperms that loses its leaves in the fall is the
   a. conifers.
   b. cycads.
   c. ginkgoes.
   d. ferns.

2. The leaves of a fern are called
   a. fronds.
   b. blades.
   c. fiddleheads.
   d. spores.

3. The underground stem of a fern is a
   a. root.
   b. rhizome.
   c. frond.
   d. rhizoid.

4. The leaves of conifers are called
   a. needles.
   b. fronds.
   c. cones.
   d. blades.

5. Plant structures common to all angiosperms are
   a. spore cases.
   b. flowers.
   c. rhizomes.
   d. monocots.

6. The number of cotyledons in a dicot is
   a. one.
   b. two.
   c. three.
   d. four.

7. The seeds of a conifer can be found in the
   a. flower.
   b. cone.
   c. needle
   d. spore.

8. Pioneer plants are usually
   a. angiosperms.
   b. gymnosperms.
   c. bryophytes.
   d. tracheophytes.

9. Pines, cedars, spruces, and hemlocks are
   a. cycads.
   b. ginkgoes.
   c. angiosperms.
   d. conifers.

10. The largest plant group is made up of
    a. gymnosperms.
    b. angiosperms.
    c. bryophytes.
    d. rhizoids.

**TRUE/FALSE** **Write *true* if the statement is true. If the statement is false, change the underlined term to make the statement true.**

11. <u>Conifers</u> are used to make many things such as lumber, turpentine, and charcoal.

12. Monocots have leaves with <u>branched</u> veins.

13. Mosses have a life cycle with <u>three</u> phases.

14. Three plants classified as <u>bryophytes</u> are mosses, liverworts, and hornworts.

15. Spore plants produce <u>flowers</u> instead of seeds.

# Concept Challenges TEST PREP

**WRITTEN RESPONSE** Answer each of the following questions in complete sentences.

1. **CONTRAST:** How do bryophytes differ from other groups of plants?
2. **COMPARE:** In what way are ferns similar to bryophytes?
3. **IDENTIFY:** What is the reproductive structure of a gymnosperm?
4. **CONTRAST:** How does a monocot differ from a dicot?
5. **PREDICT:** How would the world be different if there were no plants?

**INTERPRETING A DIAGRAM** Use Figure 3-23 to answer the following questions.

6. Both corn and beans are members of a group of plants called angiosperms. What features of the plants identify them as angiosperms?
7. Which seed is a monocot? How do you know?
8. Which seed is a dicot? How do you know?
9. How are the leaf veins in monocots and dicots different?
10. How does the flower in plant *A* differ from the flower in plant *B*?

| Plant A | Plant B |
| --- | --- |
| **Seed** 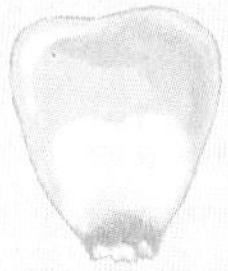 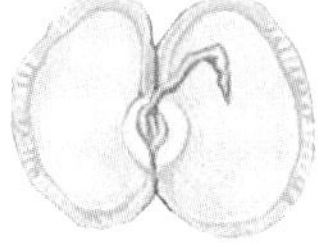 | |
| **Leaf** 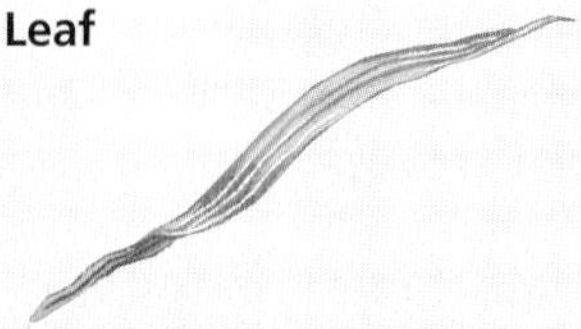  | |
| **Flower**   | |

▲ Figure 3-23

# Chapter 4  Plant Structure and Function

▲ **Figure 4-1** Hummingbirds help some flowers reproduce.

There are many different species of plants. Some are trees and some are ferns. Others are flowering plants. People admire the beauty and color of the flowers on these plants. Many birds and insects are also attracted to the bright colors of flowers. Flowers are necessary for some plants to reproduce. Birds and insects play an important role in plant reproduction.

▶ How do you think the hummingbird in Figure 4-1 helps the plant to reproduce?

## Contents

4-1     What are roots?

4-2     What are stems?

4-3     What are leaves?

4-4     What is photosynthesis?

■       **The Big Idea:** What are the physics of a tree?

4-5     What are flowers?

4-6     How do flowering plants reproduce?

4-7     What are seeds and fruits?

■       **Lab Activity:** Identifying the Parts of a Flower

4-8     What are the parts of a seed?

4-9     How do plants reproduce asexually?

4-10    What are tropisms?

# 4-1 What are roots?

## Objective
Describe the structure and the functions of roots.

## Key Terms
**fibrous** (FY-bruhs) **root system:** root system made up of many thin, branched roots

**taproot system:** root system made up of one large root and many small, thin roots

**root hair:** thin, hairlike structure on the outer layer of the root tip

**root cap:** cup-shaped mass of cells that covers and protects a root tip

**Functions of Roots** Most roots grow underground. However, some plant roots grow in water, on rocks, and even in the open air. Roots have many important functions. They anchor, or hold, a plant firmly in the soil. Roots take in water and dissolved minerals from the soil. In some plants, food is stored in the roots.

**1** ▶ LIST: What are some functions of roots?

**Kinds of Roots** The two main kinds of root systems are fibrous root systems and taproot systems. **Fibrous root systems** are made up of many thin, branched roots. Grass, wheat, and barley have fibrous roots. A **taproot system** has one large root. Many small, thin roots grow from the large root. Some taproots can store food. Carrots, radishes, and dandelions have taproots.

▲ **Figure 4-2** A fibrous root

▲ **Figure 4-3** A taproot

**2** ▶ NAME: What are two kinds of root systems?

**Parts of a Root** Roots are tubelike structures made up of three layers. The outer part of the root is made up of one layer of cells called the epidermis. Many tiny, hairlike structures called **root hairs** extend from the outer layer. Root hairs increase the surface area of the root, allowing the root to absorb more water and minerals. The second root layer, called the cortex, has soft, loose tissue. Food for the root can be stored here.

The inner part of a root contains transport tubes that are part of the vascular system. These tubes extend up through the root and into the stems and leaves. Some tubes carry water and dissolved minerals upward. Others carry food made in the leaves to all parts of the plant.

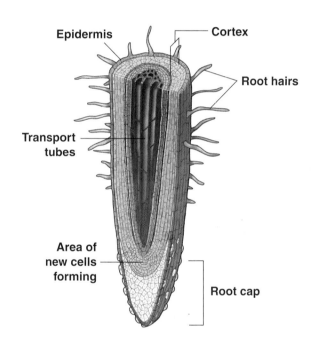

Epidermis — Cortex

Root hairs

Transport tubes

Area of new cells forming

Root cap

▲ **Figure 4-4** The parts of a root

**3** ▶ OBSERVE: Look at Figure 4-4. What is the outer layer of the root called?

**The Root Tip** Roots grow from the tip. The tip of a root is covered by a root cap. The **root cap** is a cup-shaped mass of cells. It protects the root tip from damage as the root grows into the soil. As root cap cells are worn off, new cells are produced to take their place. Behind the root cap is an area where new root cells are formed. These new cells gradually change into the different kinds of cells that make up the root.

**4** ANALYZE: Why is the root cap at the end of the root?

## ✓ CHECKING CONCEPTS

1. Roots take in water and _____ from soil.

2. A taproot system has _____ large root.

3. Structures that increase the surface area of roots are the _____.

4. The _____ part of the root contains transport tubes.

5. A root cap serves to _____ a root tip.

## 💡 THINKING CRITICALLY

6. INFER: Would a plant with a fibrous root system be easy or difficult to pull out of the ground? Explain.

7. CLASSIFY: Look at Figure 4-5. Which plants have a taproot? Which have fibrous roots?

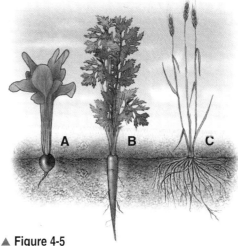

▲ **Figure 4-5**
Identify what type of root systems these plants have.

## BUILDING SCIENCE SKILLS

*Organizing Information* Make a table with the following headings: Name of Plant, Type of Root System, Depth of Roots. Use library references to find this information for the following plants: beet, oak tree, alfalfa, turnip, and corn.

## Integrating Earth Science

TOPIC: soil

### CROP ROTATION

In the one-crop system, farmers plant the same crop in the same field every year. In the crop rotation system, however, farmers plant a different crop in the same field every year. Crop rotation is a proven method for conserving soil nutrients.

▲ **Figure 4-6** Farmers alternate the crops they plant in a crop rotation system.

When planted in the same field every year, certain crops—such as corn and cotton—deplete the soil of nutrients, especially nitrogen. Using a crop rotation system, farmers plant fields with nutrient-depleting crops the first year. The next year, they plant crops that add nutrients to the soil. Plants in the legume family—such as alfalfa, peas, and beans—add nutrients to the soil. These plants have root nodules that are home to special "nitrogen-fixing" bacteria. These bacteria convert nitrogen from the air into a form that is useable by the plants.

Crop rotation also lowers the amount of pests and diseases in the soil. This reduces the amount of chemical fertilizers and pesticides that farmers sometimes use.

**Thinking Critically** A farmer rotates crops each year. If the farmer plants corn one year, what crop should the farmer plant on that same field the next year? Explain.

# 4-2 What are stems?

## Objectives

Distinguish between herbaceous and woody stems. Explain the jobs of stems.

## Key Terms

**herbaceous** (huhr-BAY-shuhs) **stem:** stem that is soft and green

**woody stem:** stem that contains wood and is thick and hard

**xylem** (ZY-luhm)**:** tissue that carries water and dissolved minerals upward from the roots

**phloem** (FLOH-em)**:** tissue that carries food from the leaves to other parts of the plant

**Kinds of Stems** Two types of plant stems are herbaceous stems and woody stems. **Herbaceous stems** are soft, smooth, and green. Usually, plants with herbaceous stems do not grow taller than 2 meters. Plants with these stems grow one season and then die. Tomato plants and bean plants have herbaceous stems. Some herbaceous plants have underground roots that survive the winter. These plants will grow new stems the next growing season.

▲ **Figure 4-7** Tomato plants have herbaceous stems.

**Woody stems** are thick, hard, and rough. The rough outer layer of the stem is the bark. Woody stems are not usually green. Plants with woody stems may live for many growing seasons. They grow taller and wider each year. All trees have woody stems. Rose bushes also have woody stems. Plants with woody stems can grow to be as tall as 83 meters. Most woody plants are gymnosperms or dicots.

▶ NAME: What are two kinds of plant stems?

**Functions of Stems** Most stems grow aboveground. The main job of stems is to support the leaves. Stems also are organs of transport. The vascular tubes within the stems carry materials between the roots and the leaves. In some plants, stems also store food. For example, the stems of sugar cane store large amounts of sugar. Potatoes are actually underground storage stems.

A tree trunk is a woody stem that has an outer layer of bark. The outer layer of bark is made of dead cells. A trunk supports very large trees and is a source of lumber.

▶ LIST: What are some functions of plant stems?

**Stem Structure** Both woody and herbaceous stems have similar tissues. However, the arrangement of the tissues is different in the two types of stems. Stems of both types contain tubes that carry water and dissolved minerals up from the roots. These tubes are made of tissue called **xylem**. Xylem carries water to the leaves. Extra water evaporates into the air through the leaves. Tissue that carries dissolved food, made in the leaves, downward to other parts of the plant is called **phloem**. Xylem and phloem make up the transport or vascular system of the plant.

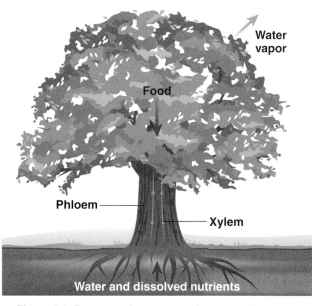

▲ **Figure 4-8** Transport tubes carry nutrients throughout a plant.

In different plants, xylem and phloem are arranged differently. In monocots, the xylem and phloem are in bundles throughout the stem. In dicots and gymnosperms, the phloem form an outer ring around an inner ring of xylem. As woody stems gets thicker each year, the inner layer of xylem gets thicker. The phloem always stay in the outer layer.

**3** ▶ **ANALYZE:** Why does a plant need xylem and phloem?

## ✓ CHECKING CONCEPTS

1. _____ stems are usually soft, smooth, and green.
2. Plants with _____ stems live for many growing seasons.
3. Roots and leaves are connected by _____.
4. Oak trees have _____ stems.
5. In monocots, xylem and phloem are found in _____.

## THINKING CRITICALLY

6. **SEQUENCE:** Make a flowchart that shows the paths of water and food in a plant.
7. **CLASSIFY:** Which plants listed have herbaceous stems? Which plants have woody stems?

   **a.** tulip      **d.** apple tree
   **b.** oak tree      **e.** sunflower
   **c.** daisy      **f.** willow

### Web InfoSearch

**Tree Rings** The xylem of a tree goes through two growth periods a year. These periods form bands called annual rings. You can determine a tree's age by counting the rings.

**SEARCH:** Use the Internet to find out more about tree rings. Then, put your findings into a report. Start your search at www.conceptsandchallenges.com. Some key search words are **annual growth rings** and **tree rings**.

## *Hands-On Activity*

### TRANSPORT IN PLANTS

*You will need a beaker, water, red or blue food coloring, a leafy celery stalk, and a knife.*

1. Put water in the beaker. Add 10–15 drops of food coloring.
2. Use the knife to cut a slice on an angle off the bottom of the celery stalk. Discard the slice. ⚠ CAUTION: Be careful when using a knife. Always cut away from yourself.
3. Put the cut end of the stalk into the water.
4. **OBSERVE:** Record your observations of the celery after 5, 10, 15, and 30 minutes.
5. **PREDICT:** What do you think will happen to the food coloring in the celery after 24 hours?
6. Keep the celery in the food coloring for 24 hours. Observe the location of the food coloring.

▲ **STEP 3** Put the cut end of the stalk into the colored water.

#### Practicing Your Skills

7. **DESCRIBE:** What happened to the food coloring in the celery?
8. **EVALUATE:** Was your prediction correct? Explain.
9. **INFER:** What life processes of a plant does this activity show?

# 4-3 What are leaves?

## INVESTIGATE

**Classifying Leaves**
HANDS-ON ACTIVITY

1. Collect a sample of several different leaves.
2. On a sheet of paper, trace the outline of each leaf. Draw in the vein pattern for each leaf.
3. Use a field guide to identify each leaf.

**THINK ABOUT IT:** How many basic leaf shapes can you identify?

STEP 1

## Objectives

Describe the structure of leaves. Classify leaves as simple or compound.

## Key Terms

**blade:** wide, flat part of a leaf

**vein:** bundle of tubes that contain the xylem and phloem in a leaf

**epidermis** (ehp-uh-DUR-mihs)**:** outer, protective layer of the leaf

**stoma** (STOH-muh), *pl.* **stomata** (STOH-muh-tuh)**:** tiny opening in the upper or lower surface of a leaf

**mesophyll** (MEHS-uh-fihl)**:** middle layer of leaf tissue in which photosynthesis occurs

**Leaf Structure** Most leaves have a stalk and a wide, flat part called the **blade**. The blade is the most important part of the leaf. Food-making takes place in the blade. The stalk supports the blade and attaches it to the stem of the plant. Throughout the leaf, there is a system of tubes called **veins** as shown in Figure 4-9. They are made up of xylem and phloem. They connect to the xylem and phloem in the stem. The xylem carries water and dissolved minerals into the leaf and the phloem carries food out of the leaf. Veins and stalks also support the leaf blade.

▶ **IDENTIFY:** What are the main parts of a leaf?

**Kinds of Leaves** In some plants, the leaf blades are in one piece. This kind of leaf is called a simple leaf. Maple, oak, and elm trees have simple leaves.

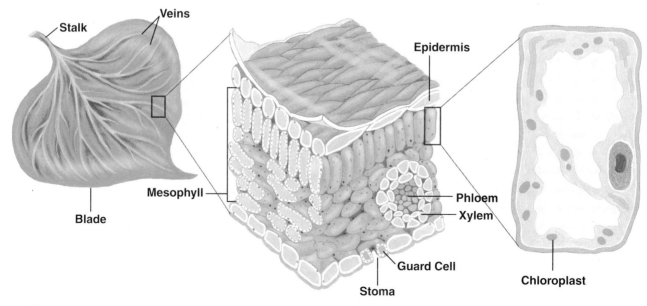

▲ **Figure 4-9** Parts of a leaf

In other plants, leaf blades are divided into pieces. This kind of leaf is called a compound leaf. The pieces that make up a compound leaf are called leaflets. Each leaflet looks like a small leaf. Poison ivy and roses have compound leaves.

 **OBSERVE:** What kind of leaf is shown in Figure 4-9?

**Leaf Tissues** Leaves are covered by a protective layer called the **epidermis** as shown in Figure 4-9. This layer prevents excess loss of water from the leaf. Scattered throughout the upper and lower epidermis are many tiny openings called **stomata**. Two guard cells control the size of each stoma. They open and close the stoma, controlling water loss. They also control the exchange of water vapor, oxygen, and carbon dioxide between the inner tissues of the leaf and the surrounding air. There are usually more stomata on the underside of a leaf than on the top.

Beneath the epidermis is a layer of tissue called the **mesophyll**. The cells in the mesophyll contain chloroplasts. Most of the food-making in the plant occurs in these cells. Veins extend throughout the mesophyll.

 **IDENTIFY:** In what tissue layer does most food-making take place in a leaf?

## Integrating Physical Science

**TOPIC: chemistry**

### THE CHEMISTRY OF CHANGING LEAVES

During the spring and summer months, the leaves on most deciduous trees appear green. That is because leaves contain chlorophyll, a pigment that reflects green light. Carotene, xanthophyll, and anthocyanin are other pigments also found in some trees. They reflect yellow and red light. The green chlorophyll masks the other pigments found in the leaves.

Sunlight causes chlorophyll to decompose. Plants constantly remake chlorophyll. To produce chlorophyll, plants need a lot of light and warm temperatures. When the temperatures get colder and the days become shorter, the trees begin to break down chlorophyll and store it for the next season. The absence of chlorophyll means the other pigments can be seen as reds, yellows, and oranges. Eventually, the leaves die and fall off the tree.

**Thinking Critically** Why do you think the trees store the chlorophyll for the next season?

▲ Figure 4-10 In autumn, the leaves of some trees change to bright reds, oranges, and yellows.

# 4-4 What is photosynthesis?

## Objective
Explain the importance of photosynthesis.

## Key Terms
**autotroph:** organism that can make its own food

**photosynthesis** (foht-oh-SIHN-thuh-sihs)**:** food-making process in plants that uses sunlight

**chlorophyll** (KLAWR-uh-fihl)**:** green material that is needed by plants for photosynthesis

**chloroplast:** organelle in plant cells that contains chlorophyll

**heterotroph:** organism that cannot make its own food

**Food Factories**　Green plants are **autotrophs**. They can make their own food in their leaves. The leaves are like "food factories." Some green stems also can make food. Food-making in plants is called **photosynthesis**. The food that plants make is a sugar called sucrose. You may know sucrose as the sugar you put on cereal. Plants change this sugar into starch, fats, and proteins. These nutrients are stored in the plants. They can be used at a later time.

**1**▶ NAME: What food do green plants make?

**Photosynthesis**　In photosynthesis, water and carbon dioxide are used to make simple sugars, such as glucose. These simple sugars are eventually made into sucrose, a more complex sugar. Roots absorb the needed water from the soil. Xylem carry the water up into the leaves. Carbon dioxide enters the plant through the stomata. Sunlight supplies the energy the plant needs to make the sugar. During photosynthesis, oxygen and water are given off as byproducts. The equation for photosynthesis is shown in Figure 4-11.

**2**▶ OBSERVE: On which side of the equation are the products shown?

**Chlorophyll**　Photosynthesis cannot occur without **chlorophyll**. Chlorophyll is a chemical pigment, or coloring, needed for photosynthesis. Other pigments in leaves are masked by chlorophyll. You see the colors of these pigments during the fall. Leaves change color. The different colors are caused by the other pigments.

Wherever there is chlorophyll in a plant, photosynthesis can occur. The chlorophyll is inside special organelles of plant cells. The organelles that contain chlorophyll are called **chloroplasts**. Leaf mesophyll cells contain many chloroplasts. Most photosynthesis takes place in the mesophyll layer.

**3**▶ NAME: What organelle contains chlorophyll?

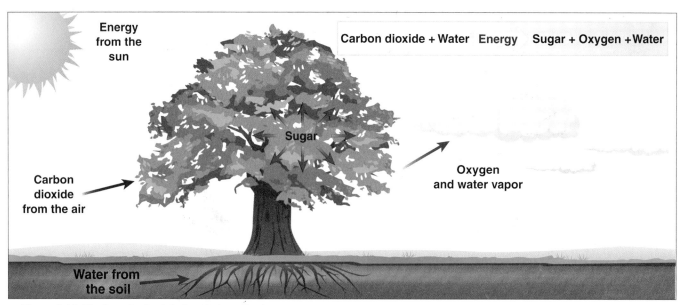

| Carbon dioxide + Water | Energy | Sugar + Oxygen + Water |

Energy from the sun

Carbon dioxide from the air

Sugar

Oxygen and water vapor

Water from the soil

▲ **Figure 4-11** Plants make food during photosynthesis.

**Plants and Animals** Animals cannot make their own food. They are **heterotrophs**. Instead, they get their energy by eating plants or by eating other animals that have eaten plants. Almost all living things, either directly or indirectly, get energy from the food made during photosynthesis.

In addition, most organisms get the oxygen they need from plants. About 21% of Earth's atmosphere is made up of oxygen. Living things need this oxygen to survive. Plants produce most of this oxygen during photosynthesis.

 **EXPLAIN:** How are plants important to people?

## ✓ CHECKING CONCEPTS

1. The food plants make is _____.
2. Chloroplasts contain the green material _____.
3. The materials a plant uses to make sugar are _____.
4. Water enters the plant through the _____.

 **THINKING CRITICALLY**

5. **EXPLAIN:** What happens to the oxygen produced during photosynthesis?
6. **APPLY:** What are two ways plants are important to you?

## INTERPRETING VISUALS

*Use Figure 4-12 to answer the following questions.*

7. **IDENTIFY:** In which layer does photosynthesis occur?
8. **IDENTIFY:** Through which structure does water for photosynthesis enter the leaf?
9. **INFER:** Which structure allows oxygen and carbon dioxide to enter and leave the leaf?

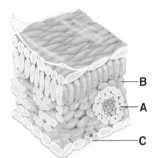

◄ Figure 4-12

 *Hands-On Activity*

## SEPARATING PIGMENTS

*You will need goggles; a paper towel; scissors; a metric ruler; timer; red, blue, and black nonpermanent felt pens; isopropyl alcohol; and a small bowl.*

1. Cut a strip of paper towel 3 cm wide and 12 cm long.
2. Use the red, blue, and black felt pens to make one dot about 5 cm from the bottom of the strip. Make only one dot on the paper towel.
3. Pour 1 cm of alcohol into the glass. ⚠ CAUTION: Do not breathe the fumes. Stand the strip of paper towel in the glass. One end of the paper towel should be over the rim.
4. **PREDICT:** What will happen to the dot on the strip?
5. **OBSERVE:** After 5 minutes, look at the strip. What happened to the dot after 5 minutes?

▲ **STEP 3** Stand the strip of paper towel in the glass.

### Practicing Your Skills

6. **INFER:** What would happen if plant pigment were used instead of ink in this experiment?
7. **HYPOTHESIZE:** If you made a dark pigment from a plant that was green and red, what colors might you see in a separation?

# THE Big IDEA

## What are the physics of a tree?

Physics is the study of force and energy. Both energy and force play an important role in the life of plants.

Chloroplasts absorb sunlight, a form of light energy. That energy helps change carbon dioxide and water into sugars and oxygen. Sugar contains chemical energy and is transferred to the fruit and leaves. Later, the energy is transferred again to birds, insects, or humans who eat the plant.

The amount of force acting on a surface is called pressure. Pressure helps explain how water travels from a plant's roots to its highest leaves. Molecules move from areas of high pressure to areas of low pressure. As leaf cells lose water through evaporation, they also lose pressure. A low-pressure cell quickly draws water from a high-pressure cell. This chain continues, pulling water from the base to the top.

Many other physical science principles are at work in the life of a tree. Look at the boxes of text that appear on this page and the next. They point out some of these processes. Follow the directions in the Science Log to learn more about "the big idea." ✦

**WRITING ACTIVITY**

*Science Log*

Look at the tree on these two pages. Which part of the tree do you think uses the most energy to do its job? In your science log, research and write about the physical science processes at work in this part of the tree. Start your search at www.conceptsandchallenges.com.

### Root

Typically, molecules move from more crowded areas to less crowded areas. That is how root hairs absorb water from soil. The process is called **osmosis**. The opposite happens when roots absorb minerals. Energy is used to pump the minerals from a less crowded area to a more crowded area. This process is called **active transport**.

Osmosis H₂O

Root hairs

Transport tubes

Active Transport

Minerals

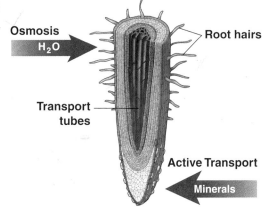

**Figure 4-13** ▶
Energy and force play an important role in the life of a tree.

**Stomata**

Water evaporates into the air in a process called **transpiration**. During transpiration, water molecules escape from the leaf through the stomata. This action causes more water molecules to be drawn up the trunk and into the leaves.

Leaf stoma

$CO_2$

$O_2$

Water vapor

**Trunk**

One of the main reasons water moves up a tree is because it is pulled upward. As water evaporates, a force called **transpiration pull** draws water up through the trunk of the tree. The water flows upward through the xylem. The strong attraction of water molecules to each other, called **cohesion**, also helps to pull water upward. Transpiration pull and cohesion are strong enough to raise water more than 300 feet.

**Inside of tree trunk**

Food

Phloem

Xylem

Water and dissolved nutrients

# 4-5 What are flowers?

## Objectives

Identify the flower as the reproductive organ of a plant. Describe the parts of a flower.

## Key Terms

**sepal** (SEE-puhl): special kind of leaf that protects the flower bud

**petal:** white or brightly colored structure above the sepal of a flower

**pistil:** female reproductive organ in a flower

**stamen** (STAY-muhn): male reproductive organ in a flower

**perfect flower:** flower with both female and male reproductive organs

**imperfect flower:** flower with either male or female reproductive organs, but not both

---

**Flowers** Not all plants have flowers. However, in plants with flowers, the flower is the organ of sexual reproduction. Flowers contain the male and female reproductive parts of a flowering plant, or an angiosperm.

**1▶ DEFINE:** What are flowers?

**Parts of a Flower** A flower is made up of several parts. The bottom of a flower is surrounded by sepals. **Sepals** are a special kind of leaf. They protect the flower bud. In some flowers, the sepals look like small green leaves. In others, they are large and brightly colored. In Figure 4-14, the sepals look similar to the petals.

The **petals** of a flower are just inside the sepals. After the sepals fold back, the petals of the flower can be seen. The petals are another kind of leaf. They may be white or brightly colored. Some flowers, such as roses and lilies, are sweet-smelling and have large, colorful petals. Unlike roses and lilies, the flowers of grass plants have very small petals that are not colorful or sweet-

smelling. Petals protect the reproductive organs of the plant and attract insects and other pollinators. Inside the petals are the reproductive organs for the plant.

**2▶ IDENTIFY:** What are two special kinds of leaves in a flower?

**Reproductive Organs** The reproductive organs in a flower are the pistil and the stamen. The **pistil** is the female reproductive organ. The **stamen** is the male reproductive organ. A flower usually has one pistil with several stamens around it. These organs are located inside the circle of petals.

▲ **Figure 4-14** The parts of a perfect flower

Some flowers have both male and female reproductive organs. These flowers are called **perfect flowers**. The lily in Figure 4-14 is an example of a perfect flower. Other flowers may have only male or only female reproductive organs. These flowers are called **imperfect flowers**. Male flowers only have stamens. Female flowers only have pistils. Look at Figure 4-15 on the next page. It shows an imperfect flower.

▲ **Figure 4-15** The zucchini plant has imperfect flowers. The male flower is shown on the left and the female on the right.

 **CLASSIFY:** The pistil and the stamen are parts of what plant system?

## ✓ CHECKING CONCEPTS

1. The organs of sexual reproduction in plants are the _____.

2. Sepals and petals are special kinds of _____.

3. The _____ is the female reproductive organ in a flower.

4. The _____ is the male reproductive organ in a flower.

## 💡 THINKING CRITICALLY

5. **MODEL:** Draw a model of a flower. Label the petals, sepals, stamen, and pistil.

6. **HYPOTHESIZE:** Why is it important for insects to be attracted to flowers?

## BUILDING SCIENCE SKILLS

*Researching* Use a dictionary or library references to find out the meaning of the terms *pistillate* and *staminate*. Research five different types of imperfect flowers. Then, classify each imperfect flower as pistillate or staminate.

 *Real-Life Science*

## BOTANICAL GARDENS

A wide variety of plants are on public display at botanical gardens. Visitors to the Missouri Botanical Gardens, for example, can explore theme gardens, educational greenhouses, and hundreds of acres of nature preserve. There is even a miniature rain forest housed in a building called the Climatron.

▲ **Figure 4-16** The Missouri Botanical Garden

Botanical gardens are necessary because many plants are becoming rare. Plant habitats often are destroyed when people develop land. Introducing new plants to an area when people travel or relocate also can endanger plants. In botanical gardens, plants are protected and displayed for people's enjoyment.

People who work in botanical gardens realize the importance of plants. Plants are an important source of food and oxygen. The chemistry of plants can help to control pests. Also, certain plants may hold the key that unlocks the cure of a fatal disease, such as cancer.

**Thinking Critically** Why are botanical gardens important to the community?

# 4-6 How do flowering plants reproduce?

## Objective

Describe how flowering plants reproduce.

## Key Terms

**filament:** stalk of the stamen

**anther:** part of the stamen that produces pollen

**pollen grain:** male reproductive cell of a plant

**fertilization** (fuhrt-uhl-ih-ZAY-shuhn)**:** joining of the nuclei of the male and female reproductive cells

**pollination** (pahl-uh-NAY-shuhn)**:** movement of pollen from a stamen to a pistil

**Stamens and Pollen** Stamens have two main parts. These parts are the filament and the anther. The **filament** is the thin stalk that holds up the anther. The **anther** is the part that produces pollen grains. **Pollen grains** are the male reproductive structures that contain sperm. Pollen is released when an anther bursts open.

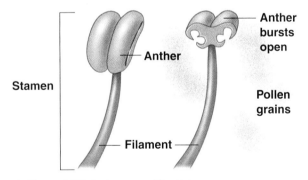

▲ **Figure 4-17** A stamen and its parts

▶ DEFINE: What is pollen?

**Fertilization** In sexual reproduction, reproductive cells from the male and female must meet. The joining of the nuclei of male and female reproductive cells is called **fertilization**. In flowering plants, fertilization takes place inside the pistil.

▶ DEFINE: What is fertilization?

**Pollination**

For fertilization to take place, pollen grains must first move from a stamen to a pistil. This is called **pollination**. Pollen often is moved by wind, insects, birds, and even bats. Sometimes, pollen is carried by water.

▲ **Figure 4-18** Bees carry pollen from plant to plant.

▶ CLASSIFY: What activity of a plant is pollination a part of?

**Self-Pollination** In many flowers, the stamens are taller than the pistil. Pollen can fall off the anther on top of a stamen and land on the pistil in the same flower. This kind of pollination is called self-pollination. Self-pollination also occurs when pollen from one flower is carried to the pistil of another flower on the same plant.

▲ **Figure 4-19** Self-pollination

▶ EXPLAIN: In what two ways may self-pollination occur?

**Cross-Pollination** Sometimes pollen is carried from the stamen of a flower on one plant to the pistil of a flower on another similar plant. This is called cross-pollination. Some plants have separate male and female flowers. Sometimes the male and female flowers are on different plants. This means they are male and female plants. These plants must cross-pollinate. Cross-pollination also can occur between two different plants that have perfect flowers.

▲ **Figure 4-20** Cross-pollination can occur between different plants with perfect flowers.

 **NAME:** What kind of pollination occurs between flowers on different plants?

## ✓ CHECKING CONCEPTS

1. The nuclei of male and female reproductive cells join in the process of _____.

2. Male reproductive cells are the _____.

3. Movement of pollen from a stamen to a pistil is _____.

4. Pollination between flowers on different plants is called _____.

5. Pollination between flowers on the same plant is called _____.

### 💡 THINKING CRITICALLY

6. **INFER:** Would flowers that depend on wind for pollination probably have flat, open flowers or tall, closed flowers? Explain.

7. **ANALYZE:** How might an insect move pollen from one flower to another?

### HEALTH AND SAFETY TIP

Hay fever is an allergic reaction to the pollen of certain plants. Large amounts of pollen in the air cause people with hay fever to sneeze. Their eyes may become red and watery. Prepare a poster that shows which plants cause hay fever, the times of the year that people suffer from hay fever, and how it can be treated.

 *People in Science*

## PLANT GENETICIST

Plant geneticists are scientists who work on ways to improve plant varieties. They study how to make plants and crops more suited to people's needs. Plant geneticists breed plants with desirable traits. They want to find out if the new breeds are more resistant to disease, more nutritious, and easier to grow.

Surinder K. Vasal, a plant geneticist from India, developed a new variety of corn. In many countries, people rely on corn as their basic food. Although corn is a good food, it is not rich in nutritionally balanced protein. Poor children who cannot get quality protein from other sources often become malnourished. Working with Evangelina Villegas, a Mexican scientist, Vasal perfected a protein-rich variety of corn called quality protein maize (QPM). This corn looks and tastes like regular corn, but it has twice as much protein and produces a larger crop. Now, QPM is grown in parts of Africa, China, Mexico, and Central America. There has been a big improvement in nutrition levels in those areas. In 2000, Vasal and Villegas received the $250,000 Millennium World Food Prize for their work on QPM.

**Thinking Critically** What are some desirable traits of a plant that a plant geneticist may be interested in reproducing?

## Objectives

Identify the parts of the pistil. Explain how seeds and fruits form.

## Key Terms

**stigma** (STIHG-muh): top part of the pistil

**style:** stalk of the pistil of a flower

**ovary** (OH-vuh-ree): bottom part of the pistil

**ovule** (AHV-yool): part of the ovary that develops into a seed after fertilization

**embryo:** undeveloped plant or animal

**fruit:** mature ovary and its seeds

**Parts of a Pistil** A pistil is made up of three parts. The top part is the **stigma**. Below the stigma is a tube called the **style**. The style connects the stigma to the bottom of the pistil. The bottom of the pistil is called the **ovary**. Inside the ovary are the **ovules**. The ovule is the part of the ovary that develops into a seed after fertilization. It contains the female reproductive cell, or egg.

**1ᐅ** IDENTIFY: What are the parts of a pistil?

**Forming a Seed** After a pollen grain lands on the stigma, it begins to change. The pollen cell grows a tube. This tube is called a pollen tube. The pollen tube grows down into the stigma. It continues to grow down through the style and the ovary. Finally, the tip of the pollen tube enters the ovule.

After the pollen tube enters the ovule, the tip of the tube dissolves. The sperm in the pollen grain move into the ovule. The nucleus of the pollen cell joins with the nucleus of the egg in the ovule. The joining of the two nuclei is called fertilization. After fertilization, the ovule develops into a seed. A new plant can grow from a seed.

**2ᐅ** ANALYZE: Why does the pollen grain grow a tube after it lands on the stigma?

**Fruits** Ovules are found inside an ovary. An ovary may have only one ovule or it may have more than one ovule. When the ovules are fertilized, they develop into seeds. Each seed contains a very young, or undeveloped, plant. Scientists call an undeveloped plant or animal an **embryo**. A seed contains a plant embryo.

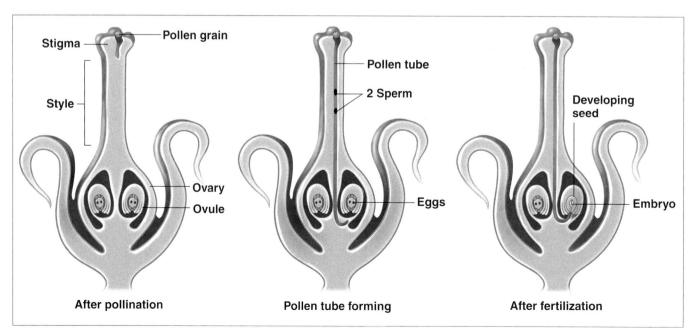

▲ **Figure 4-21** Pollination leads to fertilization and the formation of a seed.

While the seeds are forming, the ovary is changing. The ovary becomes very large. It surrounds and protects the seeds and the embryos inside the seeds. A mature ovary and its seeds are called a **fruit**. Plums and tomatoes are examples of fruits.

▲ **Figure 4-22** Apples have several seeds.

▶ DISTINGUISH: What is the relationship between the ovary and the seed?

## ✓ CHECKING CONCEPTS

1. The female reproductive cells are in the _____.

2. A seed is formed after _____.

3. The undeveloped plant inside a seed is called an _____.

4. A pollen grain that lands on a stigma grows a _____.

## THINKING CRITICALLY

5. **MODEL:** Draw and label the parts of a pistil.

6. **INFER:** The top of a stigma is usually sticky. What might be an advantage of this stickiness?

## BUILDING SCIENCE SKILLS

*Classifying* Scientists classify any plant part with seeds as fruit. Vegetables are the leaves, stems, or roots of plants. People classify fruits and vegetables differently. Classify each of the plant parts listed as if you were a scientist and then as you would every day.

a. tomato     f. celery

b. beets     g. lettuce

c. cucumber     h. papaya

d. carrot     i. green pepper

e. peach

## *Real-Life Science*

### SEED PLANTS YOU EAT

You may have eaten popcorn the last time you went to the movies. Popcorn comes from a seed plant. Have you ever had a peanut butter sandwich? Peanuts also come from a seed plant. So does the wheat used to make bread. Many of the foods we eat come from seed plants.

Apples, watermelons, and oranges are the fruits of a seed plant. The fruit of a seed plant is really a fleshy, juicy container for the seed. The fruit protects the seed. For example, inside a watermelon, there are a lot of black seeds. All the rest of the melon is protecting those seeds from water loss, disease, and insects.

Many of the foods we call vegetables and grains are really fruits of a seed plant. Anything that has seeds in it but is not a cone is a fruit. This includes tomatoes, beans, oats, and wheat. All these fruits have seeds.

**Thinking Critically** How many other fruits can you name?

▲ **Figure 4-23** Watermelons are fruits with seeds.

# LAB ACTIVITY
# Identifying the Parts of a Flower

**Materials**

Sheet of white paper

Dissecting needle

Tulip, daffodil, lily, or gladiolus flower

Hand lens

## BACKGROUND

Most flowers contain a pistil, stamens, sepals, and petals. The pistil and stamens are the reproductive organs. The sepals and petals are specialized kinds of leaves. The ovary is the place that seeds will be formed.

## PURPOSE

In this activity, you will dissect a flower and study its parts.

## PROCEDURE

1. Copy the chart in Figure 4-24 onto a sheet of paper. Label the chart.

2. Carefully remove the sepals from a flower. How many sepals does your flower have? Record your observations in your chart.

3. Remove the petals from your flower. How many petals does your flower have? What color are they? Record your observations in your chart.

4. Look at one of the stamens through a hand lens. Identify the anther and the filament.

5. Use a dissecting needle to release the pollen grains from the anther onto a sheet of white paper. Examine the pollen grains with a hand lens. Draw the pollen grains below your chart.

6. Remove the pistil from your flower. Examine it through the hand lens. Identify the stigma, the style, and the ovary. How many pistils does your flower have? Record your observations in your chart.

▲ **STEP 3** Carefully remove the petals from a flower.

▲ **STEP 4** Examine the stamens.

▲ **STEP 5** Remove pollen from anther.

▲ **STEP 7** Slice the pistil down the middle.

7. Using the dissecting needle, slice the pistil down the middle. Examine the inside of the ovary with the hand lens. ⚠ CAUTION: Be extremely careful when using dissecting needles.

8. Remove an ovule from the ovary and study it with the hand lens. Draw an ovule below your chart.

| Part | Number | Color |
|---|---|---|
| Sepals | | |
| Petals | | |
| Stamens | | |
| Pistil | | |

▲ **Figure 4-24** Copy this chart onto a sheet of paper.

## CONCLUSIONS

1. **IDENTIFY:** How are the parts of a flower arranged?

2. **OBSERVE:** Is there a pattern to the number of sepals and petals in your flower?

3. **EXPLAIN:** How do you think your flower is pollinated?

4. **APPLY:** How many seeds could have developed in the ovary?

# 4-8 What are the parts of a seed?

## *Objective*

Identify the parts of a seed.

## *Key Terms*

**seed coat:** outside covering of a seed

**hilum** (HY-luhm)**:** mark on the seed coat where the seed was attached to the ovary

**germinate** (JUR-muh-nayt)**:** to grow from a seed into an embryo plant

**Inside a Seed** Food is stored in the seed. The developing embryo uses the food as it grows. Figure 4-25 shows the inside of a green bean seed that has two large leaves, called cotyledons. In dicots they are large and cotyledons store food as starch. Monocots only have one small cotyledon. In monocots, food is stored in a special tissue called the endosperm. This food is absorbed through the cotyledon. The corn in Figure 4-25 is a monocot.

The embryo is attached to one of the seed halves. The embryo has a tiny root, a stem, and one or two cotyledons. If you plant the seed in good soil and water it, the embryo will begin to grow, or **germinate**. For some plants, as the seed germinates,

the cotyledons are pushed above ground. When the first true leaves unfold and begin photosynthesis, the cotyledons wither and die. In time, the embryo will develop into an adult plant.

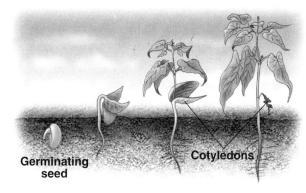

▲ **Figure 4-26** Germination

▶ **INFER:** Why would the cotyledons no longer be needed once photosynthesis begins?

**Seed Coat** All seeds have an outside covering. This outer covering is called the **seed coat**. Most seed coats are hard. The hard coat protects the embryo. Some seeds are protected so well that they can be kept for many years. They will still grow when they are planted.

▶ **NAME:** What is the outside covering of a seed called?

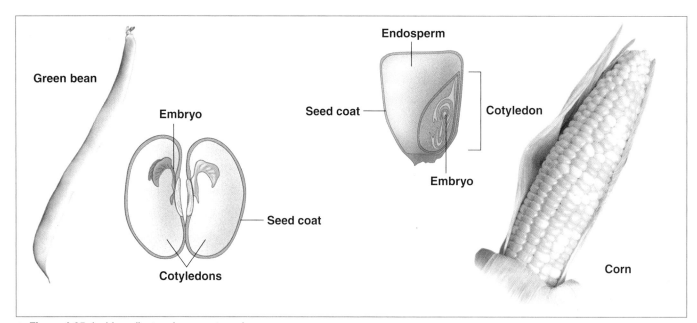

▲ **Figure 4-25** Inside a dicot and monocot seed

**Hilum** The **hilum** is a small mark, or scar, on the seed. The hilum is where the seed was attached to the ovary. Near the hilum, there is a small opening. The opening is where the pollen tube entered the ovule.

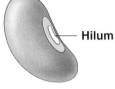
▲ Figure 4-27
A seed showing a hilum

**3** ▶ **DESCRIBE:** What is the hilum?

**Seed Dispersal** Some seeds, such as dandelion seeds, are scattered, or dispersed, by the wind. Other seeds are dispersed by water. The fruit of a coconut plant can carry its seed thousands of kilometers on ocean currents.

Animals also help disperse seeds. For example, many animals eat berries and then eliminate the seeds in their waste. Some seeds have hooklike structures that stick to a mammal's fur. As the animal moves from place to place, so do the seeds. If a seed lands in a place with enough light, water, and nutrients, it will begin to germinate.

**4** ▶ **LIST:** What are three ways seeds can be dispersed?

 **CHECKING CONCEPTS**

1. What is the outside of a seed called?
2. What part of a seed develops into an adult plant?
3. In what form is food stored in a seed?
4. What are the three parts of all seeds?
5. What is germination?

 **THINKING CRITICALLY**

6. **INFER:** All plants need water, sunlight, and nutrients to grow. Which of these does a seed not need to germinate?
7. **MODEL:** Draw a diagram showing three types of seeds that are dispersed by the following methods.
   a. water
   b. wind
   c. animal fur

 *Hands-On Activity*

**GROWING SEEDS**

*In this activity, you will need eight pinto beans, paper towels, potting soil, and two glasses.*

1. Fold a sheet of paper towel in half. Line one glass with the paper towel. Stuff a wad of paper towel into the bottom of the glass.
2. Place four pinto beans between the paper towel lining and the glass. Make sure the beans are placed an equal distance from each other.
3. Dampen the paper towels with water. Do not drench the paper towels. They should be damp to the touch.
4. Observe the glass for a week. Make sure that the paper towels are always damp. Record your observations.
5. Fill the second glass with soil. Place four pinto beans in the soil. Water the soil.

▲ **STEP 2** Make sure the beans are spaced apart equally.

**Practicing Your Skills**

6. **OBSERVE:** At the end of the week, which seeds had the most growth?
7. **INFER:** What can you tell about the best conditions to germinate seeds from this experiment?

# 4-9 How do plants reproduce asexually?

## Objective
Identify ways that plants reproduce asexually.

## Key Terms
**asexual reproduction:** reproduction needing only one parent

**vegetative propagation** (VEHJ-uh-tayt-ihv prahp-uh-GAY-shuhn)**:** kind of asexual reproduction that uses parts of plants to grow new plants

**tuber:** underground stem

**bulb:** underground stem covered with fleshy leaves

▲ **Figure 4-28** Potatoes are tubers.

**Reproduction Without Seeds** Some plants can reproduce without male and female cells joining to form seeds. This method of reproduction is called **asexual reproduction**. One type of asexual reproduction in plants is called **vegetative propagation,** or vegetative reproduction. During vegetative propagation, the growing parts of plants develop into new plants. The growing parts are roots, stems, or leaves. In vegetative propagation, the new plants that develop are genetically identical to the parent plant.

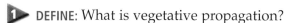 **DEFINE:** What is vegetative propagation?

**Tubers** Some plants, such as white potatoes, have underground stems. An underground stem is called a **tuber**. A white potato may have many small white buds growing on its skin. These buds are called eyes. The eyes of the potato are the organs of vegetative reproduction. When planted in soil, each eye may grow into a new potato plant. Each new plant is genetically identical to the parent plant.

When farmers plant tuber crops, they must be careful to dig them all up at the end of the growing season. If parts of the tubers are left in the ground, they will begin growing the next season and may interfere with other crops.

**DEFINE:** What is a tuber?

**Bulbs** A **bulb** is an organ of vegetative reproduction in some plants. A bulb is an underground stem. It differs from the underground stem called a tuber. A bulb is covered with thick leaves. An onion is an example of a bulb. Each onion plant produces many bulbs. When planted, each bulb may grow into a new onion plant. Other plants that grow from bulbs are daffodils, lilies, and tulips.

**NAME:** What are two plants that grow from bulbs?

**Cuttings** Some plants can grow new plants from pieces of themselves. These plant pieces are called cuttings. Roots make good cuttings. For example, the roots of asparagus are organs of vegetative reproduction. If fleshy roots are divided and planted, they will begin to grow new roots. In time, a new asparagus plant will grow. The new plant will be genetically identical to the parent.

New plants may also grow from some leaf and stem cuttings. A leaf is cut off of the plant. The leaf stalk is placed in water. Roots will grow from the stalk, and a new plant will grow. The same thing can be done with the stems of some plants.

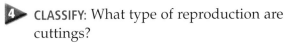
◀ **Figure 4-29** This houseplant is growing from cuttings.

**4** ▶ CLASSIFY: What type of reproduction are cuttings?

## ✓ CHECKING CONCEPTS

1. What kind of reproduction is vegetative propagation?
2. What are the growing parts of a plant?
3. What are the organs of vegetative propagation in a potato?
4. What kind of organ of reproduction is an onion?

### 💡 THINKING CRITICALLY

5. EXPLAIN: How can a houseplant be grown asexually?
6. INFER: What are the advantages of using asexual reproduction in farming?

## Web InfoSearch

**Grafting** Grafting is a kind of vegetative propagation. It is used to produce new kinds of plants. Twigs from one tree are attached to another. For example, seedless oranges cannot reproduce themselves. They can only reproduce by grafting. Twigs from a branch with seedless oranges are grafted onto a regular orange tree. Seedless oranges grow on the grafted branch.

**SEARCH:** Use the Internet to find out more about grafting. Then, write your findings in a report. Start your search at www.conceptsandchallenges.com. Some key search words are **grafting** and **seedless oranges**.

---

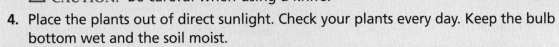

 *Hands-On Activity*

### GROWING PLANTS ASEXUALLY

*You will need safety goggles, gloves, two plastic cups, soil, water, 4 toothpicks, an onion, a potato with eyes, and a knife.*

1. Put on the goggles and gloves. Half-fill one cup with soil. Half-fill the other with water.
2. Equally space four toothpicks around the "equator" of the onion. Set the onion, root end down into the cup of water. The toothpicks should sit on the rim of the cup so the onion is touching the water, but not the bottom of the cup.
3. Cut a piece of potato that has an eye. Put it in the paper cup. Add some soil. Water the soil.
   ⚠ CAUTION:  Be careful when using a knife.
4. Place the plants out of direct sunlight. Check your plants every day. Keep the bulb bottom wet and the soil moist.

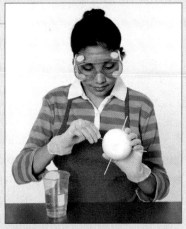
▲ **STEP 2** Push toothpicks into the onion.

#### Practicing Your Skills

5. IDENTIFY: Which plant grew roots first?
6. COMPARE: How is the reproduction of the onion and the potato similar?

# 4-10 What are tropisms?

## Observing Tropisms
### HANDS-ON ACTIVITY

STEP 3

1. Get a sample of a mimosa plant.
2. Use a hand lens to carefully observe the leaves of the plant. Draw a model of the leaves in your notebook.
3. Touch the leaves of the plant. What happens? Draw a picture or diagram of the leaves in your notebook.

**THINK ABOUT IT:** Touching the mimosa plant was a stimulus. How did the plant respond?

## Objective
Relate different stimuli to the tropisms they cause.

## Key Terms
**stimulus:** change that causes a response

**tropism** (TROH-pihz-uhm)**:** change in a plant's growth in response to a stimulus

**phototropism:** plant's response to light

**gravitropism:** plant's response to gravity

**hydrotropism:** plant's response to water

**thigmotropism:** plant's response to touch

**Plant Responses** All plants respond to changes in their environment. They may respond to light, gravity, water, or touch. Each response is caused by a stimulus. A **stimulus** is a change that causes a response. The reaction of a plant to a stimulus that causes a change in growth is called a **tropism**. Usually, a plant responds to each stimulus by growing in a certain direction. Because most tropisms happen very slowly, you may not notice them.

▶ **HYPOTHESIZE:** What stimulus do you think would make a plant grow upward?

**Light** Green plants respond to the stimulus of light. This is called **phototropism**. Most stems and leaves grow toward light. A plant left near a sunny window will bend toward the light.

Some stems even change their response to light. The flower stem of a peanut plant grows toward sunlight. After pollination, the flower stem grows away from light. It grows down into the soil, where the peanuts can develop in the dark.

▲ **Figure 4-30** This plant's response is an example of phototropism.

 **EXPLAIN:** How do most plant stems respond to light?

**Gravity** Plants respond to the stimulus of gravity. This is called **gravitropism**. Gravity is the force of attraction that exists between all objects in the universe. Roots grow down in response to gravity. If a plant in a flowerpot is tilted on its side, its roots will bend and grow down. If that plant is turned upright, its roots will bend again and grow down.

Most stems grow away from the pull of gravity. If a plant in a flowerpot is tilted on its side, its stem will respond by bending and growing up again. Rhizomes, the underground stems of some plants, grow sideways in response to gravity. They grow horizontally just under the surface of the soil.

▲ **Figure 4-31** This tree is responding to gravity.

**3** ▶ **DESCRIBE:** How does a plant root respond to gravity?

**Water** Plants respond to the stimulus of water. This is called **hydrotropism**. Roots grow toward water. In most plants, this tropism is not very strong. It occurs only when water touches the roots. In some plants, this tropism is very strong. For example, the roots of a willow tree will grow into and clog sewer and water pipes.

**4** ▶ **EXPLAIN:** How do roots respond to water?

**Touch** Plants respond to the stimulus of touch. When a vine touches a fence, it grows around it. A plant's response to touch is called **thigmotropism**.

Some plants respond immediately to stimuli. Since growth is not involved, it is not a tropism. The Venus' flytrap is a plant that responds quickly to touch. Each leaf of the Venus' flytrap is hinged so that it can close like a book. Each leaf has stiff spines on its edges. The inner surface of each leaf has six stiff hairs. When an insect walks across a leaf, it may touch the hairs. Touching only one hair causes no reaction. Touching two hairs or jiggling one hair twice makes the leaf snap

▲ **Figure 4-32** A Venus' flytrap responds to touch.

shut in one second or less. The spines interlock to form a cage. The insect is trapped inside the closed leaf. The leaf stays closed as the insect is digested.

**5** ▶ **DEFINE:** What is thigmotropism?

## ☑ CHECKING CONCEPTS

1. Something in the environment that causes a reaction to occur is a _____.
2. A change in a plant's growth in response to stimuli is a _____.
3. Green plants grow toward the stimulus of _____.
4. Roots grow down in response to _____.
5. In hydrotropism, roots grow toward _____.
6. A Venus' flytrap responds quickly to _____.
7. Plants bending toward a window is evidence of _____.

## 💡 THINKING CRITICALLY

8. **ANALYZE:** In what direction would plant stems grow in the dark? Explain your answer.
9. **HYPOTHESIZE:** What would happen to a plant's roots if you turned the plant upside down?
10. **INFER:** A drain pipe from a house seems to be clogged. A willow tree has been growing near the house for many years. What is one possible reason for the clogged drain?

## DESIGNING AN EXPERIMENT

*Design an experiment to solve the following problem. Include a hypothesis, variables, a procedure, and a type of data to study.*

PROBLEM: Luis wants to know how his houseplant will respond to stimuli, such as light, gravity, water, and touch. Pick one of these stimuli. Design an experiment that will help Luis learn how his plant will respond to this stimulus.

## Chapter Summary

### Lessons 4-1 and 4-2

- Roots hold plants in the soil, absorb water and minerals, and some store food.
- Stems support leaves and transport materials between the roots and the leaves.

### Lesson 4-3

- Most leaves have a **blade**, a stalk, and **veins**.
- The **epidermis** and the **mesophyll** are layers of leaf tissues.

### Lesson 4-4

- In **photosynthesis**, sunlight provides energy for carbon dioxide and water to form sugar. Oxygen and water are given off as byproducts.

### Lesson 4-5

- Flowers are organs of sexual reproduction.
- The reproductive organs in a flower are the **stamens** and **pistil**.

### Lesson 4-6

- **Fertilization** occurs when the nuclei of a male and a female reproductive cell join.
- **Pollination** is the movement of pollen from a stamen to a pistil. Self-pollination is pollination of flowers on the same plant. Cross-pollination is pollination between flowers on different plants.

### Lesson 4-7

- A **pollen grain** that lands on a **stigma** forms a pollen tube that grows down into the **ovary**.
- A fertilized **ovule** becomes a seed that contains an **embryo**. The ovary surrounds and protects the seeds and becomes a **fruit**.

### Lesson 4-8

- Seeds contain food that the embryo uses as it grows. The **embryo** in a seed is a tiny plant that has a tiny root, a stem, and leaves.

### Lesson 4-9

- Plants can reproduce asexually by **vegetative propagation**. **Tubers** and **bulbs** are organs of vegetative propagation.

### Lesson 4-10

- **Tropisms** are a change in a plant's growth in response to **stimuli**.

## Key Term Challenges

anther (p. 82)
asexual reproduction (p. 90)
autotroph (p. 76)
blade (p. 74)
bulb (p. 90)
chlorophyll (p. 76)
chloroplast (p. 76)
embryo (p. 84)
epidermis (p. 74)
fertilization (p. 82)
fibrous root system (p. 70)
filament (p. 82)
fruit (p. 84)
germinate (p. 88)
gravitropism (p. 92)
herbaceous stem (p. 72)
heterotroph (p. 76)
hilum (p. 88)
hydrotropism (p. 92)
imperfect flower (p. 80)
mesophyll (p. 74)
ovary (p. 84)
ovule (p. 84)
perfect flower (p. 80)

petal (p. 80)
phloem (p. 72)
photosynthesis (p. 76)
phototropism (p. 92)
pistil (p. 80)
pollen grain (p. 82)
pollination (p. 82)
root cap (p. 70)
root hair (p. 70)
seed coat (p. 88)
sepal (p. 80)
stamen (p. 80)
stigma (p. 84)
stimulus (p. 92)
stoma (p. 74)
style (p. 84)
taproot system (p. 70)
thigmotropism (p. 92)
tropism (p. 92)
tuber (p. 90)
vegetative propagation (p. 90)
vein (p. 74)
woody stem (p. 72)
xylem (p. 72)

**MATCHING** **Write the Key Term from above that best matches each description.**

1. root system made up of large root and many small thin roots

2. thin, hairlike structure on the outer layer of the root tip

3. cup-shaped mass of cells that covers and protects a root tip

4. plant's response to gravity

5. special kind of leaf that protects the flower bud

6. stem that is soft and green

7. asexual reproduction that uses parts of plants to grow new plants

8. plant's response to touch

9. organism that makes its own food

10. outside covering of a seed

# Content Challenges TEST PREP

**MULTIPLE CHOICE** Write the letter of the term or phrase that best completes each sentence.

1. In flowering plants, fertilization takes place inside the
   a. stamen.
   b. pistil.
   c. anther.
   d. sepal.

2. Most of the photosynthesis in a plant occurs in the
   a. epidermis.
   b. mesophyll.
   c. stomata.
   d. guard cells.

3. Perfect flowers have
   a. only male reproductive organs.
   b. only female reproductive organs.
   c. both male and female reproductive organs.
   d. neither male nor female reproductive organs.

4. The rough outer layer of a woody stem is the
   a. root cap.
   b. xylem.
   c. mesophyll.
   d. bark.

5. During photosynthesis, the food that plants make is a
   a. starch.
   b. protein.
   c. sugar.
   d. fat.

6. Fibrous root systems are found in
   a. grass.
   b. carrots.
   c. radishes.
   d. dandelions.

7. Chloroplasts contain the green material
   a. chlorophyll.
   b. mesophyll.
   c. xylem.
   d. phloem.

8. The small white buds growing on a potato are called
   a. bulbs.
   b. eyes.
   c. tubers.
   d. cuttings.

9. A large ovary and its seeds are called
   a. an embryo.
   b. an ovule.
   c. a fruit.
   d. a seed coat.

**TRUE/FALSE** Write *true* if the statement is true. If the statement is false, change the underlined term to make the statement true.

10. The two main parts of a <u>pistil</u> are the filament and anther.

11. Asexual reproduction in plants is called vegetative <u>pollination</u>.

12. Most seed coats are <u>soft</u>.

13. Tropisms usually happen very <u>quickly</u>.

14. In some plants, <u>food</u> can be stored in the roots.

15. Roots grow from the <u>tip</u>.

16. An onion is an example of a <u>bulb</u>.

17. Petals are a kind of <u>stem</u>.

18. The pieces that make up a <u>simple</u> leaf are called leaflets.

# Concept Challenges ~~TEST PREP~~

WRITTEN RESPONSE **Answer each of the following questions in complete sentences.**

1. **APPLY:** What would happen to the stem of a potted plant if you placed the plant on its side?

2. **HYPOTHESIZE:** What do you think might happen if a herbaceous plant grew taller than 2 m?

3. **CONTRAST:** What is the difference between pollination and fertilization?

4. **ANALYZE:** Fruit does not usually ripen until a seed is mature. Why is this important for the survival of the plant?

5. **EXPLAIN:** A slimy substance is produced by the root cap. How do you think this substance helps a plant grow?

INTERPRETING A DIAGRAM **Use Figure 4-33 to answer the following questions.**

6. Which structure is the male reproductive organ?

7. Which structure is the female reproductive organ?

8. Which structures protect the reproductive organs of a plant?

9. Which structures protect the flower bud?

10. Is the flower a perfect flower or an imperfect flower? Explain.

11. Which structure produces pollen grains?

12. Which structure contains female reproductive cells?

▲ **Figure 4-33** A lily

# Chapter 5 Animals Without Backbones

▲ **Figure 5-1** The giant clam has an outer shell but no backbone.

Giant clams live in the ocean. They usually stay in one place or move very little throughout their lives. They can grow to be 1 m in length and weigh 200 kg. They feed by taking ocean water in through a special tube and trapping tiny organisms found in the water. After a clam has absorbed the food, it releases the water. This process is called filter feeding because the clam filters food out of the water.

▶ Why do you think clams only live in water?

## Contents

**5-1**   How are animals classified?

**5-2**   What are sponges?

**5-3**   What are cnidarians?

**5-4**   What are worms?

**5-5**   What are mollusks?

**5-6**   What are echinoderms?

**5-7**   What is regeneration?

■   **Lab Activity:** Determining the Age of a Clam

**5-8**   What are arthropods?

■   **The Big Idea:** Why should coral reefs be protected?

**5-9**   What are insects?

**5-10**  How do insects develop?

# 5-1 How are animals classified?

## Objective
Identify characteristics used to classify animals.

## Key Terms
**vertebrate** (VER-tuh-briht): animal with a backbone

**endoskeleton** (ehn-doh-SKEHL-uh-tuhn): skeleton inside the body

**invertebrate** (ihn-VER-tuh-briht): animal without a backbone

**exoskeleton** (eks-oh-SKEHL-uh-tuhn): skeleton on the outside of the body

**Two Large Groups** The animal kingdom is made up of more species than the other four kingdoms combined. Scientists classify animals into two large groups. One group is made up of animals with backbones. The other group is made up of animals without backbones.

 **NAME:** What are the two groups into which the animal kingdom is divided?

**Vertebrates** Animals that have backbones are called **vertebrates.** Vertebrates belong to the phylum Chordata. They are the most complex organisms in the animal kingdom. Vertebrates are also the most widely recognized and familiar of all animals. Vertebrates include fish, frogs, snakes, birds, cats, and many other animals. Humans are vertebrates as well.

Look at Figure 5-2. It shows a killer whale. Whales are among the largest animals found on Earth. The largest animals on Earth are vertebrates. Vertebrates may grow very large because they have an **endoskeleton,** or a skeleton inside their bodies. The endoskeleton surrounds and protects soft body parts. It also helps to give shape and support to an organism. The endoskeleton is a framework that is strong enough to support large, heavy bodies. Because the endoskeleton does not limit the growth and size of an animal, vertebrates are usually larger than other kinds of animals.

▲ **Figure 5-2** Killer whales are animals with an endoskeleton.

 **DEFINE:** What is an endoskeleton?

**Invertebrates** Animals without backbones are called **invertebrates.** Most animals are invertebrates. In fact, more than 95 percent of all animals are invertebrates. There are many different phyla of invertebrate animals. Sponges and jellyfish are invertebrates. Other invertebrates include snails, clams, sea stars, spiders, and insects.

▲ **Figure 5-3** This nudibranch is an invertebrate that has no skeleton.

Some invertebrates, such as worms, do not have any skeleton at all. They are soft-bodied animals. Other invertebrates have an **exoskeleton.** An exoskeleton is a skeleton on the outside of the body. It is made up of a hard, waterproof substance. The exoskeleton protects and supports the body. Spiders, lobsters, and insects, such as the walking stick in Figure 5-4, have an exoskeleton.

▲ **Figure 5-4** Insects, such as this walking stick, have an exoskeleton.

 **LIST:** What are three kinds of animals that are invertebrates?

## ✓ CHECKING CONCEPTS

1. Animals with backbones are classified as _____.

2. An endoskeleton is a skeleton found _____ the body.

3. More than 95 percent of animals are _____.

4. Invertebrates are animals without _____.

5. A skeleton on the outside of the body is called an _____.

## THINKING CRITICALLY

6. **CLASSIFY:** Classify each of the following organisms as a vertebrate or an invertebrate.

   a. worm          d. squirrel

   b. housefly      e. sea star

   c. robin         f. clam

## BUILDING LANGUAGE ARTS SKILLS

***Building Vocabulary*** Look up the prefixes *endo-* and *exo-* in a dictionary, and write their meanings. In your own words, list and define five words that begin with the prefix *endo-* and five words that begin with the prefix *exo-*. Circle the part of each definition that relates to the meaning of the prefix.

## *People in Science*

### TAXONOMIST

Taxonomists are scientists who classify organisms. Many taxonomists only study animals. To classify animals, taxonomists compare the physical appearances of different animals. However, classification is not based on physical traits alone.

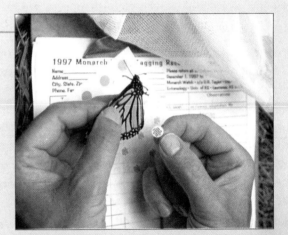

▲ **Figure 5-5** Taxonomists classify organisms.

Taxonomists also compare the chromosomes and blood proteins of different kinds of animals. Taxonomists have discovered that the chromosomes and proteins in the blood of certain animals are quite similar. If the chromosomes and blood proteins are similar, taxonomists infer that the organisms are related.

Taxonomists often study embryology. Embryology is the study of organisms in the early stages of development. Embryology helps taxonomists determine how closely some animals are related. Scientists have found that certain animals show similarities as embryos. If the embryos develop in the same way, taxonomists infer that the animals are related to each other.

**Thinking Critically** Why do you think taxonomists use several different characteristics to determine how animals are related?

# 5-2 What are sponges?

**INVESTIGATE**

### Examining Sponges
#### HANDS-ON ACTIVITY

1. Examine a natural sponge. Look at the shape, color, and texture of it. Then, use a hand lens to observe the surface and the holes in the sponge more closely.

2. Record your observations, and make a drawing of the sponge.

3. Repeat Steps 1 and 2 with an artificial sponge.

**THINK ABOUT IT:** Compare the two type of sponges. What do you think is the function of the holes?

STEP 1

## Objective
Describe the structure of a sponge.

## Key Terms
**pores:** tiny openings

**poriferan** (poh-RIHF-uhr-ran)**:** invertebrate animal with pores

**spicule** (SPIHK-yool)**:** small, hard, needlelike structure of a sponge

**Porifera** In the past, people thought that sponges were plants because they do not move from place to place like most other animals. Sponges live attached to objects on the ocean floor. However, unlike plants, sponges cannot make their own food. Today, scientists classify sponges in the animal kingdom in the phylum Porifera. The word *porifera* means "pore-bearer." If you look at a sponge, you will see it has many **pores,** or tiny openings. Sponges are sometimes called **poriferans.**

▶ IDENTIFY: In what phylum are sponges classified?

**Structure of a Sponge** Sponges are very simple animals. You can compare the body of a sponge to an empty sack. The sponge is closed at the bottom, and has a large opening at the top. The center of the sponge is hollow. The body of a sponge is made up of only two layers of cells. The outer layer is made up of thin, flat cells. The inner layer is made up of special cells called collar cells. The collar cells line the hollow center of the sponge. Each collar cell has a flagellum. A jellylike substance fills the space between the two cell layers. In the jellylike substance, there are special cells called amoebocytes. These cells carry food to other cells. They also help a sponge to reproduce.

Small, needlelike structures called **spicules** are in the jellylike layer. They link together to form a simple skeleton. Spicules support the sponge. Some spicules are made up of a rubbery, flexible material called spongin (SPUHN-jin). Spongin skeletons are dried and sold in stores as natural sponges. Most sponges you use are not natural sponges. They are factory produced.

▶ DESCRIBE: What is the shape of a sponge?

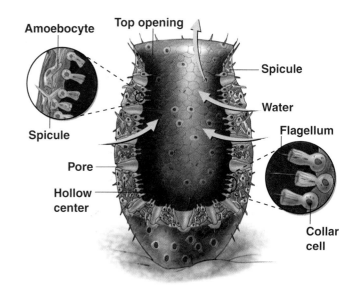

▲ **Figure 5-6** Sponges take in water through their pores.

**Life Functions** Sponges eat by filter feeding. They eat tiny organisms and bits of material in water that passes through their bodies. Water flows through the pores into a hollow center. Water flows out through a large opening at the top of a sponge. The constant beating of each flagellum keeps water moving into and out of a sponge. As water flows by, tiny bits of food are trapped by collar cells. These cells also absorb oxygen from water. Amoebocytes carry food to all cells.

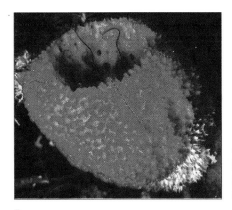

◀ **Figure 5-7** Sponges can vary greatly in color, size, and shape.

 **OBSERVE:** In how many directions does water move in a sponge?

## ✔ CHECKING CONCEPTS

1. Sponges have _____ cell layers.
2. _____ help move water through a sponge.
3. Water enters a sponge through its _____.
4. Sponges are classified in the phylum _____.
5. The rubbery material that makes up some spicules is called _____.

## 💡 THINKING CRITICALLY

6. **EXPLAIN:** Think about the structure of a sponge. Why is Porifera a good name for this phylum?
7. **HYPOTHESIZE:** Suppose each flagellum was removed from the collar cells of a sponge. What effect might this loss have on the sponge's ability to feed?

## *Real-Life Science*

### SNORKELING

Have you ever wondered what kinds of plants and animals live in the ocean? Snorkeling is a good way to find out how fish and other water animals live together.

You only need a few pieces of equipment to go snorkeling: fins, a face mask, and a snorkel. Fins help you move quickly and easily through the water. A face mask gives you a clear view through the water. A snorkel is a breathing tube that allows you to swim along the surface of the water without raising your head to breathe.

Many people like to go snorkeling in areas with coral reefs. The reefs are home to many different types of fish and sponges. The coral provides a protective habitat for these organisms. It is illegal to remove coral from reefs in the United States. Some environmental groups want to stop snorkeling near coral reefs altogether because many reefs are very fragile. If you go snorkeling, look but do not touch any part of them.

▲ **Figure 5-8** You can see a variety of sponges while snorkeling.

**Thinking Critically** Do you think snorkeling near coral reefs should be prohibited?

# 5-3 What are cnidarians?

## Objectives

Identify and describe the body forms of cnidarians.

## Key Terms

**cnidarian** (nih-DER-ee-uhn): invertebrate animal with stinging cells and a hollow central cavity

**polyp:** cuplike form of a cnidarian

**medusa** (muh-DOO-suh): umbrella-like form of a cnidarian

**Cnidarians** If you have ever seen a jellyfish, you have seen a cnidarian. **Cnidarians** are invertebrate animals with stinging cells and a hollow body cavity. Jellyfish are classified in the phylum Cnidaria. All cnidarians have tentacles, or long, armlike structures, that have special stinging cells. All cnidarians live in water. Most cnidarians, such as corals and jellyfish, live in the ocean. Other cnidarians, such as hydra, live in lakes, ponds, and streams.

▶ **CLASSIFY:** Name three cnidarians.

**Body Forms** Cnidarians have two body forms, or shapes. Some cnidarians have a tube-shaped body called a **polyp.** A hydra is an example of a polyp. A polyp does not usually move from place to place. It lives attached to a surface in the water. The mouth is at the top of the polyp and is surrounded by tentacles.

Other cnidarians, such as jellyfish, have an umbrella-shaped body called a **medusa.** Tentacles hang down from the edge of the umbrella. The mouth is in the center of the bottom surface of the medusa. A medusa can float on the surface of water or swim through water. Cnidarians may alternate between the two body forms in their lifetime. Many cnidarians begin life as a medusa and develop into a polyp. Others start life as a polyp and develop into a medusa.

▶ **CLASSIFY:** Is a jellyfish a medusa or a polyp?

**Structure of Cnidarians** Like sponges, cnidarians have two layers of cells. There is a jellylike layer in between the two layers of cells. In cnidarians, however, the cells are organized into tissues. Cnidarians have digestive, muscle, nerve, and sensory tissues. The tissues surround a central

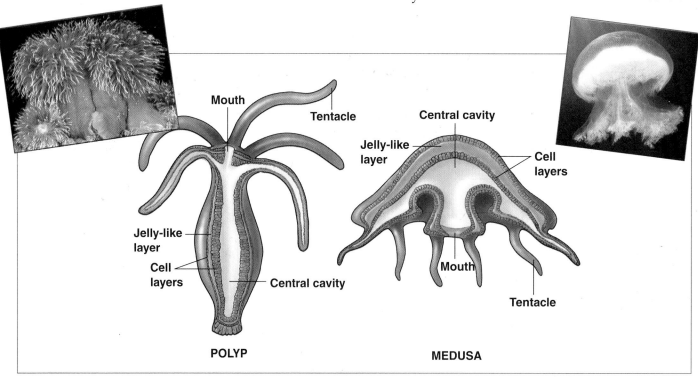

POLYP

MEDUSA

▲ **Figure 5-9** Cnidarians have two body forms, polyp and medusa.

cavity, or hollow space. A mouth opens into the cavity. The mouth is the only body opening.

 **INFER:** Why are cnidarians considered more complex than sponges?

**Getting Food** Cnidarians use their tentacles to catch food. The cells on the tentacles have stingers that contain poison. When the tentacles touch an organism, stingers shoot out very quickly, and the poison stuns or kills the organism. The tentacles wrap around the animal and pull it into the mouth and body cavity. There the food is broken down and digested.

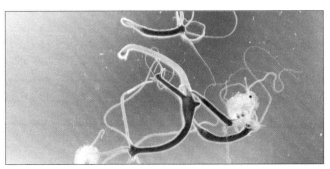
▲ **Figure 5-10** A hydra uses its tentacles to catch food.

 **EXPLAIN:** How do cnidarians get food?

 **✓ CHECKING CONCEPTS**

1. Where do cnidarians live?
2. What is the umbrella-shaped body form of a cnidarian called?
3. What types of tissue are found in cnidarians?
4. How does a cnidarian capture prey?

**💡 THINKING CRITICALLY**

*Use Figure 5-9 to answer the following questions.*

5. **ANALYZE:** Which has a larger layer of jellylike material—a polyp or a medusa?
6. **COMPARE:** How are the two body shapes of cnidarians alike?

**HEALTH AND SAFETY TIP**

Many jellyfish have poison in their stingers that is dangerous to humans. Never touch a jellyfish, even if it looks dead. It may still be able to sting you. If you are stung by a jellyfish, get first aid as soon as you can. Use a first-aid manual or other reference to find out how to treat a jellyfish sting.

🐛 *Hands-On Activity*

**OBSERVING A HYDRA**

▲ **STEP 1** Place the hydra on a slide.

*For this activity, you will need a sample of live hydra, a sample of live daphnia, a dropper, two depression slides, two cover slips, and a microscope.*

1. Use a dropper to remove a hydra from the sample. Place the hydra in the well of the depression slide.
2. Place the cover slip carefully on the slide. Then, place the slide on the stage of the microscope.
3. Use the lowest power objective of the microscope to observe the hydra. Locate the hydra's mouth and tentacles.
4. On another depression slide, place a sample of hydra and a sample of daphnia. Place the cover slip carefully on the slide. Then use the microscope to examine the behavior of the hydra and daphnia.

**Practicing Your Skills**

5. **MODELING:** Draw and label the hydra on your paper.
6. **OBSERVING:** How did the hydra respond to the daphnia?
7. **PREDICT:** What are some other factors the hydra might respond to?

# 5-4 What are worms?

## Objective
Compare the different phyla of worms.

## Key Terms
**platyhelminth** (plat-uh-HEHL-mihnth): type of worm with a flattened body

**nematode** (NEHM-uh-tohd): type of worm with a round body

**parasite** (PAR-uh-syt): organism that gets its food by living on or in the body of another organism.

**annelid** (AN-uh-lihd): type of worm with a segmented body

**setae** (SEET-ee): tiny, hairlike bristles

**closed circulatory system:** organ system in which blood moves through vessels

---

**Classification of Worms** When you think of worms, you probably think of earthworms. However, there are many different kinds of worms. They are so different from each other that they are classified into several different phyla. Three of these phyla are flatworms, roundworms, and segmented worms.

▶ **IDENTIFY:** What are the three phyla of worms?

**Flatworms** The simplest types of worms are flatworms. They are classified in the phylum Platyhelminthes. Flatworms, or **platyhelminthes,** have flattened, ribbonlike bodies. A common flatworm is the planarian (pluh-NER-ee-uhn). Planaria are small flatworms usually between 5 and 25 mm long that live in freshwater ponds and streams. They have two small eyespots that can sense light.

▲ **Figure 5-11** Planaria live in ponds and streams.

The other two groups of flatworms are called flukes and tapeworms. They are both parasites. **Parasites** live inside or on other organisms, which they feed on and harm. Some parasites have special body parts that help them live inside other organisms. They have hooks and suckers that hold them in place. In the intestines, they absorb, or take in, food as it is digested. For example, tapeworms live in the intestines of many kinds of animals, including humans. Tapeworms can grow to several meters in length.

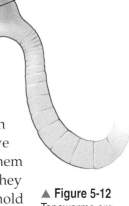

Hooks

Suckers

▲ **Figure 5-12** Tapeworms are parasitic flatworms.

▶ **CLASSIFY:** Name three examples of flatworms.

**Roundworms** Roundworms make up the phylum Nematoda. They are sometimes called **nematodes.** Roundworms can live almost anywhere. They can live in soil or in water. Some are parasites of plants or animals. Hookworms, pinworms, and *Ascaris* worms are roundworms that live in the intestines of humans. Roundworms have a threadlike body with one pointed end. They are one of the simplest animals that have a complete digestive system. Roundworms also have simple excretory and nervous systems. They do not have a circulatory or a respiratory system.

▲ **Figure 5-13** *Ascaris* worms live in the intestines of animals.

▶ **CONTRAST:** How are roundworms different from flatworms?

**Segmented Worms** The most complex worms are the segmented worms. They are classified in the phylum Annelida. Segmented worms are sometimes called **annelids.** The word *annelid* means "little rings." If you look at the body of a segmented worm, you will see that it is made up of

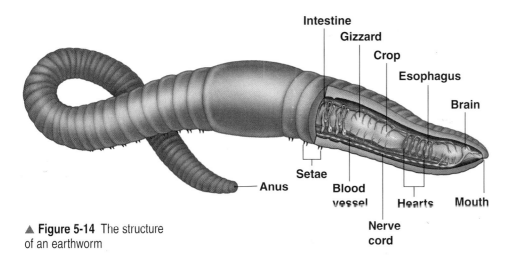

Intestine
Gizzard
Crop
Esophagus
Brain
Setae
Anus
Blood vessel
Hearts
Mouth
Nerve cord

▲ **Figure 5-14** The structure of an earthworm

many ringlike sections, or segments. There are more than 10,000 species of segmented worms. Most live in the ocean. Others live in fresh water. The best-known segmented worm is the earthworm. It lives in the soil.

**4** ▶ NAME: Where do most segmented worms live?

**Earthworms** Earthworms are the most complex worms. Look at Figure 5-14 as you read about earthworms. Like all worms, they have a head end and a tail end. Each segment except the first and last has four pairs of small bristles called **setae.** Earthworms use their setae and sets of tiny muscles to move. A list of other earthworm features follows.

- Earthworms have a complex digestive system. Food passes into the crop and gizzard where it is stored and then ground up. Food is digested and absorbed in the intestine.

- Earthworms have a **closed circulatory system.** In a closed circulatory system, blood moves through vessels, or tubes, in the body. In the head end, two large vessels meet and form five pairs of hearts, which pump blood through the vessels.

- Earthworms have a nervous system. Nerves run along the body and connect to a simple brain.

- Earthworms have male and female sex organs. A single worm, however, does not mate with itself. Earthworms reproduce sexually.

- Earthworms do not have a respiratory system. Gases pass into and out of the earthworm through its moist skin.

**5** ▶ OBSERVE: What are the two organs that store and grind up food called?

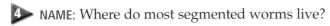

## ✔ CHECKING CONCEPTS

1. The simplest types of worms are _____.

2. Planaria are a type of _____.

3. Special body parts, such as hooks and _____, help some parasites live inside other organisms.

4. Segmented worms live in the _____, fresh water, and soil.

5. The earthworm uses small bristles called _____ for movement.

## 💡 THINKING CRITICALLY

6. COMPARE/CONTRAST: How are the three phyla of worms alike? How are they different? Make a chart that summarizes the similarities and differences among the three phyla of worms.

7. HYPOTHESIZE: A parasite often causes the organism it lives in to lose weight. Why?

## Web InfoSearch

**Leeches** Leeches are parasitic segmented worms. Many years ago, leeches were used to suck "bad blood" out of sick people. Today, doctors are using leeches again but in different ways.

**SEARCH:** Find out more about the uses of leeches in medicine. Start your search at www.conceptsandchallenges.com. Some key search terms are **leech, medicine,** and **annelid.**

# 5-5 What are mollusks?

## Objectives

Describe the features of mollusks. Give examples of different classes of mollusks.

## Key Terms

**mollusk** (MAHL-uhsk): soft-bodied organism

**mantle:** thin membrane that covers a mollusk's organs

**radula** (RAJ-oo-luh): rough, tonguelike organ of a snail

**Mollusks** Mollusks are soft-bodied animals. They are classified in the phylum Mollusca. The mollusk phylum is divided into eight classes. The three most common of these are described below. Most mollusks are covered by hard shells. Mollusks have a head, a foot, and a mass of tissue that contains a number of well-developed organ systems. These systems include excretory organs, reproductive organs, and a heart. A thin membrane covers the soft fleshy body of a mollusk. The membrane is the **mantle.** In some mollusks, the mantle forms the shell. Mollusks live in salt and fresh water and on land.

▶ **DEFINE:** What is the mantle?

**Snails and Slugs** The most common type of mollusk has a single shell or no shell at all. These mollusks belong to the class Gastropoda. This class includes snails, slugs, and sea slugs. In gastropods, the foot is used for movement. Many of these mollusks, such as snails, have a **radula**. The radula is a tonguelike organ. It is covered with toothlike structures. The radula is used to scrape food from plants and rocks.

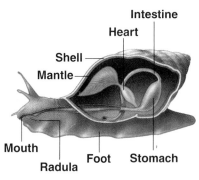

▲ **Figure 5-15** The basic structure of a snail

Labels: Intestine, Heart, Shell, Mantle, Mouth, Radula, Foot, Stomach

▶ **DEFINE:** What is a radula?

**Two-Shelled Mollusks** A second class consists of mollusks made up of two-part shells. This class is called Bivalvia. Clams, oysters, and mussels are all bivalves. The bivalves have strong muscles that are used to hold their shells closed. Bivalves feed by taking in water into their bodies through a special tube. As the water comes in, the microscopic organisms in the water are trapped. The water is then released, and the organisms are digested. This method of feeding is called filter feeding.

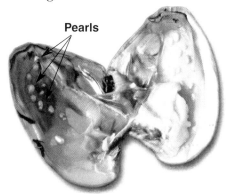

Pearls

◀ **Figure 5-16** When sand grains are caught inside the oyster, its mantle coats the sand with a shiny substance, producing pearls.

▶ **DESCRIBE:** What are the steps of filter feeding?

**Mollusks with Tentacles** A third class of mollusks contains animals that have tentacles. This class is called Cephalopoda. Squids and octopuses are included in this class. They have very complex brains and excellent eyesight. All cephalopods have tentacles which are used for movement and feeding. Each tentacle has many suction cups, used for capturing prey.

▲ **Figure 5-17** This octopus has eight tentacles.

Mollusks with tentacles can slowly crawl around rocks and through small spaces. However, they can also swim freely. Squids and octopuses swim by jet propulsion. They take in water and squirt the water back out. The force of the water squirted out pushes the animal forward. Using jet propulsion, cephalopods can quickly travel great distances.

 **EXPLAIN:** Why are cephalopods considered the most advanced mollusks?

## ✓ CHECKING CONCEPTS

1. A _____ covers the internal organs of a mollusk.
2. A _____ is the tonguelike organ found in snails.
3. Snails and slugs belong to the class _____.
4. Squids and octopuses use _____ for feeding and movement.
5. Bivalves take in water through a _____.

## THINKING CRITICALLY

6. **INFER:** Newton's Third Law of Motion states that for every action there is an equal and opposite reaction. How does this law relate to jet propulsion by squids and octopuses?
7. **CONTRAST:** How are the feeding methods of the three types of mollusks different?

## BUILDING SCIENCE SKILLS

*Researching* The world's largest known invertebrate is the giant squid. The giant squid reaches lengths of up to 18 meters, or 60 feet. Scientists have been unable to photograph or capture a live specimen, but they are still searching. Use library references and scientific journals to find out more about the search for the giant squid. Write a report about your findings.

## *Hands-On Activity*
### MODELING SQUID JET PROPULSION

*You will need a plastic straw, scissors, a fishing line, cellophane tape, an elongated balloon, and 2 desk chairs.*

1. Use the scissors to cut a 10-cm long piece of straw.
   ⚠ CAUTION: Be careful when using scissors.
2. Place the two chairs back to back about 2 m apart.
3. Tie one end of the line to the back of one of the chairs. Thread the line through the piece of straw. Tie the other end of the line to the other chair. Make sure the line is pulled tight between the two chairs.
4. Blow up the balloon, but do not tie a knot. Tape the balloon to the piece of straw on the fishing line while still holding the balloon closed. Let go of the balloon. Observe the direction in which it moves.

▲ **STEP 4** Tape the balloon to the straw on the fishing line. Then, let go.

### Practicing Your Skills

5. **IDENTIFY:** In which direction did the balloon move?
6. **COMPARE:** How does the movement of the balloon compare to the movement of the squid?
7. **ANALYZE:** Do you think the amount of water taken in by the squid affects its movement? Explain.

# 5-6 What are echinoderms?

## Objectives

List the common characteristics of echinoderms.
Name some echinoderms.

## Key Terms

**echinoderm** (ee-KY-noh-duhrm): spiny-skinned
animal

**water-vascular system:** system of tubes used
to transport water

**tube feet:** small structures of echinoderms used
for movement and feeding

**Echinoderms**   **Echinoderms** are spiny-skinned
animals classified in the phylum Echinodermata.
Sea stars are the best-known echinoderms. Other
echinoderms are sea urchins, sand dollars, brittle
stars, and sea cucumbers. Some echinoderms
move by crawling slowly on the ocean floor.
Others attach themselves to rocks or other objects
and do not move at all.

▶ **LIST:** Name three echinoderms.

**Anatomy of Echinoderms**   Echinoderms have
an endoskeleton, or an internal skeleton. The
endoskeleton is made up of spines. The most
noticeable thing about echinoderms is their spiny
skin. In fact, the name *echinoderm* means "spiny
skin." In some echinoderms, such as the sea stars,
the spines are hard, rounded lumps. In the sea
urchins, the spines are like long needles. The skin
of the sea cucumber is soft and leathery.

▲ **Figure 5-18** This sea urchin has long needlelike
spines to protect it.

Echinoderms do not have a left side or a right
side. Most have rays, or arms, around a central
point. Their body structures are arranged like the
spokes of a wheel around a central body point.
Echinoderms do not have circulatory, excretory, or
respiratory systems. They have a nervous system,
but echinoderms do not have a brain. Echinoderms
also have a system called the **water-vascular system.**
This system controls movement and respiration. The
water-vascular system is a network of tubes that
moves water throughout the body of the
echinoderm. Water enters the echinoderm through
an opening on the upper surface.

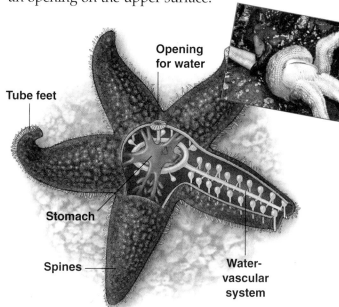

Tube feet

Opening
for water

Stomach

Spines

Water-
vascular
system

▲ **Figure 5-19** The anatomy of a sea star

▶ **OBSERVE:** What is the most noticeable thing
about the echinoderms in Figure 5-18?

**Tube Feet**   Sea stars move using hundreds of
small structures called **tube feet.** Tube feet are part
of the water-vascular system that works to pull a
sea star forward. Each tube foot is like a suction
cup. Using its tube feet, a sea star can move slowly
across the ocean floor.

Tube feet are also used to get food. Sea stars
usually eat mollusks. They use their tube feet to
pull open shells of mollusks, such as clams. The
clam uses its muscles to keep its shell closed.
Eventually, the clam's muscles will tire, and the

shell will open a bit. The sea star will then push its stomach out of its mouth and into the clam. When the clam is digested, the sea star will pull its stomach back inside its body.

**3** ▶ NAME: For what two purposes does a sea star use its tube feet?

## ✔ CHECKING CONCEPTS

1. Name four echinoderms.
2. What kind of skeleton do echinoderms have?
3. Which echinoderm has long needlelike spines?
4. What are tube feet?
5. What type of organisms do sea stars usually eat?
6. To what phylum do sea stars belong?

## THINKING CRITICALLY

7. INFER: Why do you think a sea star would have trouble moving over sand or mud?
8. INFER: If all the sea stars in a clam bed were destroyed, what would happen?

*Understanding Symmetry* Animals have different kinds of symmetry. For example, sea stars have radial symmetry. Some animals have no symmetry at all. Use a dictionary or science references to define bilateral symmetry and radial symmetry. Then, trace the outlines of the animals shown below. What kind of symmetry does each animal have?

▲ **Figure 5-20** Different animals have different kinds of symmetry.

## Integrating Physical Science

**TOPICS: hydraulics, force, pressure**

### HYDRAULIC SYSTEMS IN SEA STARS

A sea star's tube feet are connected to its water-vascular system. Water enters the system through a small round opening on the upper surface. This opening leads to a ring-shaped tube with branches leading out into the sea star's arms. Along the underside of each arm are two rows of tube feet. Muscles push water into the tube feet, making them longer. When the muscles relax, the water is released, and the tube feet get shorter. This action allows the sea star to move.

▲ **Figure 5-21** The tube feet of a sea star are part of its water-vascular system.

A sea star's water-vascular system works very much like the hydraulic brake system in a car. Hydraulic machines, such as brakes, use liquid to function. When a force exerts pressure on one part of the system, the pressure is transmitted through the liquid in the tubes. In a car's brakes, the driver's foot on the brake pedal creates pressure that travels through the hydraulic brake system to the wheels. The pressure then makes pistons press on brake pads to stop the wheels from turning.

**Thinking Critically** Explain how the water-vascular system of a sea star is similar to the braking system of a car.

# 5-7 What is regeneration?

## Objective

Explain how some organisms can regrow lost parts.

## Key Term

**regeneration** (rih-jehn-uh-RAY-shuhn)**:** ability to regrow lost parts

**Regeneration** New plants can grow from a part of a plant by vegetative propagation. Does this kind of asexual reproduction also take place in animals? Some animals have the ability to regrow lost parts. This ability is called **regeneration.** Some animals can develop a whole new animal from just a part of the original animal's body. If an entire new animal develops from a part, regeneration is considered a kind of asexual reproduction.

▶ **DEFINE:** What is regeneration?

**Regeneration of Body Parts** Not all animals have the same ability to regenerate, or regrow, lost body parts. A few kinds of animals can regenerate a large body part. Most animals, however, can regrow only a small part. Lobsters and crabs, for example, can regenerate claws that have broken off.

Most sea stars have five arms, or rays. If a ray is cut off, a new ray grows back. Sea stars can even regenerate all five rays as long as the central body region is still intact.

▲ **Figure 5-22** Crabs can regenerate lost claws.

Many animals use their ability to regenerate lost parts as a defense against predators. When an animal is being threatened or attacked, it can shed a body part without causing harm to itself. This ability allows it to escape while the predator is feeding on the lost body part. For example, the glass lizard can regenerate its tail. If the lizard is attacked and grabbed by its tail, its tail breaks off. The lizard escapes, and gradually, its tail grows back.

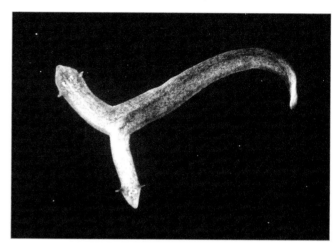

▲ **Figure 5-23** Under laboratory conditions, the flatworm planarian can even regenerate a second head!

▶ **EXPLAIN:** How is the ability to regenerate helpful to an organism?

**Asexual Reproduction** Some animals can reproduce asexually by regeneration. The flatworm planarian is one example of an organism that can reproduce through regeneration under natural conditions. The planarian attaches to a stick or rock and then begins stretching its head region forward. It continues stretching until it splits in two. Then, the two parts develop into new organisms. Because each part of the planarian keeps its original genetic material, the two new organisms are genetically identical.

Sponges can also reproduce by regeneration. If a sponge is cut into pieces, each piece can develop into a new sponge. The process is slow, and it takes many months for the new sponge to grow as large as the parent sponge.

▶ **NAME:** What are two organisms that can reproduce by regeneration?

## ✓ CHECKING CONCEPTS

1. What are some animals that can regenerate lost body parts?
2. How does regeneration help the glass lizard?
3. What type of reproduction is regeneration?
4. How does a planarian reproduce through regeneration?
5. What body parts can crabs and lobsters regenerate?

## 💡 THINKING CRITICALLY

6. **RELATE:** How are vegetative propagation and regeneration similar?
7. **INFER:** Why is regeneration of a lobster's claw not a kind of asexual reproduction?
8. **CONTRAST:** How is regeneration in a lobster different from regeneration in a sponge?

## Web InfoSearch

**Regeneration of Human Tissue** Humans do not have the same ability as some invertebrates to regenerate. We cannot regrow lost limbs. However, some of our tissues do have the ability to regenerate.

**SEARCH:** Use the Internet to find out which tissues in humans can regenerate. Write a report about your findings. Explain how the ability to regenerate tissue plays a role in medicine. Start your search at www.conceptsandchallenges.com. Some key search words are **tissue regeneration** and **skin regeneration.**

## *Real-Life Science*

### REGENERATION IN SEA STARS

Sea stars feed on mollusks, such as clams, mussels, and oysters. The more of these mollusks that are eaten by the sea stars, the fewer there are for humans to harvest. This feeding pattern was a problem for people who made their living catching and selling mollusks. In the nineteenth century, these people thought they had a solution. Whenever they caught a sea star, they chopped it in half and threw the "dead" pieces back into the sea. What they did not realize was that they were helping the sea stars to multiply!

▲ **Figure 5-24** This sea star is in the process of regenerating three of its arms.

Sea stars have the ability to regenerate. If a sea star is cut into two pieces, each piece can regenerate the missing half to create two sea stars out of one. This process usually takes about a year. When a sea star regenerates from a single arm, the new rays are much smaller. This kind of sea star is called a comet. People who caught sea stars that were regenerating lost parts finally figured out what the oyster harvesters were doing wrong.

**Thinking Critically** Why do invertebrates, such as sea stars, regenerate more easily than vertebrates?

# LAB ACTIVITY
# Determining the Age of a Clam

Materials

4 Different size clam shells of the same species

Masking tape

Hand lens

Metric ruler

## BACKGROUND

Mollusks, such as clams and oysters, have hard protective shells. Clams grow in size each year. However, they do not shed their shells every year. Their shells have to grow with them. A new layer is added to the shell of a clam every year as it grows. This growth can be seen on the outside of the shell in the form of large ridges, or bands, that form at the end of each year's growth spurt. These ridges can help determine a clam's age.

## PURPOSE

In this activity, you will examine the shells of clams to determine their ages.

## PROCEDURE

1. Obtain four clam shells of different sizes, but of the same species. Arrange the shells on your desk in order from largest to smallest.

2. Use the masking tape to make four labels for the shells. Label the shells *A*, *B*, *C*, and *D*. Label your largest shell *A* and your smallest shell *D*.

3. Copy the chart in Figure 5-25 onto your paper. Look at the outside of the shell for ridges and bands. On shell *A*, use a ruler to measure the width of five different bands in millimeters. The bands are formed by groups of smaller ridges. Record your measurements on your chart.

4. Find the average width of the five bands by adding the measurements together and dividing by five. Record the average value on your chart.

▲ **STEP 1** Obtain four clam shells of different sizes.

▲ **STEP 3** Measure the width of five bands.

5. Repeat Steps 3 and 4 for shells *B, C,* and *D.*

6. Use the hand lens to look at the bands more closely. Count the number of bands on each shell starting at the crown of the shell. Record the number of bands on each shell on your chart.

▲ **STEP 6** Use a hand lens to examine the bands.

7. The number of bands on the shell represents the approximate age of the clam. Record the approximate age of each clam on your chart.

### Structure of Clam Shells

| Shell | Width of Five Bands | Average Number of Bands | Total Number of Bands | Age |
|-------|--------------------|-----------------------|----------------------|-----|
| A | | | | |
| B | | | | |
| C | | | | |
| D | | | | |

▲ **Figure 5-25** Copy this chart onto a sheet of paper.

## CONCLUSIONS

1. **OBSERVE:** Which shells had the wider bands?

2. **OBSERVE:** Which shells had the most bands?

3. **CALCULATE:** Which clam was the oldest? How can you tell?

4. **HYPOTHESIZE:** Why do you think some bands are wider than others on the same shell? What might the width of one particular band tell you about that year in the clam's life?

# 5-8 What are arthropods?

## Objectives

List the main features of arthropods and give examples of some arthropods.

## Key Terms

**arthropod** (AHR-throh-pahd): animal with an exoskeleton and jointed legs

**chitin** (KY-tin): hard material that makes up the exoskeleton of arthropods

**open circulatory system:** circulatory system in which blood does not flow constantly through tubes

**molting:** process by which an animal sheds its outer covering

**Classifying Arthropods** **Arthropods** are animals that have jointed legs and an exoskeleton. They are classified in the phylum Arthropoda. Arthropods make up the largest phylum of animals. Scientists think that there are more than one million species of organisms in the phylum Arthropoda.

Arthropods are divided into several groups, which are shown in Figure 5-26. The three largest groups are the crustaceans (kruhs-TAY-shuhnz), arachnids (uh-RAK-nidz), and insects. Crustaceans include lobsters, crabs, and shrimp. Arachnids include spiders, ticks, mites, and scorpions. Insects include flies, butterflies, moths, ants, bees, mosquitoes, and cockroaches. There are two other groups of arthropods which together are called myriapods (MYR-ee-uh-pahdz). Myriapods include centipedes and millipedes.

▶ **1** IDENTIFY: Name the three largest groups of arthropods.

**Arthropod Characteristics** All arthropods have an exoskeleton and a segmented body. The exoskeleton protects and supports the soft, inner body parts. The exoskeleton is made of a material called **chitin.** Chitin is tough, but light in weight. Arthropods have jointed legs that are made of several sections. The sections are connected by joints that can bend and are moved by muscles attached to the exoskeleton. Arthropods have an **open circulatory system.** Blood moves through open spaces in their bodies. It does not flow through vessels, or tubes.

▶ **2** IDENTIFY: Of what material is the exoskeleton of an arthropod made?

**Molting** When you grow, your bones grow. Your skeleton grows along with the rest of your body. An exoskeleton, however, cannot grow. It is not made of living material. As an arthropod grows, it becomes too big for its exoskeleton and must shed it. This process is called **molting.** The exoskeleton

---

### THE MAJOR GROUPS OF ARTHROPODS

**Crustaceans**
- Crustaceans usually have two body parts and five pairs of legs.
- Most crustaceans live in water.
- Some examples are lobsters, crayfish, crabs, and shrimp.

**Insects**
- Insects have three body parts and three pairs of legs.
- There are more species of insects than of any other animal.
- Some examples are bees, ants, houseflies, beetles, and grasshoppers.

**Arachnids**
- Most arachnids have two body parts and four pairs of legs.
- Most arachnids live on land.
- Some examples are spiders, ticks, mites, and scorpions.

**Myriapods**
- Centipedes have one pair of legs per body segment. Some centipedes are poisonous.
- Millipedes have two pairs of legs per body segment.

▲ Figure 5-26

splits open, and the animal works its way out. Gradually, a new, larger exoskeleton forms and hardens.

 **DEFINE:** What is molting?

**Special Body Parts** Depending on where they live, what they eat, and how they move, arthropods have different body parts. Insects have special mouth parts that help them get food. These mouth parts may be used for biting, chewing, or sucking, based on how the insect feeds. Most insects also have wings. Some crustaceans, such as lobsters and crabs, have large front claws. They use the claws to get food and to protect themselves. Spiders have silk glands that make silk for their webs.

 **LIST:** What are some special body parts of arthropods?

## ✔ CHECKING CONCEPTS

1. What is an exoskeleton made of?
2. Describe the characteristics of arthropods.

3. What is the name of the largest animal phylum?
4. What is molting?
5. How are large claws helpful for a crustacean?

 **THINKING CRITICALLY**

6. **ANALYZE:** Can you tell which of the arthropods in Figure 5-26 can fly? How?
7. **INFER:** How are the grasshopper's large back legs suited to how it moves?

**HEALTH AND SAFETY TIP**

**Arthropods and Disease** Some arthropods have been known to carry diseases. Deer ticks may carry the bacteria that causes Lyme disease. Mosquitoes have been known to carry several diseases, including malaria and the West Nile virus. To protect yourself from these diseases, it is a good idea to wear insect repellent anytime you plan to be outside in the summer. It is also helpful to wear long pants when hiking or camping.

 ## Science and Technology
### USES OF CHITIN

What do crab shells, some contact lenses, and certain types of varnish have in common? They are all made of chitin. Scientists are finding new uses for the tough, protective chitin.

Chitin is especially good as a material for medical uses because it does not cause allergic reactions in most people. For this reason, chitin is used to make some kinds of contact lenses. Chitin is also used to make artificial skin that can be used to protect badly burned parts of the human body until new skin can form. A type of thread made from chitin is used for sewing wounds or incisions. This type of thread dissolves in the body and does not need to be removed.

▲ **Figure 5-27** Chitin is a material that can be found in the shells of crabs.

Researchers have found many other uses for chitin. Varnish made of chitin makes an excellent finish for some musical instruments. Seeds coated with chitin are protected from infection. Chitin has also been used in filters to clean water in swimming pools. Research on the uses of chitin continues. Chitin is now being tested as a coating for fabrics and paper. Who knows? Some day you may be wearing chitin-treated T-shirts and reading books printed on chitin-coated paper!

**Thinking Critically** Why is chitin a good material to use in surgery?

# THE Big IDEA

## Why should coral reefs be protected?

Environmental science is the study of how humans interact with their surroundings. It looks at how we use and conserve natural resources. The protection of ecosystems is also a major concern of environmental scientists.

Many environmental scientists are concerned about coral reefs, which are home to one-fourth of all marine plants and animals, including sponges, worms, mollusks, crustaceans, and fish.

Many countries depend on coral reefs for economic reasons. The reefs provide fishing grounds for food and produce income from tourism and recreation. Reefs also shield about one-sixth of the world's coasts from storm damage.

Coral reefs around the world are in danger. Human activities and natural factors are damaging them. There are many diseases that kill coral. Some are related to water quality.

In some places, poor fishing practices threaten reefs. Many reef organisms depend on each other for food or protection. Removing one species from the ecosystem affects the other species living there. Pollution, coral mining, and careless divers or boaters also damage reefs. Many efforts are now under way to protect coral reefs, and several programs have been developed to map and monitor reefs. Countries are now working together to promote good fishing practices. Some reefs have become preserves.

Look at the boxes of text that appear on these two pages. They point out some reef invertebrates and their relationship to humans. Follow the directions in the Science Log to learn more about "the big idea."✦

### Queen Conch

The queen conch is a mollusk. A large, spiral shell protects its soft body. Many people collect conch shells because of their beauty. The shells also are used to make jewelry and lamps. Conch is a popular food in Florida and islands in the Caribbean. There is concern that strong demand may lead to the extinction of the conch.

### Sponge

For hundreds of years, people have used sponges for bathing, painting, and mopping. They also provide hiding places for small reef creatures, such as shrimp. Scientists are now studying the use of certain sponges in medicine. They have found that one sponge species produces a chemical that kills cancer cells.

▲ **Figure 5-28** Coral reefs are home to hundreds of different animal species.

## Sea Urchins

Sea urchins play an important role in many coral reefs. By eating algae, they prevent it from smothering the coral. Many people eat sea urchins and their eggs.

## Spiny Lobster

Spiny lobsters are a valuable seafood export for many countries. These crustaceans are also known as rock lobsters. During the spiny lobster's first year, it hides in reef crevices to avoid predators.

## Coral

Some corals look like plants, but they are animals. They are classified as cnidarians. As each coral polyp grows, it forms a hard external skeleton. Billions of skeletons covered by a layer of living coral make up a coral reef.

### WRITING ACTIVITY

*science Log*

Which kind of organism from the coral reef would you like to see up close? Research and write about one of the invertebrates in the reef community. Explain why they should be protected. Start your search at www.conceptsandchallenges.com.

# 5-9 What are insects?

## Objective

Describe the features of insects.

## Key Terms

**antenna** (an-TEHN-uh), *pl.* **antennae:** structure used for touch, taste, and smell

**thorax** (THAWR-aks)**:** middle section of an insect's body

**abdomen** (AB-duh-muhn)**:** third section of an insect's body

**spiracle** (SPIR-uh-kuhl)**:** opening to an air tube of a grasshopper

**tympanum** (TIHM-puh-nuhm)**:** hearing organ in a grasshopper

**Insects** Insects are the largest class of arthropods. There are more different kinds of insects than of any other kind of animals. In fact, more than one million insects have been identified. Insects live almost everywhere, except in the oceans. They live in the air, the soil, on plants, and even in the walls of buildings. Beetles, fleas, termites, moths, and ants are all insects.

 **CLASSIFY:** What is the largest class of arthropods?

### The Grasshopper

The grasshopper is a good model to use when you study insects. Like all arthropods, a grasshopper has jointed legs, a segmented body, and an exoskeleton.

▲ **Figure 5-29** Grasshoppers use their hind legs to jump.

A grasshopper has three pairs of legs and one pair of **antennae.** Antennae are sensory structures that detect touch, taste, and smell. All insects have three body segments—the head, the thorax, and the abdomen. The **thorax** is the middle section of an insect's body. The three pairs of legs are attached to the thorax. The **abdomen** is the third section of an insect's body. Like most insects, the adult grasshopper also has wings.

Look at the grasshopper in Figure 5-30. Find the **spiracles.** The spiracles are openings to air tubes inside the grasshopper. The grasshopper breathes by moving air in and out through the spiracles. Find the **tympanum.** It is used for hearing.

 **STATE:** What are three features of all insects?

**Social Insects** Some insects live together in colonies. Insects that live in colonies are called social insects. Ants and honeybees are social insects. In a honeybee hive, there are three kinds of honeybees.

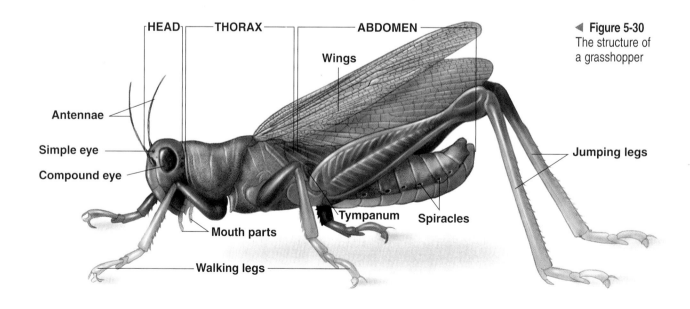
◀ **Figure 5-30** The structure of a grasshopper

HEAD — THORAX — ABDOMEN

Wings

Antennae

Simple eye

Compound eye

Jumping legs

Mouth parts

Tympanum    Spiracles

Walking legs

They are the queen, the drones, and the workers. Each one has its own job in the beehive. The queen bee lays eggs. The drones fertilize the eggs. The workers take care of the eggs and feed the queen and the drones. Workers also gather nectar and pollen and build and protect the hive.

▲ **Figure 5-31** Bees are social insects.

 **NAME:** Name the three kinds of honeybees.

## ✓ CHECKING CONCEPTS

1. What are three body parts of an insect?
2. How many legs do insects have?
3. What are the openings to air tubes on a grasshopper called?

4. What do grasshoppers use for hearing?
5. What are insects that live in colonies called?

## 💡 THINKING CRITICALLY

6. **INFER:** Why do you think insects are the most common kind of animal?
7. **COMPARE:** Explain the difference between breathing in earthworms and breathing in insects
8. **PREDICT:** What might happen to a colony of bees if all the worker bees were removed?
9. **MODEL:** Draw and label a diagram of an insect.

## INTERPRETING VISUALS

*Look at the diagram in Figure 5-30. Determine whether the parts listed below are used for moving, feeding, breathing, or sensing the environment.*

| | |
|---|---|
| **a.** simple eye | **e.** spiracles |
| **b.** mouth parts | **f.** wings |
| **c.** walking legs | **g.** tympanum |
| **d.** antennae | **h.** jumping legs |

 *How Do They Know That?*

## SOCIAL INSECTS FORM A SOCIETY

In 1975, American sociobiologist Edward Osborne Wilson proposed an interesting hypothesis. Wilson believed that insects, like humans, behaved in certain ways because of genetics.

▲ **Figure 5-32** Each kind of ant in a colony has its own job to do.

Wilson proved that social insects live in groups divided by class. These insects displayed three major characteristics. First, the mother, along with other individuals, took care of the young together. Second, some individuals in the group were born to work, rather than to reproduce. Lastly, there was the presence of overlapping generations in which the younger generation took care of the older one. These social systems have been proven to exist among many types of insects including ants, bees, wasps, and termites.

Today, researchers continue to study the behavior of social insects. For example, a recent study found that honeybees could understand abstract thoughts, such as "sameness" and "difference." Scientists may now take this information and apply it to the study of humans.

**Thinking Critically** How is human behavior similar to that of social insects?

# 5-10  How do insects develop?

## Objective

Identify and describe the stages of metamorphosis.

## Key Terms

**metamorphosis** (meht-uh-MAWR-fuh-sihs): series of developmental changes of an organism

**nymph** (NIHMF): young insect that looks like the adult

**larva** (LAHR-vuh), *pl.* **larvae**: immature stage of many animals that usually looks different from the adult form

**pupa** (PYOO-puh): resting stage during complete metamorphosis

**cocoon** (kuh-KOON): protective covering around the pupa

**Metamorphosis**   All insects lay eggs. The developing insect, or embryo, feeds on yolk stored in the egg. The eggs are laid on or near a food supply. After the eggs hatch, the young insects use this food.

When an insect hatches from its egg, it may not look at all like the adult insect. For example, a small butterfly does not hatch from a butterfly egg. After the insect hatches from the egg, it goes through changes in form and size. The series of developmental changes is called **metamorphosis.**

▶ **1** DEFINE: What is metamorphosis?

**Complete Metamorphosis**   Some insects, such as butterflies, moths, and houseflies, undergo complete metamorphosis. Complete metamorphosis has four stages. There is a change in body form in each stage of development.

The egg hatches into a **larva.** The larva is a newly hatched organism that usually looks very different from the adult form. Larvae eat a lot of food and grow very quickly. After a time, the larva goes into a resting stage called the **pupa.** During this stage, many insects spin a covering called a **cocoon** around themselves. In the pupa stage, the insect does not eat. Many body changes take place inside the cocoon. The structures of the adult, including the wings, form. When the adult is formed, it comes out of its cocoon. Look at the left side of Figure 5-33 to learn about the stages of complete metamorphosis.

▶ **2** SEQUENCE: Name the stages of complete metamorphosis in the correct order.

**Incomplete Metamorphosis**   Some insects, such as grasshoppers, crickets, and termites, undergo incomplete metamorphosis. In incomplete metamorphosis, an insect hatches from an egg and gradually develops into an adult. There are three basic stages—egg, **nymph,** and adult. First, the eggs hatch into nymphs. Nymphs look very much like a small adult. However, nymphs do not have working wings and have no reproductive organs.

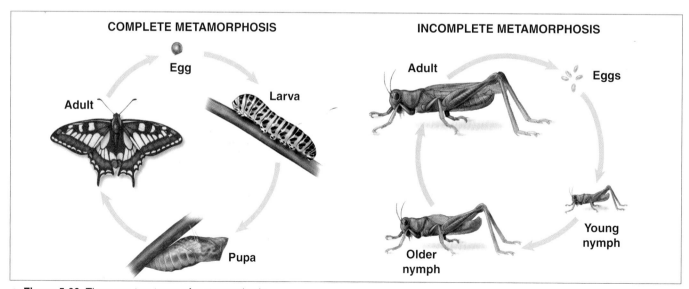

COMPLETE METAMORPHOSIS

Egg

Larva

Adult

Pupa

INCOMPLETE METAMORPHOSIS

Adult

Eggs

Young nymph

Older nymph

▲ **Figure 5-33** There are two types of metamorphosis.

Then, nymphs gradually change and grow into adult insects. They do so by molting several times. Nymphs eventually reach adult size and develop wings. Look at the right side of Figure 5-33 to learn about the stages of incomplete metamorphosis.

**3** ▶ LIST: What are the three stages of incomplete metamorphosis?

## ✓ CHECKING CONCEPTS

1. In insects, the third stage in complete metamorphosis is the _____.

2. In insects, the first stage of metamorphosis is always an _____.

3. A caterpillar is the _____ stage of a butterfly.

4. Nymphs develop into adults by _____.

5. The stage of incomplete metamorphosis in which some insects look like a small adult is the _____.

## THINKING CRITICALLY

6. INFER: Why is the pupa called the resting stage?

7. COMPARE: Explain the differences between incomplete and complete metamorphosis.

## INTERPRETING VISUALS

*Look at Figure 5-34 to answer the question.*

8. Place the stages in the development of the housefly in the correct order. Then, write a paragraph explaining what is happening at each stage.

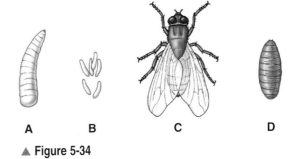

A       B       C       D

▲ Figure 5-34

# Hands-On Activity

## OBSERVING METAMORPHOSIS

*You will need a butterfly-raising kit from your teacher.*

1. Set up the kit according to your teacher's instructions.

2. Create a science journal to record your observations. Draw the eggs in your science journal.

3. After 2–3 days, observe the eggs hatching into larvae. Draw the larvae and record the date in your science journal.

4. Place several leaves in the container for the larvae to eat.

5. After several more days, the larvae will begin to form pupas. Observe the pupas. Record the date and your observations in your science journal.

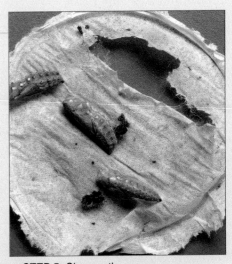

▲ STEP 5 Observe the pupas.

6. After another day, young butterflies will emerge from the cocoons. Observe the butterflies. Record the date and your observations in your science journal.

### Practicing Your Skills

7. OBSERVE: Explain the developmental changes that took place during the life cycle of the butterfly.

8. CALCULATE: Based on the dates you recorded in your science journal, approximately how long does the complete metamorphosis of a butterfly take?

## Chapter Summary

### Lesson 5-1

- **Vertebrates** are animals with backbones. **Invertebrates** are animals without backbones. Some invertebrates are soft-bodied; others have an **exoskeleton**.

### Lesson 5-2

- Sponges are classified in the phylum *Porifera*. **Poriferans** have many **pores**. **Spicules** form a simple skeleton and support the sponge.

### Lesson 5-3

- All **cnidarians** have tentacles and live in water. The two body forms of cnidarians are **polyps** and **medusas.**

### Lesson 5-4

- Worms are classified into several different phyla, including flatworms, roundworms, and segmented worms. The earthworm is typical of segmented worms. Earthworms have a **closed circulatory system** and a complex digestive system.

### Lesson 5-5

- **Mollusks** are soft-bodied animals with a head, a foot, and a **mantle.** Many mollusks have a **radula** used for getting food.

### Lessons 5-6 and 5-7

- **Echinoderms** are spiny-skinned animals. Echinoderms have **tube feet** that are part of a **water-vascular system** used to move and to get food. The ability of an animal to regrow lost parts is called **regeneration.**

### Lessons 5-8, 5-9, and 5-10

- **Arthropods** are animals with jointed legs and an exoskeleton. The three largest arthropod groups are the insects, crustaceans, and arachnids.
- Insects are the most common type of animal on Earth. All insects have three pairs of legs, three body segments, and two antennae.
- The series of developmental changes of an insect is called **metamorphosis.** The three stages of incomplete metamorphosis in insects are egg, **nymph,** and adult. The four stages of complete metamorphosis in insects are egg, **larva, pupa,** and adult.

## Key Term Challenges

abdomen (p. 118)
antenna (p. 118)
arthropod (p. 114)
annelid (p. 104)
chitin (p. 114)
closed circulatory system (p. 104)
cnidarian (p. 102)
cocoon (p. 120)
echinoderm (p. 108)
endoskeleton (p. 98)
exoskeleton (p. 98)
invertebrate (p. 98)
larva (p. 120)
mantle (p. 106)
medusa (p. 102)
metamorphosis (p. 120)
mollusk (p. 106)
molting (p. 114)
nematode (p. 104)

nymph (p. 120)
open circulatory system (p. 114)
parasite (p. 104)
platyhelminthe (p. 104)
polyp (p. 102)
pores (p. 100)
poriferan (p. 100)
pupa (p. 120)
radula (p. 106)
regeneration (p. 110)
setae (p. 104)
spicule (p. 100)
spiracle (p. 118)
thorax (p. 118)
tube feet (p. 108)
tympanum (p. 118)
vertebrate (p. 98)
water-vascular system (p. 108)

**MATCHING** Write the Key Term from above that best matches each description.

1. tiny openings

2. small, hard needlelike structures of a sponge

3. animal without a backbone

4. thin membrane that covers the mollusk's body

5. tough, lightweight material that makes up an arthropod's exoskeleton

6. structures on an echinoderm used for movement and feeding

**FILL IN** Write the Key Term from above that best completes each statement.

7. The protective covering of a pupa is called a _____.

8. A _____ is a soft-bodied organism.

9. The two forms of a cnidarian are the _____ and the medusa.

10. The ability to regrow body parts is called _____.

# Content Challenges TEST PREP

**MULTIPLE CHOICE** **Write the letter of the term or phrase that best completes each statement.**

1. Spicules are found in a sponge's
   a. jellylike substance.
   b. hollow center.
   c. endoskeleton.
   d. cell layer.

2. All porifera and cnidarians have
   a. four cell layers.
   b. three cell layers.
   c. two cell layers.
   d. one cell layer.

3. The simplest worms are the
   a. segmented worm.
   b. roundworms.
   c. flatworms.
   d. earthworms.

4. Roundworms belong to the phylum
   a. Platyhelminthes.
   b. Porifera.
   c. Nematoda.
   d. Annelida.

5. Sea stars and sea urchins belong to the phylum
   a. Porifera.
   b. Echinodermata.
   c. Annelida.
   d. Mollusca.

6. All insects have
   a. two body parts.
   b. four pairs of legs.
   c. an exoskeleton.
   d. wings.

7. Clams and oysters belong to the class of mollusks that have
   a. no shell.
   b. a one-part shell.
   c. a two-part shell.
   d. a three-part shell.

8. Complete metamorphosis has
   a. two stages.
   b. three stages.
   c. four stages.
   d. five stages.

9. The largest group of arthropods is the
   a. insects.
   b. crustaceans.
   c. arachnids.
   d. myriapods.

**TRUE/FALSE** **Write *true* if the statement is true. If the statement is false, change the underlined term to make the statement true.**

10. The organ used by a grasshopper for hearing is the <u>tympanum</u>.

11. Both hydra and <u>sponges</u> have tentacles.

12. The umbrella-like form of a cnidarian is called a <u>polyp</u>.

13. An earthworm uses its setae and muscles to <u>move</u>.

14. Sponges take in water through their <u>pores</u>.

15. All arthropods have an <u>endoskeleton</u>.

16. Insects develop through a series of stages of development called <u>mimicry</u>.

# Concept Challenges TEST PREP

**WRITTEN RESPONSE** **Answer each of the following questions in complete sentences.**

1. **INFER:** Until the mid-nineteenth century, most scientists thought that sponges were plants. Why might scientists have considered sponges to be part of the plant kingdom?

2. **INFER:** Why do you think earthworms avoid sunlight?

3. **RELATE:** How is the ability to regenerate related to an animal's ability to survive?

4. **INFER:** Why do you think insects are able to survive in so many different types of habitats?

5. **CONTRAST:** What are the differences between an open circulatory system and a closed circulatory system?

**INTERPRETING A DIAGRAM** **Use Figure 5-35 to answer the following questions.**

6. Identify each of the parts labeled below.

7. What letter represents a grasshopper's hearing organ?

8. Which letter represents the openings to air tubes?

9. Which letter represents the segment to which a grasshopper's legs attach?

10. Which part is not fully developed in a nymph?

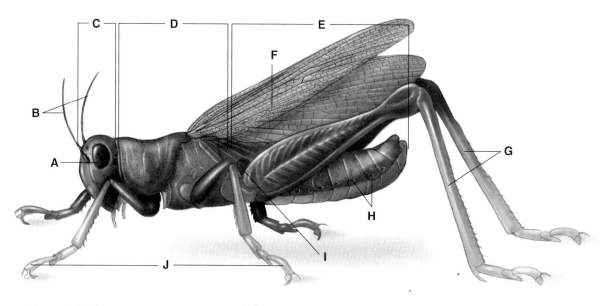

▲ **Figure 5-35** A grasshopper

# Chapter 6 Animals With Backbones

▲ **Figure 6-1** Some animals, such as this horned owl, have a backbone.

What do a fish, an owl, and a giraffe have in common? They all have endoskeletons with backbones. The skeleton gives a body its shape and protects organs. Some bones in the skeleton help animals move. Other bones limit an animal's movement. An owl's eyes are held in place by bony structures in its skull. That means an owl cannot move its eyes. Flexible joints in its neck allow the owl to turn its head almost three-quarters of the way around so it can see behind itself.

▶What part of an owl's skeleton helps the owl see behind itself?

## Contents

6-1   What are chordates?

6-2   What are fish?

6-3   What are amphibians?

6-4   How do amphibians develop?

6-5   What are reptiles?

6-6   What are birds?

■   **Lab Activity:** Investigating an Owl Pellet

6-7   What are mammals?

■   **The Big Idea:** How are the skeletons of vertebrates like levers?

6-8   How do animal embryos develop?

6-9   What are innate and learned behaviors?

6-10  What are social behaviors?

# 6-1 What are chordates?

## Objective
Identify the structure of chordates.

## Key Terms
**notochord** (NOHT-uh-kawrd): strong, rodlike structure in chordates that can bend

**chordate** (kawr-DAYT): animal with a notochord at some time during its development

**vertebrate** (VER-tuh-briht): animal with a backbone

**Phylum Chordata** Fish, frogs, snakes, birds, cats, and many other animals all have something in common. They have a notochord at some time during their development. A **notochord** is a strong, rodlike structure that can bend. It is used for support. The notochord is located just below the nerve cord that runs down the back of the animal. An animal with a notochord is called a **chordate**. They are classified in the phylum Chordata, some of which are shown in Figure 6-2.

 **DEFINE:** What is a chordate?

**Other Chordate Features** Besides a notochord, chordates have a hollow nerve cord. It runs down the back of the animal. The nerve cord carries messages between all the nerves in the body and the brain. Chordates also have paired gill slits at some time during their development. In fish, the gill slits become gills. Gills are used to take in oxygen dissolved in water. In most other chordates, the gill slits are on an embryo but disappear as the embryo develops.

 **NAME:** What are two chordate features besides a notochord?

**Body Plan of Chordates** Chordates have a bilateral symmetry. An animal with bilateral symmetry can be divided into similar halves at only one place. Each half is a mirror image of the other. Chordates also have a tail at some point in their development. In humans, the tail is reduced to the tailbone.

Chordates have many organ systems. One of these organ systems is a closed circulatory system. It is made up of a heart and many blood vessels. Chordates also have the most highly developed nervous systems of all animals.

 **INFER:** Based upon the body plan of chordates, why are you classified as a chordate?

| TYPES OF CHORDATES | | |
|---|---|---|
| **Lancelets** Lancelets are a simple chordate with no backbone. These fishlike animals keep their notochords throughout their lifetime.  | **Fish** Fish are simple vertebrates. They have a closed circulatory system with a two-chambered heart. Sharks, tuna, and trout are examples of fish.  | **Amphibians** Amphibians are vertebrates that live part of their lives in water and part on land. They have a closed circulatory system with a three-chambered heart. Frogs, toads, and salamanders are examples of amphibians.  |
| **Reptiles** Reptiles are land vertebrates. They have a closed circulatory system with a three- or four-chambered heart. Snakes, turtles, and alligators are examples of reptiles.  | **Birds** Birds are the only animals with feathers. They have a closed circulatory system with a four-chambered heart. Eagles, hawks, and parrots are examples of birds.  | **Mammals** Mammals are vertebrates with body hair. They have a closed circulatory system with a four-chambered heart. Opossums, elephants, and humans are examples of mammals.  |

▲ Figure 6-2

**Lancelets** In most adult chordates, the notochord is replaced by the backbone. Only a few kinds of simple chordates, such as lancelets, do not have a backbone. Lancelets are small, fishlike animals. A lancelet keeps its notochord throughout its life. It is never replaced by a backbone.

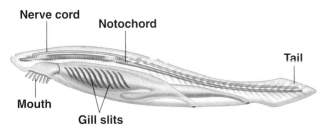

Nerve cord

Notochord

Tail

Mouth

Gill slits

▲ **Figure 6-3** A lancelet keeps its notochord throughout its life.

 **ANALYZE:** Look at the lancelet in Figure 6-3. Why is it classified as a chordate?

**Vertebrates** Animals that have a backbone are called **vertebrates.** There are five major groups of vertebrates: fish, amphibians, reptiles, birds, and mammals. Vertebrates also have an endoskeleton, or a skeleton inside the body. The endoskeleton protects the organs and gives the body its shape and support.

 **DEFINE:** What are vertebrates?

## ✓ CHECKING CONCEPTS

1. A notochord is a strong, flexible _____ structure.
2. The nerve cord of a chordate runs down the _____ of the animal.
3. Animals with backbones are called _____.
4. An endoskeleton protects organs and gives the body _____.
5. Chordates have a _____ circulatory system.

## THINKING CRITICALLY

6. **INFER:** What structure do you think replaces the notochord in vertebrates?
7. **CONTRAST:** Identify two features of vertebrates that invertebrates do not have.

## INTERPRETING VISUALS

*Use Figure 6-2 to answer the question.*

8. **INFER:** What makes all of these animals chordates?

▲ **Figure 6-4** Zoo veterinarians work with many wild animals.

 *People in Science*

### VETERINARIAN

Treating an elephant's foot infection, cleaning and polishing a bear's teeth, and checking bison for complications after surgery are all in a day's work for a zoo veterinarian. Veterinarians are doctors who treat animals. They may treat household pets or farm animals. Zoo veterinarians specialize in the treatment of wildlife species that live in zoos.

A large part of a zoo veterinarian's job is knowing how to restrain and soothe wild animals such as tigers and gorillas. They give routine exams to healthy animals and they treat and perform surgery on animals with health problems. Also, zoo veterinarians help animals—especially endangered species—give birth and raise their young.

In order to become a veterinarian, students must first attend college and earn a bachelor's degree. Many students hoping to become veterinarians take courses in biology, chemistry, and mathematics. After college, students must attend a veterinary medial school for approximately four years.

**Thinking Critically** Would you enjoy a career as a veterinarian? Why or why not?

# 6-2 What are fish?

## Objective

Give examples of the different types of fish.

## Key Terms

**ectotherm:** animal whose body temperature changes with its environment; coldblooded animal

**gill:** organ that absorbs dissolved oxygen from water

**cartilage** (KAHRT-uhl-ihj)**:** tough, flexible connective tissue

**swim bladder:** organ of a fish that allows the fish to remain at a specific depth in the water

**Fish** Fish are the oldest group of vertebrates. Fish first appeared more than 500 million years ago. Today, fish live in most of Earth's waters.

Fish are **ectotherms,** or coldblooded animals. The body temperature of an ectothermic animal changes with the temperature of its surroundings. When the water temperature drops, the body temperature of a fish also drops.

**1** PREDICT: How would the body temperature of a fish change if the water temperature rose?

**Gills** Fish breathe through organs called **gills.** Gills are protected by a hard covering called a gill cover. Fish take water in through their mouths and get rid of it through their gills. Dissolved oxygen in the water is absorbed by the gills. The oxygen passes into the blood through the walls of the gills. Blood carries the oxygen to all the cells in the fish's body. Carbon dioxide passes out of the blood in the gills, and then into the water. Look at Figure 6-5 to learn about the parts of a fish.

▲ Figure 6-6
Like all fish, a seahorse has gills.

**2** IDENTIFY: What organs do fish use to breathe?

**Four Classes** Fish are the largest group of vertebrates. They have a two-chambered heart. The top chamber is the atrium, and the bottom chamber is the ventricle. Fish are grouped into four classes: lampreys, hagfish, cartilaginous fish, and bony fish.

Lampreys and hagfish are both jawless fish. They look very different from most fish. These fish are long and snakelike. They do not have scales.

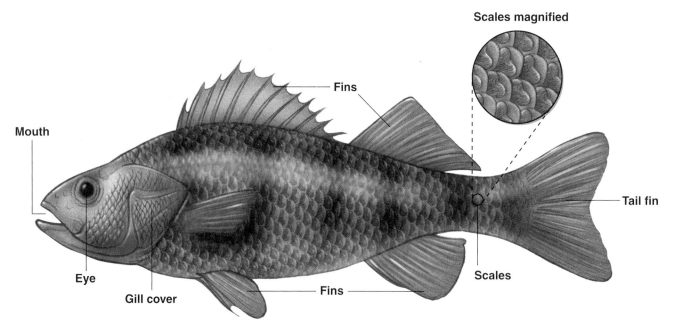

▲ Figure 6-5 The basic anatomy of a fish

The cartilaginous fish include sharks, rays, and skates. These fish have skeletons made of cartilage. **Cartilage** is a strong, flexible tissue. The tip of your nose and your ears are made of cartilage. Cartilaginous fish also have specialized fins for steering and balance.

▲ **Figure 6-7** A hammerhead shark is a cartilaginous fish.

Bony fish have skeletons made of bone. Tuna, salmon, bass, and flounder are all examples of bony fish. Bony fish are suited to many different environments. Most have streamlined bodies for easy movement through the water. They also have different kinds of fins that are used for steering and balance. Their bodies are covered with tough, overlapping scales that protect their skin.

Bony fish also have a **swim bladder**. The swim bladder adjusts the average density of the fish. The fish can control the amount of gas in the swim bladder to equal the pressure of the water. As a result, the fish can remain at any depth in the water.

 **CLASSIFY:** What are the four classes of fish?

 ## Hands-On Activity

### MODELING A SWIM BLADDER

*You will need safety goggles, two balloons, a large bowl filled with water, and extra water.*

1. Inflate a balloon with air. Then place it in a bowl of water.
2. Fill the second balloon half-way with water. Then, blow air into it until it is approximately the same size as the first balloon.
3. Place the second balloon in the bowl of water.

**Practicing Your Skills**

4. **IDENTIFY:** Which balloon is floating on the surface of the water? Which is floating below the surface of the water?
5. **APPLY:** How do the balloons model a swim bladder?

▲ **STEP 3** Place the balloons in a bowl of water.

## ✔ CHECKING CONCEPTS

1. What is an ectothermic animal?
2. How do fish breathe?
3. How many chambers does a fish's heart have?
4. What are the only two kinds of jawless fish?
5. What is the main characteristic of a cartilaginous fish?

## THINKING CRITICALLY

6. **CLASSIFY:** Place each of the following fish into its correct class:

   a. tuna
   b. bass
   c. sea skate
   d. hammerhead shark
   e. salmon
   f. whale shark

## BUILDING SCIENCE SKILLS

***Inferring*** When you infer, you form a conclusion based on facts. Both of a flounder's eyes are on one side of its head. A flounder is also the color of sand or mud. Both of these features are adaptations. How do you think a sandy color and eyes on one side of its head make a flounder suited to life on the ocean floor?

# 6-3 What are amphibians?

## Objective

Identify the characteristics of amphibians.

## Key Term

**amphibian** (am-FIHB-ee-uhn): animal that lives part of its life in water and part on land

**Amphibians** An **amphibian** is an animal that lives part of its life in water and part on land. In fact, the word *amphibian* comes from a Greek word meaning "double life." The young of most amphibians live in water. As they grow, they undergo changes. Adult amphibians usually live on land and only return to the water to lay eggs. Scientists think that the first amphibians developed from fish that could stay out of water for long periods of time. These fish had lungs and could breathe air.

Amphibians are ectothermic. Look at Figures 6-8 and 6-9. Except for toads, amphibians, such as the leopard frog, have smooth, moist skin. Toads have bumpy skin. Most amphibians also have webbed feet. Because they live part of their life in water and part on land, they use gills, lungs, and their skin to exchange oxygen and carbon dioxide. Amphibian eggs do not have shells and are usually laid in water.

▲ **Figure 6-8** A leopard frog

▲ **Figure 6-9** A toad

▶ **PREDICT:** As the temperature of the mud that a toad is in drops, what will happen to its body temperature?

**Classify Amphibians** Scientists have classified more than 4,000 different species of amphibians. Scientists classify amphibians into three orders based on their body structures. The best-known amphibians are frogs and toads. They are the order of tailless amphibians. Salamanders and newts belong to the order of amphibians with tails. The third order of amphibians is the caecilians (see-SIL-ee-uhns), which do not have legs. Caecilians are wormlike animals that live mainly in the forests of South America.

▲ **Figure 6-10** Salamanders are amphibians with tails.

▶ **LIST:** What are the three orders of amphibians?

**More About Amphibians** Amphibians have a three-chambered heart that is part of a closed circulatory system. The heart has two atria and one ventricle.

Almost all amphibians have gills during the early stages of development. As adults, they have lungs. Some water salamanders have gills throughout their lives. Many amphibians also breathe through their skin. Their skin must stay moist so that oxygen and carbon dioxide can be exchanged through it.

▶ **INFER:** If a type of amphibian needed to keep its skin moist, in what kind of environment would it live?

## ✔ CHECKING CONCEPTS

1. What does the word *amphibian* mean?
2. From what animals do most scientists think amphibians developed?
3. What kind of skin do toads have?
4. What kind of amphibians are frogs and toads?
5. Why must amphibians keep their skin moist?

## 💡 THINKING CRITICALLY

6. CONTRAST: How does the body structure of a frog differ from that of a salamander?
7. INFER: Why do you think most amphibians have webbed feet?
8. IDENTIFY: List four characteristics of amphibians.

## Web InfoSearch

**Caecilians** Caecilians are amphibians without legs. Caecilians look like long, colorful earthworms. Like earthworms, caecilians live in soil. Some caecilians have very small eyes. Most caecilians, however, are considered blind.

▲ **Figure 6-11** A caecilian

**SEARCH:** Use the Internet to find out more about caecilians. Use your findings to make a model of a caecilian and its environment. Start your search at www.conceptsandchallenges.com. Some key search words are **amphibian** and **caecilian.**

## Science and Technology

### COMPUTER DISSECTIONS

Computers have become useful tools in science. They can be used to store data, make calculations, add color to photographs, and help keep track of research. Computers can also be used to run simulations, or moving models.

In many schools, animal dissections are no longer done on preserved animals. Instead, computers are used to run a dissection simulation. A special computer program may be on a CD-ROM, a DVD, or even the Internet. For example, you can dissect a frog by using a dissection simulation program. On the computer screen, you use laboratory equipment to open the frog and explore the different organ systems.

Many people prefer using computer dissection. They do not think animals should be killed for dissections. Other people think that dissection on preserved specimens is important to the study of life science. Medical students still practice surgery on preserved animals, however. What do you think?

▲ **Figure 6-12** Some schools use dissection simulation programs instead of dissecting preserved animals.

**Thinking Critically** What are some benefits of using a computer dissection program?

# 6-4 How do amphibians develop?

## Objective
Explain metamorphosis in frogs.

## Key Terms
**larva** (LAHR-vuh): immature stage of many animals that usually looks different from the adult form

**tadpole:** larval stage of a frog

**Metamorphosis**  The series of developmental changes of an organism is called metamorphosis. Like some insects, the appearance of amphibians changes dramatically during their life cycles. During the early stages, amphibians can live only in water. They breathe through gills. As adults, most amphibians live on land. They use their lungs to breathe. When under water, adult amphibians absorb oxygen through their moist skin because most of them no longer have gills.

▶ **NAME:** What are two groups of animals that change during their life cycle?

**Amphibian Eggs**  All amphibians lay eggs. Amphibian eggs do not have a shell. Instead, they are covered with a clear, jellylike substance that protects the embryo. This substance also helps the eggs cling to each other or to water plants.

Amphibians usually lay their eggs in water. For example, frogs and toads lay their eggs in freshwater lakes, ponds, and other bodies of water. They lay their eggs in the spring. Toads lay long strings of eggs. Frogs lay clumps of eggs.

▶ **IDENTIFY:** Do frogs lay many eggs, a few eggs, or one egg?

**Larva**  Usually in about 12 days, amphibian eggs hatch into larvae. A **larva** is a newly hatched organism that usually looks very different from the adult form. Frog eggs hatch into tadpoles. **Tadpoles** are the larval stage of a frog. Tadpoles do not look like adult frogs at all. They look like very small fish. Their bodies are streamlined, they have a thin tail, and they breathe with gills.

Unlike tadpoles, most salamander larvae do not look very different from adult salamanders. Salamander larvae have small legs and a tail. The big difference between salamander larvae and adult salamanders is that the larvae have external gills.

▶ **NAME:** What is the early stage of a frog called?

**Larva to Adult**  As a tadpole grows, its body changes. Legs begin to develop. As the tadpole begins to develop into a young frog, its tail shrinks and gradually disappears. Lungs develop and the gills disappear. At this point, the young frog leaves the water. It is adapted, or suited, to a life on land.

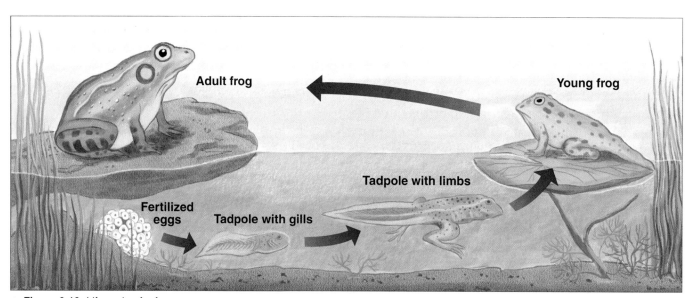

▲ **Figure 6-13** Life cycle of a frog

For salamander larvae, the change is not as dramatic. When a salamander larva metamorphoses, it loses its gills. The lungs develop and the salamander is adapted to life on land.

 **INFER:** What adaptation does a young amphibian have for breathing air?

## ✓ CHECKING CONCEPTS

1. During the early stages in their development, amphibians breathe with _____.

2. Amphibians and insects undergo _____.

3. Most amphibians lay their eggs in _____.

4. The larval stage in the development of a frog is a _____.

5. Frog eggs hatch into tadpoles in about 12 _____.

6. The eggs of frogs are surrounded by a _____.

## THINKING CRITICALLY

7. **MODEL:** Make a flowchart that shows the stages in frog development.

8. **INFER:** Why do you think frogs lay so many eggs at one time?

9. **HYPOTHESIZE:** Why do you think amphibians lay their eggs in water?

## BUILDING SCIENCE SKILLS

***Comparing and Contrasting*** When you compare and contrast things, you look at how they are alike and how they are different. Use library resources to find out more about the metamorphosis of insects and amphibians. How do they compare? What are the similarities? What are the differences?

## *Integrating Earth Science*

**TOPICS: storm water, water pollution**

## POLLUTANTS AND FROG DEVELOPMENT

Water pollution is the release of harmful substances into Earth's waters. One way that pollutants get in the water is through storm water, or water than runs off our houses and streets when it rains. This water is caught in gutters, drains, creeks, and rivers, and eventually makes its way to the sea. Pollutants, such as litter, fertilizers, and chemicals used to wash cars, get picked up by storm water.

Environmental scientists believe that pollutants in the water affect the development of frogs. In 1995, science students on a field trip in Minnesota

▲ **Figure 6-14** Pollutants in water may have led to mutations in this frog.

discovered more than two dozen frogs with severe mutations, including extra limbs and eye mutations. To find the cause of the mutations, scientists conducted an experiment. A group of 40 tadpoles were placed in either water from water sources in Minnesota or purified water. More than half of the frogs that developed in the water from Minnesota had mutations. As a result, the Minnesota water was analyzed. A chemical called methoprene was found. Methoprene is a pesticide used to kill mosquitoes. Scientists believe that this chemical, when heated by the sun, caused mutations in the frog-egg genes.

**Thinking Critically** How could humans help to decrease mutations found in frogs?

# 6-5 What are reptiles?

## Objectives

Explain how reptiles are adapted to life on land. Describe the four orders of reptiles.

**Life on Land** Reptiles were the first true land animals. Unlike amphibians, most reptiles do not need water for reproduction. They lay their eggs on land. Most reptile eggs are covered with a leathery shell. The shell keeps the eggs from drying out. Young reptiles develop in the eggs.

Reptiles have lungs throughout their lives. They have hard, dry skin covered with scales. The skin is waterproof. The waterproof skin reduces water loss from the body.

▲ **Figure 6-15** A komodo dragon is a reptile.

**1** EXPLAIN: How are reptiles adapted for life on land?

**Reptiles** Reptiles are ectothermic. They have a three-chambered or four-chambered heart. Most reptiles also have two pairs of legs and clawed feet.

More than 100 million years ago, reptiles were the major group of animals on Earth. By about 65 million years ago, most of those reptiles had died out. Today, there are almost 8,000 different species of reptiles.

**2** NAME: What are some of the characteristics of reptiles?

**Orders of Reptiles** The smallest order of reptiles includes the tuataras (too-uh-TAH-ruhz). In fact, this order is so small it has only two species—both types of tuataras. They are sometimes called living fossils because they have many features of ancient reptiles. These animals have changed very little since they first appeared about 200 million years ago. Tuataras look like lizards, but have spikes on their backs.

The largest order of reptiles includes snakes and lizards. When snakes and lizards grow, they shed their skins. Most snakes and lizards live in warm areas. The main difference between snakes and lizards is that snakes do not have legs. There are more than 4,500 different kinds of snakes and lizards.

◀ **Figure 6-16** This viper is well suited for life in the trees.

Turtles and tortoises make up another order of reptiles. This group of animals has shells. Instead of teeth, most reptiles in this order have beaks. Turtles live mostly in water. Tortoises live mostly on land. Turtles have flat, streamlined shells. Tortoises have high, domed shells.

▲ **Figure 6-17** How is this green sea turtle adapted to life under water?

The fourth order of reptiles includes crocodiles and alligators. These animals spend much of their time in water. You can tell the difference between them by looking at their heads. Alligators have broad, rounded heads. Crocodiles have more triangular heads.

▲ **Figure 6-18** A crocodile

▲ **Figure 6-19** An alligator

 **INFER:** Why do you think a flat, streamlined shell is helpful to a turtle in water?

## ✓ CHECKING CONCEPTS

1. Where do young reptiles develop?
2. Why are tuataras called living fossils?

3. Which animals are members of the largest order of reptiles?
4. Where do most tortoises live?
5. How can you tell an alligator from a crocodile?

## 💡 THINKING CRITICALLY

6. **CONTRAST:** How do snakes differ from all other reptiles?

### Web InfoSearch

**Whiptail Lizards** Most animals reproduce sexually. One animal that reproduces asexually is the whiptail lizard. Whiptail lizards reproduce by parthenogenesis, or the production of offspring from unfertilized eggs. All whiptail lizards are female.

**SEARCH:** Use the Internet to find out more about whiptail lizards. Write your findings in a report. You can start your search at www.conceptsandchallenges.com. Some key search words are **whiptail lizards** and **parthenogenesis.**

## *Real-Life Science*

### HELPFUL SNAKES

Most people do not want to get too close to a venomous snake. Some scientists, however, have been researching possible medical uses of snake venom. Snake venom may contain many helpful chemicals and proteins.

▲ **Figure 6-20** Snake venom is collected by a process called milking.

For example, stroke victims usually have problems with their circulatory system. Venom from the Malayan pit viper has been used in new drugs that thin the blood and prevent blood clots from forming. Because cobra venom contains an enzyme that breaks down virus cell walls, scientists have been researching possible medical uses for it. Snake venom also greatly affects the nervous system. As a result, medical researchers are studying snake venom to find medications for people who have Alzheimer's disease or epilepsy.

To study venom, first scientists must remove it from the snake. This process is known as milking the snake. When working with venomous snakes, scientists must be careful. Snake venom can be fatal to humans.

**Thinking Critically** Should snake venom be used in medical research? Explain.

# 6-6 What are birds?

## Objectives

Describe the characteristics of birds. Classify different kinds of birds.

## Key Term

**endotherm:** vertebrate whose body temperature remains about the same; a warmblooded animal

**Features of Birds** Unlike fish, amphibians, and reptiles, birds are **endotherms,** or warmblooded. The body temperature of an endothermic animal remains about the same. It does not change when the temperature of the animal's surroundings changes. Birds maintain their body temperatures by using heat produced by the breakdown of food.

Birds are very easy to recognize. They are the only animals with feathers. Birds also have other characteristics.

- Birds have two wings and two legs.
- Birds have lightweight bones.
- Birds have a beak without teeth.
- Birds lay hard-shelled eggs.

Birds have well-developed organ systems. Their respiratory system, in particular, works very well. It supplies the wing muscles with large amounts of oxygen during flight. Birds also have a four-chambered heart. The two upper chambers are the atria. The two lower chambers are the ventricles.

 **COMPARE:** What is the difference between ectothermic and endothermic animals?

**Five Groups** All birds are classified in the class Aves (AH-vays). They can be further classified by comparing their beaks and feet. Figure 6-21 shows some characteristics that different birds share. All swimming birds, such as ducks, have webbed feet for paddling through water. Hawks and other meat-eating birds, or birds of prey, have long, sharp claws to capture animals. Wading birds have long legs.

Look at the structure of the bill, or beak, in each group. The beak varies with eating habits. Birds that feed on seeds have short, strong beaks. Hunting birds, such as hawks, owls, and eagles, have curved beaks for tearing meat. Wading birds have long beaks.

 **INFER:** Why do you think hunting birds need strong beaks?

**Feathers** Birds have different types of feathers. Different feathers have different functions. Down feathers insulate, or keep warm, a bird's body. They are soft and fluffy. Contour feathers streamline a bird's body and help it fly. Contour

| TYPES OF BIRDS | | | | |
|---|---|---|---|---|
| **Birds of Prey** | **Perching Birds** | **Nonperching Birds** | **Swimming Birds** | **Wading Birds** |
| **Body features:** Sharp, curved claws Strong, sharp beak **Examples:** Hawks, owls, eagles, falcons | **Body features:** Curved toes Small beaks **Examples:** Cardinals, sparrows, crows, lorikeets | **Body feature:** Long, clinging toes **Examples:** Turkeys, hummingbirds, grouse, chickens | **Body feature:** Webbed feet **Examples:** Ducks, geese, swans, loons, gulls | **Body features:** Long legs Long, sharp beaks **Examples:** Herons, flamingoes, sandpipers, cranes |

▲ Figure 6-21

feathers are made up of a shaft and many branches called barbs.

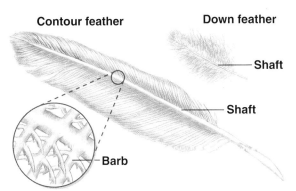

**Contour feather**  **Down feather**

— Shaft

— Shaft

— Barb

▲ **Figure 6-22** Each type of feather has a specific function.

 **STATE:** What is the purpose of down feathers?

## ✓ CHECKING CONCEPTS

1. Unlike reptiles and fish, birds are _____ animals.
2. Birds are the only animals with _____.
3. Perching birds have _____ toes.
4. Birds have _____ feathers to help insulate them.

## 💡 THINKING CRITICALLY

5. **CLASSIFY:** *Use Figure 6-21 to classify each of the birds listed.*
   a. hawk       d. heron
   b. duck       e. eagle
   c. cardinal
6. **APPLY:** Sea gulls live near oceans. Describe what kind of feet and beaks you think sea gulls have.
7. **INFER:** People, like birds, have four-chambered hearts. What do you think the upper and lower chambers of the human heart are called?
8. **APPLY:** What characteristic can you use to classify an animal as a bird?

## HEALTH AND SAFETY TIP

The meat and eggs of poultry might contain bacteria called *Salmonella. Salmonella* causes food poisoning. Use library references to find out what the symptoms of *Salmonella* poisoning are. Also find out two ways to help reduce your risk of poisoning from this bacteria.

## ◈ *Integrating Physical Science*

**TOPICS: gravity, force, air pressure**

### THE MECHANICS OF BIRD FLIGHT

Four different forces act on a flying bird. One is weight, the force of gravity that pulls an object downward. A bird's weight is opposed by a force called lift, which is produced when a bird flaps its wings. As the wings move downward, the pressure from air above the wings decreases, while the pressure from air below them increases. A bird's forward motion adds to this pressure difference. The higher air pressure below a flying bird pushes it up. As the bird flaps its wings, it tilts its main flight feathers so that the lower air pressure is toward the front. This movement produces a force called thrust, which propels the bird forward. Thrust is opposed by drag from the air through which the bird is moving.

Very strong chest muscles power the wings, and feathers can be turned to different angles to help a bird steer. A bird's body has a streamlined shape. Air flows around it smoothly, reducing drag. A bird uses drag to slow down and land by spreading its tail and lowering its feet.

**Thinking Critically** Do you think an animal without feathers could fly? Explain.

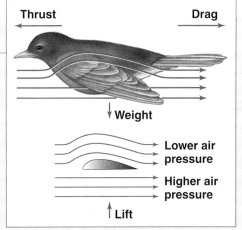

Thrust          Drag

↓ Weight

→ Lower air pressure

→ Higher air pressure

↑ Lift

▲ **Figure 6-23** A bird's body is built for flight.

# LAB ACTIVITY
## Investigating an Owl Pellet

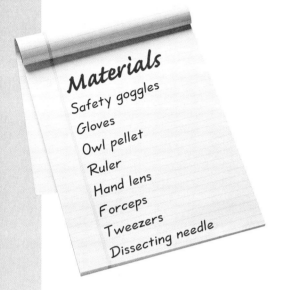

**Materials**
Safety goggles
Gloves
Owl pellet
Ruler
Hand lens
Forceps
Tweezers
Dissecting needle

### BACKGROUND

Owls are carnivores. Carnivores feed on other animals. Because birds do not have teeth, their food remains partially intact before it is digested. An owl pellet is the undigested materials an owl coughs up after it eats.

### PURPOSE

In this activity, you will learn about an owl's diet by examining an owl pellet.

### PROCEDURE

1. Observe the outside of an owl pellet with a hand lens. Record your observations.

2. Using the forceps, hold the owl pellet in place. Hold the forceps with one hand.

3. Use the dissecting needle to separate the owl pellet. ⚠ CAUTION: Be very careful when using dissecting needles.

4. Remove the bones from the owl pellet. If there is any fur attached to the bones, remove it with tweezers.

5. Group the bones together based on similarities. Observe the bones with a hand lens.

6. Record the number of skulls you find. Observe the skulls with a hand lens. Record the shape of the skulls and the number of teeth each skull has.

▲ **STEP 1** Observe the outside of a pellet with a hand lens.

▲ **STEP 3** Use the dissecting needle to separate the owl pellet.

▲ **STEP 4** Remove any bones from the pellet.

▲ **STEP 6** Observe the skulls with a hand lens.

7. Measure the skulls with a ruler. Record the measurement of each skull.

8. Use Figure 6-24 to identify the types of skulls you found. Record this information.

9. Use the bones and skulls you have found to reconstruct a skeleton of one of the organisms eaten by the owl.

▲ **STEP 7** Measure the skulls.

| IDENTIFYING FEATURES OF OWL PELLET REMAINS | | | | |
|---|---|---|---|---|
| **Shrew** | **Mouse** | **Vole** | **Mole** | **Rat** |
| Upper jaw has at least 18 teeth. | Upper jaw has two biting teeth and extends over lower jaw. | Upper jaw has two biting teeth and does not extend over lower jaw. | Upper jaw has at least 18 teeth. | Upper jaw has two biting teeth and extends over lower jaw. |
| Skull is less than 23 mm long. | Skull is less than 22 mm long. | Skull is more than 23 mm long. | Skull is more than 23 mm long. | Skull is more than 22 mm long. |

▲ **Figure 6-24** Use this chart to determine what an owl eats.

## CONCLUSIONS

1. **IDENTIFY:** How many animal remains did you find in the owl pellet?

2. **CALCULATE:** If owls cough up approximately two pellets a day, about how many animals might an owl eat in a week?

3. **INFER:** Compare your results with the results of two classmates. Based on your combined data, what animal do owls eat most frequently? Are they also vertebrates? How do you know?

# 6-7 What are mammals?

## INVESTIGATE

### Modeling Insulation
**HANDS-ON ACTIVITY**

1. Put on a pair of rubber gloves.
2. Spread a thick coat of shortening over one glove. Do not coat the other glove.
3. Remove the glove you used to spread the shortening over the first glove. Put on a clean glove. One glove should have shortening on it, the other glove should be clean.
4. Place both hands in a bowl of cold water for three minutes.

**THINK ABOUT IT:** Which hand got colder faster? Explain.

STEP 4

## Objective

Describe the characteristics of mammals.

## Key Terms

**mammary** (MAM-uh-ree) **gland:** gland that produces milk in female mammals

**monotreme:** mammal that lays eggs

**marsupial:** mammal whose young develops in pouches

**placenta** (pluh-SEHN-tuh)**:** structure through which materials are exchanged between the mother and the developing embryo

**Conquerors of the Earth** More than 250 million years ago, animals called therapsids (thuh-RAP-sihdz) roamed the Earth. Fossils show this animal had characteristics of reptiles and mammals. Some biologists infer that all modern mammals came from the therapsids. When the dinosaurs became extinct, early mammals no longer had to compete with them for food and living space. The mammals adapted to the new environment and reproduced. Today, mammals are one of the most successful groups of animals on Earth.

▶ **ANALYZE:** Why did mammals survive after the dinosaurs died out?

**Characteristics of Mammals** Mammals are a class of vertebrates that include humans and most of the best-known large animals. Mammals are endothermic. Because they are warmblooded,

mammals can live almost everywhere. They live on the plains, in forests, in deserts, and in swamps. Some live in oceans and a few can even fly.

Besides being endothermic, mammals have the following characteristics.

- Mammals have body hair. Body hair provides insulation that helps keep body heat from escaping.

- Mammals have a four-chambered heart.

- Mammals have specialized teeth to help them chew their food. Most mammals have four different types of teeth.

◀ **Figure 6-25**
Mammals have specialized teeth.

- Most mammals have a highly developed brain and nervous system.

- Female mammals nurse their young with milk. The milk is produced by **mammary glands**.

▶ **LIST:** What are the characteristics of mammals?

**Kinds of Mammals** There are over 4,600 species of mammals. They are sometimes grouped according to how they give birth to their young. There are three basic mammal groups. One group is made up of egg-laying mammals, or **monotremes.** There are only three kinds of animals in this group. These are the duckbill platypus (PLAT-uh-puhs) and two types of spiny anteater. In these animals, the young develop in an egg surrounded by a shell.

▲ **Figure 6-26** Monotremes, such as this duckbill platypus, are mammals that lay eggs.

The second mammal group is the pouched mammals, or **marsupials.** In marsupials, the young are born at a very early stage of development. They then crawl into a pouch, or pocket, on the belly of the mother. They remain in the pouch until they are big enough to survive on their own. Kangaroos, opossums, and koalas are pouched mammals.

◀ **Figure 6-27**
Koala bears carry their young in pouches.

The third and largest group of mammals is the placental mammals. In these animals, a special structure called the **placenta** develops in the female during pregnancy. The placenta is a structure through which materials are exchanged between the mother and the developing embryo.

Dogs, cats, cattle, seals, whales, bats, apes, and humans are placental mammals.

▲ **Figure 6-28** White-tailed deer are placental mammals.

**3** **LIST:** What are the three groups of mammals?

## ✔ CHECKING CONCEPTS

1. Mammals have _____ on their bodies.
2. Female mammals produce milk in _____ glands.
3. Materials are exchanged between a mother and an embryo through a _____.
4. The young of spiny anteaters develop inside an _____.
5. Kangaroos are _____ mammals.

## 💡 THINKING CRITICALLY

6. **CONTRAST:** How do spiny anteaters and duckbill platypuses differ from reptiles?
7. **COMPARE:** What characteristics are used to classify mammals into each of their groups?

### Web InfoSearch

**Marine Mammals** Dolphins and whales are marine mammals. Marine mammals live in water but come to the surface for oxygen.

**SEARCH:** Use the Internet to find out more about marine mammals. Then, write your findings in a report. Start your search at www.conceptsandchallenges.com. Some key search words are **marine mammals, dolphins,** and **whales.**

# THE Big IDEA

## How are the skeletons of vertebrates like levers?

Physical science involves the study of machines and the study of motion. Did you know the bones in your neck, arms, and legs are like machines?

A machine makes it easier to do work. A lever is a simple machine. A lever is a bar that turns on a fixed point called the fulcrum. See Figure 6-29. Something pushes or pulls the lever to lift a weight. The weight is called the load. The push or pull is the effort force. Many bones and muscles work as levers to move your body.

Effort force

Load

Fulcrum

**Figure 6-29** Lever

Your forearm is a lever. Your elbow joint is the fulcrum, and the weight of your wrist and hand is the load. When your bicep muscle applies the effort force on your forearm, your wrist and hand are lifted up.

Bones and joints have different shapes, depending on their purpose. Knee and elbow joints are hinges. Shoulder and hip joints are a ball and socket. Joints are coated with a slippery fluid and smooth tissue to reduce friction. This makes movement easier.

The skeleton of each animal affects how it moves. Look at the images that appear on this page and the next. They show how the skeletons of some vertebrates allow them to move in special ways. Follow the directions in the Science Log to learn more about "the big idea." ◆

### Bird

A bird is designed for flight. Its short backbone makes its body compact and stiff. This provides strength and stability as the bird flies. Its neck, however, is flexible. This allows the bird to reach for food and twist to preen its feathers. Powerful flight muscles are anchored to a large breastbone. The flight muscles power a bird's wings.

### Cheetah

The cheetah is the fastest land animal. Its leg bones are long and thin, and its backbone is flexible. When the cheetah's strong muscles pull on these bones, its backbone arches and springs back like a bow. The vertebrae in its backbone and the bones in its legs act as levers.

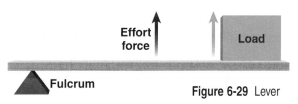

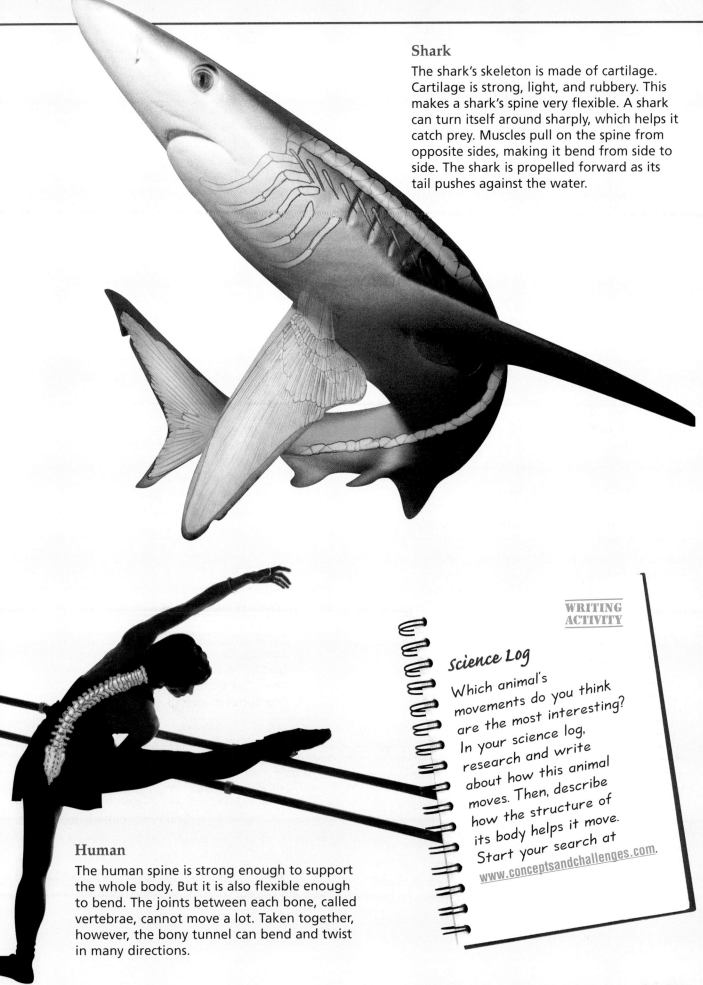

## Shark

The shark's skeleton is made of cartilage. Cartilage is strong, light, and rubbery. This makes a shark's spine very flexible. A shark can turn itself around sharply, which helps it catch prey. Muscles pull on the spine from opposite sides, making it bend from side to side. The shark is propelled forward as its tail pushes against the water.

### WRITING ACTIVITY

*science Log*

Which animal's movements do you think are the most interesting? In your science log, research and write about how this animal moves. Then, describe how the structure of its body helps it move. Start your search at www.conceptsandchallenges.com.

## Human

The human spine is strong enough to support the whole body. But it is also flexible enough to bend. The joints between each bone, called vertebrae, cannot move a lot. Taken together, however, the bony tunnel can bend and twist in many directions.

# 6-8 How do animal embryos develop?

## Objective

Recognize how the development of mammals differs from that of other animals.

## Key Terms

**egg:** female reproductive cell

**sperm:** male reproductive cell

**fertilization** (fuhrt-uhl-ih-ZAY-shuhn)**:** joining of the nuclei of the male and female reproductive cells

**gestation** (jehs-TAY-shuhn)**:** time it takes an embryo to fully develop inside its mother's body

**Water Animals** Most fish and amphibians lay their eggs in water. An **egg** is a female reproductive cell. The male animal deposits sperm on the eggs. **Sperm** are male reproductive cells. The union of a sperm cell nucleus and an egg cell nucleus is called **fertilization.** Only one sperm cell joins with each egg. In these animals, the eggs are fertilized outside the female's body. After fertilization, the embryo begins to develop inside the egg. Remember, the egg is outside the female's body. The embryo uses food stored in the egg.

◄ **Figure 6-30**
Salmon eggs are laid in water.

▶ **1** INFER: Where do the embryos of frogs develop?

**Land Animals** The eggs of reptiles, birds, and mammals are fertilized inside the body of the female. In some animals, such as snakes and birds, the eggs develop a shell after fertilization and are then laid. The embryos develop in the eggs outside the body of the female. The embryo uses the food stored in the egg. You know the food as the yolk.

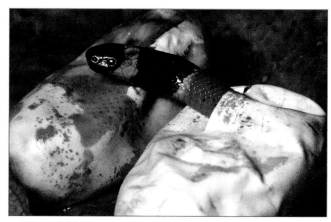

▲ **Figure 6-31** Young snakes develop in eggs with leathery shells.

▶ **2** STATE: Where are the eggs of mammals fertilized?

**Embryo Development in Mammals** In all mammals, fertilization takes place inside the body of the female, or mother. Monotremes are the only mammals that lay eggs. Marsupials and placental mammals do not. In these mammals, the embryo develops inside the mother's body. Most mammals give birth to living young.

◄ **Figure 6-32**
A kangaroo embryo develops in its mother's pouch.

The time it takes for an embryo to fully develop inside its mother's body is called **gestation**. Gestation periods are different for different types of animals. The gestation period of a dog is nine weeks. The gestation period of a human is nine months. An elephant's gestation period is 22 months.

▶ **3** STATE: Where do the embryos of most mammals develop?

**Embryo Nutrition** The embryos of placental mammals get their food from the mother through the placenta. Digested food and oxygen from the mother's blood pass into the bloodstream of the embryo. The embryo uses this food and oxygen for growth and development. Waste substances produced by the embryo pass into the mother's blood. These wastes are then excreted from the mother's body together with her own waste products.

 **STATE:** Where do mammal embryos get their food supply?

## ☑ CHECKING CONCEPTS

1. What is an egg?
2. What are sperm?
3. What is fertilization?
4. What is an embryo?

5. Where does an embryo that develops inside an egg get its food?
6. Where do the embryos of placental mammals get their food?
7. Where do the embryos of most mammals develop?

## 💡 THINKING CRITICALLY

8. **CONTRAST:** How is the development of the embryos of most animals different from the development of a mammal embryo?

## BUILDING SCIENCE SKILLS

*Researching* When you do research, you gather information about a topic. Use library references to find out the gestation periods for the following mammals: whale, mouse, dog, cat, human, horse, and cow. Present your findings in a graph.

## *Hands-On Activity*

### OBSERVING A BIRD EGG

*You will need a chicken egg, a hand lens, and a small dish.*

1. Obtain a raw chicken egg.
2. Use the hand lens to observe the shell of the chicken egg. Describe the shell of the chicken egg.
3. Crack open the egg into the dish.
4. Look at the inside of the shell. Find the shell membrane and the air space. Draw a model of the inside of the egg shell. Label the parts.
5. Look at the egg in the dish. Draw a model of the inside of the egg. Label the yolk and the egg white.

▲ **STEP 2** Examine the shell of the egg.

### Practicing Your Skills

6. **OBSERVE:** What color is the egg shell? Is the shell smooth or slightly bumpy?
7. **IDENTIFY:** What part of the egg is the embryo?
8. **IDENTIFY:** What two parts make up most of the bird egg?
9. **INFER:** What is the function of the shell? The egg white?
10. **HYPOTHESIZE:** Why do you think birds make nests for their eggs?

# 6-9 What are innate and learned behaviors?

**INVESTIGATE**

## Observing Learning
### HANDS-ON ACTIVITY

**1.** Stand with your back to a partner, who will stand on a chair.

**2.** Your partner will drop a meter stick in front of you. Try to catch the meter stick.

**3.** Repeat Step 2 several times. How high was the meter stick when you caught it?

**THINK ABOUT IT:** Were you able to catch the meter stick the first time? How did your reaction change each time?

STEP 2

## Objective

Describe innate and learned behaviors.

## Key Terms

**innate behavior:** behavior an animal is born with

**instinct:** innate behavior that animals perform correctly the first time

**learned behavior:** behavior an animal practices and learns

**Innate Behavior** The way an animal reacts to its environment is called behavior. One type of behavior is **innate behavior,** or behavior an animal is born with. Reflexes are innate behaviors and do not involve any learning or thought and cannot be controlled. Swallowing is a reflex. Another innate behavior is an **instinct.** Animals perform instinctive behaviors correctly the first time. A spider spinning a web is an example of an instinctive behavior.

▶ **1 IDENTIFY:** What kind of behavior is a reflex?

**Learned Behavior** Behavior that is not innate must be learned. These behaviors are called **learned behaviors.** Learned behaviors are not present at birth. They may not be performed correctly the first time. Learned behaviors usually need to be practiced. Throwing a ball and birds flying are examples of learned behaviors.

▶ **2 DESCRIBE:** What are learned behaviors?

**Imprinting** Imprinting is another way some animals learn behaviors. Imprinting is a permanent behavior that comes from observations made by an animal during the early stages of development. For example, a newborn animal forms an attachment to the first animal it sees, usually its mother. The newborn then imitates this animal. By imitation, the newborn learns how to find food. Scientists have also learned that imprinting is the means by which an animal recognizes members of its species.

◀ **Figure 6-33** In imprinting, newborns develop an attachment to the first thing they see. These geese imprinted on a human.

▶ **3 DEFINE:** What is imprinting?

**Trial and Error** Animals also learn behaviors through trial and error. Have you ever tried a new recipe? Each time you make the recipe, you experiment with the ingredients until the finished dish tastes exactly like you want it. This is learning through trial and error. When animals learn behaviors through trial and error, they learn from repeated practice and from their errors until they can perform their new skill perfectly.

**4 ▶ DESCRIBE:** What is trial and error?

**Conditioning** Conditioning is one way some animals learn behaviors. In conditioning, behaviors are changed so that a response associated with one stimulus becomes associated with a new stimulus. The response to the new stimulus is a conditioned response. Ivan Pavlov performed an experiment about stimulus and response in dogs. Figure 6-34 shows his experiment.

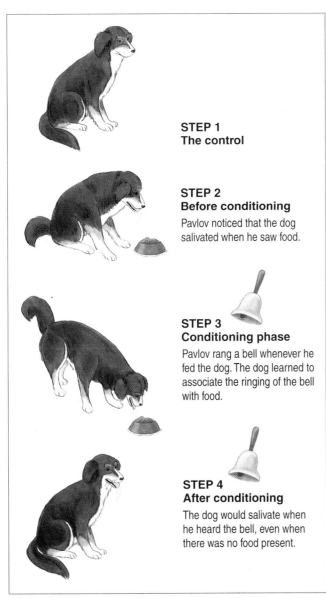

**STEP 1**
**The control**

**STEP 2**
**Before conditioning**
Pavlov noticed that the dog salivated when he saw food.

**STEP 3**
**Conditioning phase**
Pavlov rang a bell whenever he fed the dog. The dog learned to associate the ringing of the bell with food.

**STEP 4**
**After conditioning**
The dog would salivate when he heard the bell, even when there was no food present.

▲ **Figure 6-34** Pavlov experimented with conditioning.

**5 ▶ EXPLAIN:** What is conditioning?

**Rewards and Punishment** Rewards can help animals learn new behaviors. B. F. Skinner performed an experiment. He placed a rat in a box with a lever. Behind the lever was food. When the rat accidentally touched the lever, food dropped into the box. The rat learned that pressing the lever caused a reward, the food, to appear.

Punishments can help stop bad behaviors. For example, if your parents punish you for taking an item that does not belong to you, you will learn not to take other people's belongings again.

**6 ▶ IDENTIFY:** Who was B. F. Skinner?

**Insight** Animals also use insight to learn new behaviors. With insight, animals use what they have already learned about a similar problem to solve a new problem. In insight learning, animals perform a task by using what they already know without a period of trial and error.

**7 ▶ APPLY:** What is insight?

## ✓ CHECKING CONCEPTS

1. What are the main types of behavior?
2. What is conditioning?
3. How do rewards help animals learn new behaviors?
4. What is a conditioned response?

## THINKING CRITICALLY

5. **ANALYZE:** When have you used insight to solve a problem?
6. **PREDICT:** How would students learn to behave if each time they were late, the teacher awarded the students an A for the day?

## DESIGNING AN EXPERIMENT

*Design an experiment to solve the following problem. Include a hypothesis, variables, a procedure, and a type of data to study.*

PROBLEM: Lara wants her dog to roll over. She gives the dog a command to roll over, but the dog does not respond. How can Lara teach her dog to roll over?

# 6-10 What are social behaviors?

## Objective
Describe social behaviors.

**Social Behaviors** Animals interact with other animals. These interactions and reactions to other animals are called social behaviors. Most social behaviors are innate behaviors.

Communication is a very important part of social behaviors. Communication is the process of sharing information. Animals communicate in many different ways. Some communicate with sound. A wolf may growl or howl to let other wolves know its position in the pack. Other animals use movement to communicate. When a bee has found food, it returns to the hive and performs a "dance." This allows other bees to know that food has been found and where it is.

▶ 1 IDENTIFY: What forms of communication have you used today?

**Courtship and Parenting** Before animals of the same species mate, they engage in courtship behaviors. Courtship behaviors allow males and females to recognize each other. Courtship behaviors also signal that both animals are ready to mate and reproduce.

One way animals communicate that they are ready to mate is visually. When a male peacock is seeking a mate, he spreads out the colorful feathers on his lower back.

▲ **Figure 6-35** Male peacocks display their colorful feathers when they are ready to mate.

Animals mate to reproduce. Many fish, amphibians, and reptiles do not care for their young. The young are on their own once they are born. Other animals, such as birds and mammals, care for their offspring. They feed and protect them. In addition, they teach them how to survive on their own.

▶ 2 EXPLAIN: What are courtship behaviors?

**Territory** All animals need space in which to live, reproduce, and find food. This space is called an animal's territory. Many animals claim a territory as their own. They defend their territories from other members of the same species.

Many animals make substances in special scent glands. Some mammals rub against trees and bushes to spread their scent and mark their territory. Scent-marking is a form of communication. By scent-marking its territory, an animal warns others in its species to keep away.

▶ 3 DEFINE: What is a territory?

**Aggression** Animals often compete for territory and other limited resources, such as food, water, and mates. Sometimes when animals compete, they display aggressive behaviors. Aggressive behaviors are threatening behaviors. Animals use aggressive behaviors to intimidate and control other animals. Some aggressive behaviors are visual. The skin around an Australian frill lizard's neck fans out when it is faced with danger. Some animals use sound. When faced with a threat, a dog may growl.

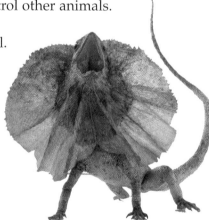

▲ **Figure 6-36** This lizard expands its frills when it is threatened.

▶ 4 EXPLAIN: How do animals use aggressive behaviors?

**Societies** Animals often live in groups with other members of their species. These groups are called societies. In societies, animals work together for the benefit of the whole society. Each member of the society has a specific job. For example, in a honeybee society, the job of the drone is to mate with the queen bee. Most societies have leaders. In a society of gorillas, the strongest male is usually the leader.

▲ **Figure 6-37** The silverback is often the head of a gorilla society.

 **APPLY:** How is a sports team like a society?

## ✓ CHECKING CONCEPTS

1. What is communication?
2. How do bees communicate with each other?
3. How do peacocks display courtship behaviors?
4. What is scent-marking?
5. What is a society?

## THINKING CRITICALLY

6. **EXPLAIN:** Why is communication an important part of social behaviors?
7. **APPLY:** What are some benefits to living in a society?
8. **IDENTIFY:** What are some social behaviors humans engage in?
9. **INFER:** Look at the photos of animals on these two pages. What adaptations have they evolved to help their social behaviors?

---

## *Integrating Physical Science*

**TOPIC: chemistry**

### PHEROMONES

Scent is another way animals in the same species communicate. Pheromones are chemical scents that are made by one animal and influence the behavior of other animals in the same species. Pheromones are unique. Pheromones are made up of long chains of atoms. Each pheromone has a different set of atoms and a unique chemical structure when the atoms combine. This means that no two species have the same pheromone. In fact, some species have several pheromones that identify members of different societies.

▲ **Figure 6-38** The sensors on the antennae of this male Atlas silkworm can pick up the scent of a female Atlas silkworm's pheromones.

Animals use pheromones to establish their territories, find mates, and identify members of their society. When scent-marking a territory, dogs use pheromones. The female Atlas silkworm uses pheromones to let males know she is ready to mate. If an ant wanders into a different colony, its pheromone alerts the members of the colony to its presence. The members of the colony then attack the stranger.

**Thinking Critically** How could pheromones be used to help control insects at a picnic?

## Chapter Summary

### Lesson 6-1

- Chordates are animals that have a **notochord** at some time during their development. Animals with a backbone are **vertebrates.**

### Lesson 6-2

- Fish are **ectothermic** marine animals that breathe through **gills.** Some types of fish are jawless fish, cartilaginous fish, and bony fish.

### Lessons 6-3 and 6-4

- **Amphibians** are ectothermic animals that live part of their lives in water and part on land. They usually have smooth skin and webbed feet.
- Amphibians lay eggs without shells in water. As a **larva** develops into an adult, it develops legs, loses its tail, develops lungs, and loses its gills.

### Lesson 6-5

- Reptiles are ectothermic land animals that lay eggs. They have lungs and scaly, waterproof skin.
- Reptiles are classified into four orders: tuataras, snakes and lizards, turtles and tortoises, and alligators and crocodiles.

### Lesson 6-6

- Birds are **endotherms.** They are the only animals with feathers.
- Birds can be classified by comparing the shapes of their beaks and feet.

### Lesson 6-7

- Mammals are endotherms that have body hair, a four-chambered heart, and a highly developed nervous system. They nurse their young with milk produced in **mammary glands.**

### Lesson 6-8

- The **eggs** of land and sea mammals are fertilized inside the body of the mother. In most mammals, the embryo develops inside the mother's body.

### Lessons 6-9 and 6-10

- A reflex is an **innate behavior. Learned behavior** must be practiced.
- Social behaviors, such as courtship, are how animals interact with other animals.

## Key Term Challenges

amphibian (p. 130)
cartilage (p. 128)
chordate (p. 126)
ectotherm (p. 128)
egg (p. 144)
endotherm (p. 136)
fertilization (p. 144)
gestation (p. 144)
gill (p. 128)
innate behavior (p. 146)
instinct (p. 146)
larva (p. 132)
learned behavior (p. 146)
mammary gland (p. 140)
marsupial (p. 140)
monotreme (p. 140)
notochord (p. 126)
placenta (p. 140)
sperm (p. 144)
swim bladder (p. 128)
tadpole (p. 132)
vertebrate (p. 126)

**MATCHING** Write the Key Term from above that best matches each description.

1. union of a sperm cell nucleus and an egg cell nucleus

2. organ used for obtaining oxygen dissolved in water

3. animal with a backbone

4. organ in female mammals that produces milk

5. organ through which materials are exchanged between the mother and the developing embryo

6. organ that allows a fish to remain at any depth in the water

**APPLYING DEFINITIONS** Explain the difference between the terms in each pair. Write your answers in complete sentences.

7. sperm, egg

8. ectotherm, endotherm

9. amphibians, reptiles

10. cartilage, bone

11. marsupials, monotremes

12. notochord, nerve cord

13. gills, lungs

14. larva, tadpole

15. innate behavior, learned behavior

# Content Challenges TEST PREP

**MULTIPLE CHOICE** **Write the letter of the term or phrase that best completes each statement.**

1. The three features common to all chordates are a hollow nerve cord, gill slits at some time during their development, and
   a. cartilage.
   b. a notochord.
   c. an endoskeleton.
   d. a placenta.

2. In most adult chordates, the notochord is replaced by
   a. gills slits.
   b. lungs.
   c. a backbone.
   d. an endoskeleton.

3. Fish are classified as either hagfish, lampreys, cartilaginous fish, or
   a. bony fish.
   b. tailless fish.
   c. tailed fish.
   d. venomous fish.

4. Fish, amphibians, and reptiles all
   a. are ectotherms.
   b. are endotherms.
   c. have a three-chambered heart.
   d. have smooth, moist skin.

5. Amphibians are classified into three orders based on their
   a. heart chambers.
   b. lungs.
   c. body structures.
   d. skin.

6. In the larval stage, a frog is called
   a. a toad.
   b. an egg.
   c. an adult.
   d. a tadpole.

7. The largest order of reptiles is made up of
   a. tuataras.
   b. snakes and lizards.
   c. turtles and tortoises.
   d. alligators and crocodiles.

8. Both birds and mammals
   a. have lightweight bones.
   b. have mammary glands.
   c. are endotherms.
   d. are ectotherms.

9. The duckbill platypus is
   a. a placental mammal.
   b. a pouched mammal.
   c. an egg-laying mammal.
   d. a marine mammal.

10. Biologists believe mammals come from a group of animals called
    a. dinosaurs.
    b. therapsids.
    c. carnivores.
    d. marsupials.

11. Blinking is
    a. a learned behavior.
    b. a conditioned response.
    c. an innate behavior.
    d. a stimulus.

**TRUE/FALSE** **Write** *true* **if the statement is true. If the statement is false, change the underlined term to make the statement true.**

12. Fish, amphibians, reptiles, birds, and mammals are <u>invertebrates</u>.

13. When you use what you already know to solve a problem, you are using <u>trial and error</u>.

14. Animals are born with <u>learned</u> behaviors.

15. Communication is a very important part of <u>social</u> behaviors.

# Concept Challenges TEST PREP

**WRITTEN RESPONSE** Answer each of the following questions in complete sentences.

1. **DISCUSS:** How do ectothermic animals differ from endothermic animals? Are humans ectotherms or endotherms? Explain.
2. **DESCRIBE:** What are the major characteristics of an amphibian? Explain the characteristics that help it survive in its environment.
3. **CONTRAST:** What are three differences between amphibians and reptiles?
4. **INFER:** Why do you think birds that feed on seeds have short, strong beaks?
5. **COMPARE:** In what two ways are birds and mammals alike?
6. **CONTRAST:** How is insight different from trial-and-error learning?

**INTERPRETING A DIAGRAM** Use Figure 6-39 to answer the following questions.

7. What is the part of the fish labeled *B*?
8. What is the part of the fish labeled *C*?
9. What does the part labeled *C* protect?
10. Which parts help the fish swim through the water?
11. What is the part of the fish labeled *E*?
12. What is the function of the part labeled *E*?

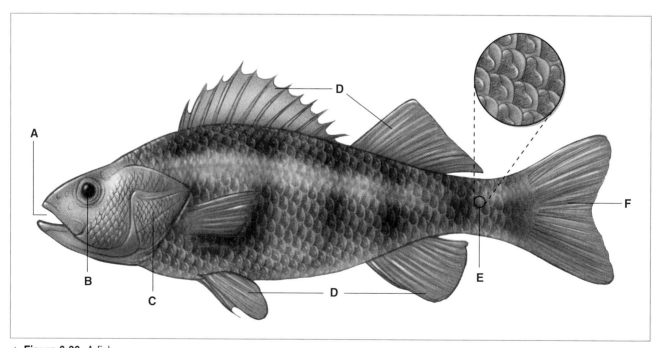

▲ **Figure 6-39** A fish

# Appendix A — Metric System

## The Metric System and SI Units

The metric system is an international system of measurement based on units of ten. More than 90% of the nations of the world use the metric system. In the United States, both the English system and the metric system are used.

The *Système International*, or SI, has been used as the international measurement system since 1960. The SI is a modernized version of the metric system. Like the metric system, the SI is a decimal system based on units of ten. When you want to change from one unit in the metric system to another unit, you multiply or divide by a multiple of ten.

- When you change from a smaller unit to a larger unit, you divide.

- When you change from a larger unit to a smaller unit, you multiply.

### METRIC UNITS

| LENGTH | SYMBOL | RELATIONSHIP |
|---|---|---|
| kilometer | km | 1 km = 1,000 m |
| meter | m | 1 m = 100 cm |
| centimeter | cm | 1 cm = 10 mm |
| millimeter | mm | 1 mm = 0.1 cm |
| **AREA** | **SYMBOL** | |
| square kilometer | $km^2$ | $1\ km^2 = 1{,}000{,}000\ m^2$ |
| square meter | $m^2$ | $1\ m^2 = 1{,}000{,}000\ mm^2$ |
| square centimeter | $cm^2$ | $1\ cm^2 = 0.0001\ m^2$ |
| square millimeter | $mm^2$ | $1\ mm^2 = 0.000001\ m^2$ |
| **VOLUME** | **SYMBOL** | |
| cubic meter | $m^3$ | $1\ m^3 = 1{,}000{,}000\ cm^3$ |
| cubic centimeter | $cm^3$ | $1\ cm^3 = 0.000001\ m^3$ |
| liter | L | 1 L = 1,000 mL |
| milliliter | mL | 1 mL = 0.001 L |
| **MASS** | **SYMBOL** | |
| metric ton | t | 1 t = 1,000 kg |
| kilogram | kg | 1 kg = 1,000 g |
| gram | g | 1 g = 1,000 mg |
| centigram | cg | 1 cg = 10 mg |
| milligram | mg | 1 mg = 0.001 g |
| **TEMPERATURE** | **SYMBOL** | |
| Kelvin | K | |
| degree Celsius | °C | |

▲ Figure 1

### COMMON METRIC PREFIXES

| | | | |
|---|---|---|---|
| micro- | 0.000001 or 1/1,000,000 | deka- | 10 |
| milli- | 0.001 or 1/1,000 | hecto- | 100 |
| centi- | 0.01 or 1/100 | kilo- | 1,000 |
| deci- | 0.1 or 1/10 | mega- | 1,000,000 |

▲ Figure 2

### METRIC-STANDARD EQUIVALENTS

| SI to English | English to SI |
|---|---|
| **LENGTH** | |
| 1 kilometer = 0.621 mile (mi) | 1 mi = 1.61 km |
| 1 meter = 1.094 yards (yd) | 1 yd = 0.914 m |
| 1 meter = 3.28 feet (ft) | 1 ft = 0.305 m |
| 1 centimeter = 0.394 inch (in.) | 1 in. = 2.54 cm |
| 1 millimeter = 0.039 inch | 1 in. = 25.4 mm |
| **AREA** | |
| 1 square kilometer = 0.3861 square mile | $1\ mi^2 = 2.590\ km^2$ |
| 1 square meter = 1.1960 square yards | $1\ yd^2 = 0.8361\ m^2$ |
| 1 square meter = 10.763 square feet | $1\ ft^2 = 0.0929\ m^2$ |
| 1 square centimeter = 0.155 square inch | $1\ in.^2 = 6.452\ cm^2$ |
| **VOLUME** | |
| 1 cubic meter = 1.3080 cubic yards | $1\ yd^3 = 0.7646\ m^3$ |
| 1 cubic meter = 35.315 cubic feet | $1\ ft^3 = 0.0283\ m^3$ |
| 1 cubic centimeter = 0.0610 cubic inch | $1\ in.^3 = 16.39\ cm^3$ |
| 1 liter = 0.2642 gallon (gal) | 1 gal = 3.79 L |
| 1 liter = 1.06 quarts (qt) | 1 qt = 0.946 L |
| 1 liter = 2.11 pints (pt) | 1 pt = 0.47 L |
| 1 milliliter = 0.034 fluid ounce (fl oz) | 1 fl oz = 29.57 mL |
| **MASS** | |
| 1 metric ton = 0.984 ton | 1 ton = 1.016 t |
| 1 kilogram = 2.205 pounds (lb) | 1 lb = 0.4536 kg |
| 1 gram = 0.0353 ounce (oz) | 1 oz = 28.35 g |
| **TEMPERATURE** | |
| Celsius = 5/9(°F – 32) | Fahrenheit = 9/5°C + 32 |
| 0°C = 32°F (Freezing point of water) | 72°F = 22°C (Room temperature) |
| 100°C = 212°F (Boiling point of water) | 98.6°F = 37°C (Human body temperature) |
| Kelvin = (°F + 459.67)/1.8 | Fahrenheit = (K × 1.8) – 459.67 |

▲ Figure 3

# Appendix B  Science Terms

## Analyzing Science Terms

You can often unlock the meaning of an unfamiliar science term by analyzing its word parts. Prefixes and suffixes, for example, each carry a meaning that comes from a word root. This word root usually comes from the Latin or Greek language. The following list of prefixes and suffixes provides clues to the meaning of many science terms.

| WORD PART | MEANING | EXAMPLE |
|---|---|---|
| a- | not, without | abiotic |
| aero- | air | aerobic |
| anti- | against | antibodies |
| bi- | two | biceps, binary fission |
| bio- | life | biotechnology, biology |
| carn- | meat, flesh | carnivore |
| chemo- | of, with, or by chemicals | chemosynthesis |
| chlor- | green | chloroplasts |
| cyt- | cell | cytoplasm |
| -derm | skin, covering | echinoderm, dermatology |
| di- | twice, double | dicot, disaccharide |
| eco- | environment, habitat | ecosystem, ecology |
| ecto- | outer | ectoderm, ectotherm |
| endo- | inside | endospore, endoskeleton |
| epi- | on, on the outside | epidermis, epiphyte |
| exo- | outside | exocrine, exoskeleton |
| -gen | produce, generate | pathogen, antigen |
| geo- | earth | geologic, geographic |
| hemo- | blood | hemoglobin |
| hydro- | water | hydroponics, hydrophilic |
| -itis | disease of | appendicitis, dermititis |
| leuko- | white | leukocyte |
| -logy | study of, science of | biology, zoology |
| mono- | one | monocot, monosaccharide |
| -ose | carbohydrate | glucose, cellulose |
| photo- | light | photosynthesis, phototropism |
| -phyll | leaf | mesophyll |
| -phyte | a plant | bryophyte, anthophyte |
| -scope | instrument for viewing | microscope |
| syn- | to put together, with | synthetic, photosynthesis |
| thigmo- | touch | thigmotropism |
| trans- | across | transpiration |
| trop- | turn, respond to | tropism |
| uni- | one | unicellular |

▲ Figure 4

# Appendix C The Microscope

## Parts of the Microscope

One of the most important tools in biology is the microscope. A microscope enables scientists to view and study objects or structures not visible to the unaided eye. The compound microscope is used most often in biology classes.

A compound microscope has two or more lenses. One lens is located in the eyepiece. The eyepiece lens usually has a magnification of 10×. An object viewed through this lens would appear ten times larger than it would look with the unaided eye.

The second lens is called the objective lens. Compound microscopes may have many objective lenses. Most compound microscopes, however, have two objective lenses. Each objective lens has a different magnification. The magnification is printed on each objective lens.

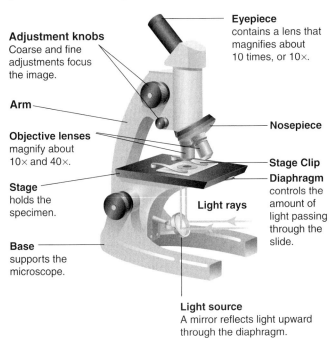

**Adjustment knobs**
Coarse and fine adjustments focus the image.

**Arm**

**Objective lenses**
magnify about 10× and 40×.

**Stage**
holds the specimen.

**Base**
supports the microscope.

**Eyepiece**
contains a lens that magnifies about 10 times, or 10×.

**Nosepiece**

**Stage Clip**

**Diaphragm**
controls the amount of light passing through the slide.

**Light rays**

**Light source**
A mirror reflects light upward through the diaphragm.

▲ **Figure 5** A compound microscope

## Calculating Power of Magnification

When you use a microscope, you must determine the total power of magnification. To find the total magnification of a microscope, use the following equation.

$$\text{eyepiece lens magnification} \times \text{objective lens magnification} = \text{total magnification}$$

For example, if the eyepiece lens has a magnification of 10× and the objective lens you are using has a magnification of 10×, the total magnification would be 100×. Looking at an object under this total magnification, you would be seeing the object 100 times larger than the object would look with the unaided eye.

A microscope is a delicate, but relatively uncomplicated, easy-to-use tool. Before you try to use a microscope, however, you should know the parts of a microscope and what each part does. Study Figure 5 to learn about the parts of the microscope and their functions.

### HEALTH AND SAFETY TIP

1. ⚠ **CAUTION** Always carry a microscope with two hands.

2. Use caution when handling glass slides—they can break easily and cause injury.

3. Be careful when handling electric cords, outlets, and light bulbs. After using a microscope the light bulb may be hot to the touch.

4. Always carry a microscope with one hand under the base and one hand holding the arm.

## *Hands-On Activity*

### USING A MICROSCOPE

*You will need a microscope, a slide, a cover slip, and material to be examined. You may also need an eye dropper or pipette, and some type of stain.*

1. Place the material to be examined on a clean slide. If you are examining a liquid, use an eye dropper or pipette.

2. You may need to add 1–2 drops of water or liquid stain. Follow the directions in the lab or your teacher's instructions.

3. Carefully place one edge of the cover slip onto the slide, next to your sample. Gently lower the cover slip so that it covers the sample.

4. You may need to clean up excess liquid from the slide. To do this, place a small piece of tissue or paper towel next to the edge of the cover slip.

5. Now you are ready to observe your slide under the microscope! Always begin by using the lowest power objective lens.

6. Make sure the sample is centered over the opening in the stage.

7. Slowly move the slide back and forth or up and down while looking through the eyepiece.

8. Focus using the coarse adjustment knob first and then the fine adjustment.
   ⚠ CAUTION! Never use the coarse adjustment when you are on high power.

9. Make sure there is enough light coming through the opening in the stage. To adjust the amount of light, turn the diaphragm.

▲ **STEP 2**   Add two drops of water to the slide.

▲ **STEP 8**   Focus the microscope.

### Practicing Your Skills

10. **OBSERVE:** Draw what you see at low power.

11. **COMPARE:** What details can you see at high power?

12. **ANALYZE:** How does a microscope help you to learn more about something?

# Appendix D — The Classification of Life

This appendix gives the taxonomic classification based on a five-kingdom system. Other classification systems have been suggested but are not yet formally recognized. Classification continuously changes as new information about organisms is discovered. Common names are given in parentheses next to the scientific names. Because of the large amount of organisms, not all groups are listed. *Note: The term *division* is used by many scientists in place of *phylum* for the plant and fungi kingdom.

## KINGDOM MONERA

*Mostly one-celled organisms without membrane-bound organelles*

Subkingdom Archaebacteria (bacteria that live in extreme environments)

Subkingdom Eubacteria (other bacteria)

## KINGDOM PROTISTA

*Mostly one-celled organisms that have organelles and may move freely*

Animal-like Protists

Phylum Rhizopoda (amoeba)

Phylum Ciliophora (paramecium)

Plantlike Protists

Phylum Chrysophyta (golden algae)

Phylum Euglenophyta (euglena)

Funguslike Protists

Phylum Myxomycota (slime mold)

Phylum Oomycota (water mold)

## KINGDOM FUNGI

*Many-celled organisms that are heterotrophic and reproduce by spores*

*Division Zygomycota (bread mold)

Division Ascomycota (yeast, truffles)

Division Basidiomycota (mushrooms)

## KINGDOM PLANTAE

*Many-celled organisms that are autotrophic and have cell walls*

Division Bryophyta (mosses, liverworts)

Division Pterophyta (ferns)

Division Coniferophyta (conifers)

Division Cycadophyta (cycads)

Division Ginkgophyta (ginkgoes)

Division Anthophyta (flowering plants)

## KINGDOM ANIMALIA

*Many-celled organisms that are heterotrophic and lack cell walls; most animals have complex tissues and can move freely.*

Phylum Porifera (sponges)

Phylum Cnidaria (hydras, jellyfish)

Phylum Platyhelminthes (flatworms)

Phylum Nematoda (roundworms)

Phylum Annelida (segmented worms)

Phylum Mollusca (mollusks)

Phylum Echinodermata (echinoderms)

Phylum Arthropoda (arthropods)

Phylum Chordata (chordates)

Subphylum Vertebrata (vertebrates)

Class Agnatha (jawless fish)

Class Chondrichthyes (cartilaginous fish)

Class Osteichthyes (bony fish)

Class Amphibia (amphibians)

Class Reptilia (reptiles)

Class Aves (birds)

Class Mammalia (mammals)

# Glossary

Pronunciation and syllabication have been derived from *Webster's New World Dictionary*, Second College Edition, Revised School Printing (Prentice Hall, 1985). Syllables printed in capital letters are given primary stress. (Numbers in parentheses indicate the page number, or page numbers, on which the term is defined.)

| | | PRONUNCIATION KEY | | | |
|---|---|---|---|---|---|
| Symbol | Example | Respelling | Symbol | Example | Respelling |
| a | amber | (AM-bur) | ks | thorax | (THAWR-aks) |
| ah | molecule | (MAHL-ih-kyool) | oh | embryo | (EM-bree-oh) |
| aw | absorption | (ab-SAWRP-shuhn) | oi | joint | (JOINT) |
| ay | adaptation | (ad-uhp-TAY-shuhn) | oo | asexual | (ay-SEK-shoo-uhl) |
| eh | energy | (EHN-uhr-jee) | sh | circulation | (sur-kyoo-LAY-shuhn) |
| ee | ecology | (ee-KAHL-uh-jee) | u | urine | (YUR-ihn) |
| f | phloem | (FLOH-em) | uh | data | (DAYT-uh) |
| g | gamete | (GAM-eet) | y, eye | biome, iris | (BY-ohm), (EYE-ris) |
| I | specialization | (spesh-uhl-ih-ZAY-shuhn) | z | organism | (AWR-guh-nihz-uhm) |
| j | genes | (JEENZ) | zh | diffusion | (dih-FYOO-zhuhn) |
| k | Calorie | (KAL-uh-ree) | | | |

## A

**abdomen** (AB-duh-muhn):  third section of an insect's body (p. 118)

**amphibian** (am-FIHB-ee-uhn):  animal that lives part of its life in water and part on land (p. 130)

**angiosperm** (AN-jee-oh-spuhrm):  type of vascular flowering plant (p. 62)

**annelid** (AN-uh-lihd):  type of worm with a segmented body (p. 104)

**antenna** (an-TEHN-uh) *pl.* **antennae**:  structure used for touch, taste, and smell (p. 118)

**anther**:  part of the stamen that produces pollen (p. 82)

**arthropod** (AHR-throh-pahd):  animal with an exoskeleton and jointed legs (p. 114)

**asexual** (ay-SEK-shoo-uhl) **reproduction**:  reproduction needing only one parent (p. 90)

**autotroph** (AW-toh-trahf):  organism that can make its own food (p. 76)

## B

**bacillus** (buh-SIHL-uhs) *pl.* **bacilli**:  rod-shaped bacterium (p. 32)

**bacteriology** (bak-tihr-ee-AHL-uh-jee):  study of bacteria (p. 34)

**bacteriophage** (bak-TIHR-ee-uh-fayj):  virus that infects bacteria (p. 26)

**blade**:  wide, flat part of a leaf (p. 74)

**bryophytes** (BRY-oh-fyts):  group of plants that do not have transport tubes (p. 52)

**budding**:  kind of asexual reproduction in which a new organism forms from a bud on a parent (p. 46)

**bulb**:  underground stem covered with fleshy leaves (p. 90)

## C

**cap**:  umbrella-shaped top of a mushroom (p. 42)

**capsid** (KAP-sihd):  protein covering of a virus (p. 26)

**cartilage** (KAHRT-uhl-ihj):  tough, flexible connective tissue (p. 128)

**chitin** (KY-tihn):  hard material that makes up the exoskeleton of arthropods (p. 114)

**chlorophyll** (KLAWR-uh-fihl):  green material in chloroplasts that is needed by plants for photosynthesis (p. 76)

**chloroplast:** organelle in a plant cell that contains chlorophyll (p. 76)

**chordate** (kawr-DAYT): animal with a notochord at some time during its development (p. 126)

**cilium** (SIHL-ee-uhm) *pl.* **cilia:** tiny, hairlike structure (p. 36)

**classification** (klas-uh-fih-KAY-shuhn): grouping things according to similarities (p. 16)

**closed circulatory system:** organ system in which blood moves through vessels (p. 104)

**cnidarian** (nih-DER-ee-uhn): invertebrate animal with stinging cells and a hollow central cavity (p. 102)

**coccus** (KAHK-uhs) *pl.* **cocci:** spherical-shaped bacterium (p. 32)

**cocoon** (kuh-KOON): protective covering around the pupa (p. 120)

**coldblooded:** having a body temperature that changes with the temperature of the surroundings (p. 128)

**communication:** sharing information (p. 8)

**conditioned response:** learned behavior in which a new stimulus causes the same response that an old one did (p. 147)

**conifer** (KAHN-uh-fuhr): tree that produces cones and has needlelike leaves (p. 60)

**constant:** something that does not change (p. 11)

**controlled experiment:** experiment in which all the conditions except one are kept constant (p. 11)

**cotyledon** (kaht-uh-LEED-uhn): leaflike structure inside a seed that contains food for the developing plant (p. 62)

## D

**data:** information you collect when you observe something (p. 3)

**decomposition:** breakdown of dead material by simple organisms (p. 34)

**dicot:** flowering plant with two cotyledons, or seed leaves, in its seeds (p. 62)

## E

**echinoderm** (ee-KY-noh-duhrm): spiny-skinned animal (p. 108)

**ectotherm:** animal whose body temperature changes with its environment; coldblooded animal (p. 128)

**egg:** female reproductive cell (p. 144)

**embryo** (EHM-bree-oh): undeveloped plant or animal (p. 84)

**endoskeleton** (ehn-doh-SKEHL-uh-tuhn): skeleton inside the body (p. 98)

**endospore:** inactive bacterium surrounded by a thick wall (p. 32)

**endotherm:** vertebrate whose body temperature remains about the same; warmblooded animal (p. 136)

**epidermis** (ehp-uh-DUR-mihs): outer, protective layer of the leaf (p. 74)

**exoskeleton** (eks-oh-SKEHL-uh-tuhn): skeleton on the outside of the body (p. 98)

## F

**fermentation:** process by which a cell releases energy from food without using oxygen (p. 42)

**fertilization** (furt-uhl-ih-ZAY-shuhn): joining of the nuclei of a male and a female reproductive cell (pp. 82, 144)

**fibrous** (FY-bruhs) **root system:** root system made up of many thin, branched roots (p. 70)

**filament:** stalk of the stamen (p. 82)

**flagellum** (fluh-JEHL-uhm) *pl.* **flagella:** whiplike structure on a cell (p. 32)

**frond:** leaf of a fern (p. 56)

**fruit:** mature ovary and its seeds (p. 84)

**fungus** (FUHN-guhs) *pl.* **fungi:** plantlike organism that lacks chlorophyll (p. 22)

## G

**genus** (JEE-nuhs): classification group made up of related species (p. 18)

**germinate** (JUR-muh-nayt): to grow from a seed into an embryo plant (p. 88)

**gestation** (jehs-TAY-shuhn): time it takes an embryo to fully develop inside its mother's body (p. 144)

**gill:** structure in a mushroom that produces spores (p. 42); organ that absorbs dissolved oxygen from water (p. 128)

**gram:** basic unit of mass (p. 4)

**gravitropism:** plant's response to gravity (p. 92)

**gymnosperm** (JIHM-noh-spuhrm): type of land plant that has uncovered seeds (p. 60)

**H**

**herbaceous** (huhr-BAY-shuhs) **stem:** stem that is soft and green (p. 72)

**heterotroph** (HEHT-uhr-oh-trahf): organism that cannot make its own food (p. 76)

**hilum** (HY-luhm): mark on the seed coat where the seed was attached to the ovary (p. 88)

**hydrotropism:** plant's response to water (p. 92)

**hypha** (HY-fuh): threadlike structure that makes up the body of molds and mushrooms (p. 42)

**hypothesis:** suggested answer to a question or problem (p. 10)

**I**

**imperfect flower:** flower with either male or female reproductive organs, but not both (p. 80)

**innate behavior:** behavior an animal is born with (p. 146)

**instinct:** innate behavior that animals perform correctly the first time (p. 146)

**invertebrate** (ihn-VER-tuh-briht): animal without a backbone (p. 98)

**K**

**kingdom:** classification group made up of related phyla (p. 18)

**L**

**larva** (LAHR-vuh): immature stage of many animals that usually looks different from the adult form (pp. 120, 132)

**leaflet:** smaller division of a leaf (p. 56)

**learned behavior:** behavior an animal practices and learns (p. 146)

**liter:** basic unit of liquid volume (p. 4)

**M**

**mammary** (MAM-uh-ree) **gland:** gland that produces milk in female mammals (p. 140)

**mantle:** thin membrane that covers a mollusk's organs (p. 106)

**marsupial:** mammal whose young develops in a pouch (p. 140)

**mass:** amount of matter in something (p. 4)

**medusa** (muh-DOO-suh): umbrella-like form of a cnidarian (p. 102)

**meniscus:** curve at the surface of a liquid in a thin tube (p. 4)

**mesophyll** (MEHS-uh-fihl): middle layer of leaf tissue in which photosynthesis occurs (p. 74)

**metamorphosis** (meht-uh-MAWR-fuh-sihs): series of developmental changes of an organism (p. 120)

**meter:** basic unit of length or distance (p. 4)

**model:** tool scientists use to represent an object or a process (p. 3)

**mollusk** (MAHL-uhsk): soft-bodied organism (p. 106)

**molting:** process by which an animal sheds its outer covering (p. 114)

**moneran** (muh-NEER-uhn): single-celled organism that does not have a true nucleus (p. 22)

**monocot:** flowering plant with only one cotyledon, or seed leaf, in its seeds (p. 62)

**monotreme:** mammal that lays eggs (p. 140)

**N**

**nematode** (NEHM-uh-tohd): type of worm with a round body (p. 104)

**nonvascular plant:** plant that does not have transport tubes (p. 52)

**notochord** (NOHT-uh-kawrd): strong, rodlike structure in chordates that can bend (p. 126)

**nymph** (NIHMF): young insect that looks like the adult (p. 120)

**O**

**open circulatory system:** circulatory system in which blood does not flow constantly through tubes (p. 114)

**ovary** (OH-vuh-ree): in a plant, the bottom part of the pistil that produces seeds (p. 84)

**ovule** (AHV-yool): part of the ovary that develops into a seed after fertilization (p. 84)

**P**

**parasite** (PAR-uh-syt): organism that gets its food by living on or in the body of another organism (p. 104)

**perfect flower:** flower with both male and female reproductive organs (p. 80)

**petal:** white or brightly colored structure above the sepal of a flower (p. 80)

**phloem** (FLOH-em): tissue that carries food from the leaves to other parts of the plant (p. 72)

**photosynthesis** (foht-oh-SIHN-thuh-sihs): food-making process in plants that uses sunlight (p. 76)

**phototropism:** plant's response to light (p. 92)

**phylum** (FY-luhm) *pl.* **phyla:** classification group made up of related classes (p. 18)

**pistil:** female reproductive organ in a flower (p. 80)

**placenta** (pluh-SEHN-tuh): structure through which materials are exchanged between the mother and the developing embryo (p. 140)

**plankton** (PLANK-tuhn): microscopic organisms that float on or near the water's surface (p. 40)

**platyhelminth** (plat-uh-HEHL-mihnth): type of worm with a flattened body (p. 104)

**pollen grain:** male reproductive cell of a plant (p. 82)

**pollination** (pahl-uh-NAY-shuhn): movement of pollen from a stamen to a pistil (p. 82)

**polyp** (PAHL-ihp): cuplike form of a cnidarian (p. 102)

**pore:** tiny opening (p. 100)

**poriferan** (poh-RIHF-uhr-uhn): invertebrate animal with pores (p. 100)

**protist** (PROHT-ihst): simple organism that has cells with nuclei (p. 22)

**protozoan** (proht-uh-ZOH-uhn): one-celled, animal-like protist (p. 36)

**pseudopod** (SOO-doh-pahd): fingerlike extension of cytoplasm (p. 36)

**pupa** (PYOO-puh): resting stage during complete metamorphosis (p. 120)

**R**

**radula** (RAJ-oo-luh): rough, tonguelike organ of a snail (p. 106)

**regeneration** (rih-jehn-uh-RAY-shuhn): ability to regrow lost parts (p. 110)

**rhizoid** (RY-zoid): fine, hairlike structure that acts as a root (p. 54)

**rhizome** (RY-zohm): horizontal underground stem (p. 56)

**root cap:** cup-shaped mass of cells that covers and protects a root tip (p. 70)

**root hair:** thin, hairlike structure on the outer layer of the root tip (p. 70)

**S**

**seed:** structure that contains a tiny living plant and food for its growth; a reproductive cell (p. 60)

**seed coat:** outside covering of a seed (p. 88)

**sepal** (SEE-puhl): special kind of leaf that protects the flower bud (p. 80)

**setae** (SEET-ee): tiny, hairlike bristles (p. 104)

**simulation:** computer model that usually shows a process (p. 3)

**species:** group of organisms that look alike and can reproduce among themselves (p. 18)

**sperm:** male reproductive cell (p. 144)

**spicule** (SPIHK-yool): small, hard, needlelike structure of a sponge (p. 100)

**spiracle** (SPIR-uh-kuhl): opening to an air tube of a grasshopper (p. 118)

**spirillum** (spy-RIHL-uhm) *pl.* **spirilla:** spiral-shaped bacterium (p. 32)

**spore:** reproductive structure found in fungi and some plants (pp. 42, 54)

**spore case:** structure that contains spores (p. 46)

**sporulation** (spawr-yoo-LAY-shuhn): kind of asexual reproduction in which a new organism forms from spores released from a parent (p. 46)

**stalk:** stemlike part of a mushroom (p. 42)

**stamen** (STAY-muhn): male reproductive organ in a flower (p. 80)

**stigma** (STIHG-muh): top part of the pistil (p. 84)

**stimulus** (STIHM-yuh-luhs): change that causes a response (p. 92)

**stoma** (STOH-muh) *pl.* **stomata:** tiny opening in the upper or lower surface of a leaf (p. 74)

**style:** stalk of the pistil of a flower (p. 84)

**swim bladder:** organ of a fish that allows the fish to remain at a specific depth in the water (p. 128)

**T**

**tadpole:** larval stage of a frog (p. 132)

**taproot system:** root system made up of one large root and many small, thin roots (p. 70)

**taxonomy** (tak-SAHN-uh-mee): science of classifying living things (p. 16)

**temperature:** measurement of the amount of heat energy something contains (p. 4)

**tentacles:** long, armlike structures (p. 102)

**theory:** set of hypotheses that have been supported by testing over and over again (p. 10)

**thigmotropism:** plant's response to touch (p. 92)

**thorax** (THAWR-aks): middle section of an insect's body (p. 118)

**tracheophytes** (TRAY-kee-uh-fyts): group of plants that have transport tubes (p. 52)

**tropism** (TROH-pihz-uhm): change in a plant's growth in response to a stimulus (p. 92)

**tube feet:** small structures of echinoderms used for movement and feeding (p. 108)

**tuber:** underground stem (p. 90)

**tympanum** (TIHM-puh-nuhm): hearing organ in a grasshopper (p. 118)

**unit:** amount used to measure something (p. 4)

**variable:** anything that can affect the outcome of an experiment (p. 11)

**vascular plant:** plant that contains transport tubes (p. 52)

**vegetative propagation** (VEHJ-uh-tayt-ihv prahp-uh-GAY-shuhn): kind of asexual reproduction that uses parts of plants to grow new plants (p. 90)

**vein** (VAYN): bundle of tubes that contains the xylem and phloem in a leaf (p. 74)

**vertebrate** (VER-tuh-briht): animal with a backbone (pp. 98, 126)

**virus** (VY-ruhs): nonliving particle made up of a piece of nucleic acid covered with a protein (p. 26)

**volume:** amount of space an object takes up (p. 4)

**warm-blooded animal:** animal having a body temperature that remains about the same (p. 136)

**water-vascular system:** system of tubes used to transport water (p. 108)

**woody stem:** stem that contains wood and is thick and hard (p. 72)

**xylem** (ZY-luhm): tissue that carries water and dissolved minerals upward from the roots (p. 72)

# Index

## A

abdomen, 118
active transport, 78
adaptations, 129
African sleeping sickness, 37
aggression, 148
air pressure, 137
algae, 36, 40
  brown, 40
  golden brown, 40
algal blooms, 41
alligators, 126, 135
amoeba, 22, 36
amoebocytes, 100–101
amphibians, 126–127, 130–131,
  148
  development of, 132–133
angiosperms, 62–63
  characteristics of, 62
animal kingdom, 18, 23, 98
animal-like protists, 36
animals
  with backbones, 125–149
  without backbones, 97–121
  classification of, 98–99
  coldblooded, 128
  embryo development in, 144–145
  in seed dispersal, 89
  viruses of, 26
  warmblooded, 136
annelids, 104–105
anteater, spiny, 141
antennae, 118
anther, 82
anthocyanin, 75
ants, 114, 118
arachnids, 114
archaebacteria, 22, 33
arthropods, 114–115, 118
  characteristics of, 114
  classifying, 114
Ascaris worms, 104
asexual reproduction, 46, 90–91,
  110, 135
asthma, 33
athlete's foot, 43
atmosphere, 77
autotrophs, 76
Aves, 136

## B

bacilli, 32
bacteria, 41
  blue-green, 33
  foods and, 34, 44–45
  grouping, 32
  movement in, 32
  needs of, 32–33
  nitrogen-fixing, 71
  scientific study of, 34–35
  soil and, 34
bacterial cell, 32
bacterial diseases, 33, 35
bacteriologists, 33
bacteriology, 33–34
bacteriophage, 26
bass, 129
bees, 114
beetles, 114, 118
behaviors
  innate, 146
  learned, 146
  social, 148–149
bilateral symmetry, 109, 126
binary fission, 32
biologists, 140
birds, 126–127, 136–137, 148
  mechanics of flight in, 137
  types of, 136
Bivalvia, 106
blades, 74
blue-green bacteria, 33
bony fish, 128–129
Borella burgdorferi, 35
botanical gardens, 81
botanists, 52–53
botulism, 35
brittle stars, 108
bryophytes, 52–55
  life cycle of, 54–55
  structure of, 54
budding, 46
bulbs, 90
butterflies, 114, 120

## C

caecilians, 130–131
calcium carbonate, 37
cap, 42
capsid, 26
carbon dioxide, 76
Carboniferous Period, 57
careers
  bacteriologists, 33
  biologists, 140
  botanists, 52–53
  environmental scientists, 116,
    133
  plant geneticists, 83
  public health scientists, 33
  taxonomists, 16, 99
  veterinarians, 127
carnivores, 138
carotene, 75
cartilage, 128–129
cartilaginous fish, 128–129
cedars, 60
cell membrane, 32
cells
  bacterial, 32
  collar, 100
  plant, 52
  sperm, 144
cellular respiration, 43
cell walls, 32
centipedes, 114
Cephalopoda, 106
cheese, 44
cheetah, 142
chemistry, 149
chitin, 114–115
chlorophyll, 23, 40, 42, 52, 75–76
chloroplasts, 23, 42, 52, 76, 78
chordata, 18, 98
chordates, 126–127
  body plan of, 126
chromosomes, 99
clams, 97–98, 106, 108–109, 111
  determining age of, 112–113
classes, 18
classification, 16–17
  early systems of, 16–17
  of plants, 52–53
  of shells, 20–21
climatron, 81
closed circulatory system,
  104–105, 130
cnidarians, 102–103, 117
  food for, 103
  structure of, 102–103
coal, 57
cocci, 32
cockroaches, 114
cocoon, 120–121
coldblooded animals, 128
cold sore, 26
collar cells, 100
complete metamorphosis,
  120–121
compound leaf, 74–75
computer dissections, 131
conch, 116
conditioned response, 147
conditioning, 147
cones, 60–61
conifers, 60
coral reefs, 101
  protecting, 116–117
corals, 102
corn, 64–65
corn smut, 43
cortex, 70
cotyledons, 62, 88
courtship, 148

crabs, 110, 114–115
crayfish, 114
Cretaceous Period, 37
crickets, 120
crocodiles, 135
crop rotation, 71
cross-pollination, 82–83
crustaceans, 114–115
cuttings, 90–91
cyanobacteria, 33
cycads, 60–61
cytoplasm, 32, 43

**D**

decomposition, 34
deep-sea vents, 33
deer ticks, 115
deoxyribonucleic acid (DNA), 16
   in classifying organisms, 19
   virus, 27
diatomaceous earth, 31
diatoms, 31, 40
dicots, 62–63, 72–73, 88
dicotyledons, 63
dietary supplements, 61
digestive tract
   bacteria in, 34
dinosaurs, 140
diseases
   bacterial, 33, 35
   spread of, 115
   viral, 26–27
dolphins, 141
drag, 137
duckbill platypus, 141

**E**

eagles, 126
earth, diatomaceous, 31
earthworms, 105
echinoderms, 108
economics, 64–65
economy, effect of plants on,
   64–65
ectotherms, 128, 134
eggs, 144–145
electricity, 57
elephants, 126
embryo, 84, 132, 144–145
   nutrition, 145
embryology, 99
endoskeleton, 98, 127
endosperm, 88
endospore, 32–33, 35
endotherms, 136, 140
environment, plant responses to
   changes in, 92–93
environmental science, 116
environmental scientists, 116, 133
epidermis, 70, 74–75
eubacteria, 22
euglena, 22, 40
evergreens, 60–61

exoskeleton, 98, 114–115, 118
eyespot, 40

**F**

families, 18
farming, crop rotation in, 71
feathers, 136–137
fermentation, 42–43
ferns, 56–57
   life cycle of, 57
   prehistoric, 57
   structure of, 56, 58–59
fertilization, 54, 82, 84, 144
fertilizers, 71
fibrous root systems, 70
fiddleheads, 56
filament, 82
filter feeding, 97, 106
fish, 127–129, 148
fission, binary, 32
five-kingdom classification
   system, 22
flagellates, 37
flagellum, 32, 37, 40, 100–101
flatworms, 104, 110
fleas, 118
Fleming, Alexander, 47
flies, 114
flounder, 129
flowers, 62–63, 69, 80–81
   parts of, 80–81, 86–87
   reproduction of, 80–83
flukes, 104
foods, bacteria and, 34, 44–45
force, 137
fossil fuels, 57
frogs, 126, 130
fronds, 56
fruits, 60, 62, 84–85
fuel, peat as, 55
fungal infections, 43
fungi, 22–23, 42–43
   sexual reproduction in, 46–47
fungicides, 43
fungi kingdom, 42–47
funguslike protist molds, 41

**G**

gastropods, 106
genus, 18
geologic time, 57
germination, 88–89
gestation, 144
giant redwood trees, 60
giant tree ferns, 57
*Giardia lambia*, 45
gills, 42, 126, 128, 130
*Ginkgo biloba*, 61
ginkgoes, 60–61
ginseng, 61
golden-brown algae, 40
grafting, 91
grasshoppers, 114, 118, 120

gravitropism, 92
gravity, 92–93, 137
gross domestic product (GDP), 64
gymnosperms, 60–62, 73

**H**

hagfish, 128
hawks, 126, 136
hay fever, 83
hemlocks, 60
herbaceous stems, 72
herbal supplements, 61
heterotrophs, 76–77
hilum, 88
Hominid, 18
*Homo sapiens*, 18–19
honeybees, 118–119
hookworms, 104
hornworts, 54
human immunodeficiency virus
   (HIV), 26
humans, 143
hummingbird, 69
hydra, 102–103
hydrotropism, 92–93
hypha, 42

**I**

ice cream, 45
imperfect flowers, 80–81
imprinting, 146
incomplete metamorphosis,
   120–121
infections, fungal, 43
innate behaviors, 146
insects, 98, 114, 118–119
   development of, 120–121
insight, 147
instinct, 146
invertebrates, 98

**J**

jawless fish, 128
jellyfish, 98, 102–103
jet propulsion, 107
joints, 142

**K**

kangaroos, 141
kelp, 40
kingdom, 18
koalas, 141

**L**

*Lactobacillus bulgaricus*, 44
lampreys, 128
lancelets, 126–127
larva, 120–121, 132–133
learned behavior, 146
learning, 146–147
leaves, 52–53, 70, 74–75
   chemistry of changing, 75

kinds of, 74–75
structure of, 74
tissues of, 75
leeches, 105
legume family, 71
leopard frog, 130
life cycle
of bryophytes, 54–55
of ferns, 57
lift, 137
light, 92
Linnaeus, Carolus, 17, 19
liverworts, 54
living things, classifying, 16, 18–19
lizards, 110, 134–135, 148
lobsters, 98, 110, 114–115
Lyme disease, 35, 115

**M**

mammals, 126–127, 140–141, 148
characteristics of, 140
embryo development in, 144
kinds of, 141
marine, 141
placental, 141, 144–145
mammary glands, 140
mantle, 106
maple syrup, 65
marine mammals, 141
marsupials, 140–141, 144
McFarland, Louise, 33
medicines, 47, 64
medusa, 102
meningitis, 33
mesophyll, 74–76
metamorphosis, 120–121, 132
complete, 120–121
incomplete, 120–121
methoprene, 133
microscopes, 22, 38–39
millipedes, 114
Missouri Botanical Gardens, 81
mites, 114
molds, 42–43, 47
mollusks, 106–107, 116
molting, 114–115
monerans, 22, 32–33
monocots, 62–63, 88
monocotyledons, 63
monotremes, 140–141, 144
mosquitoes, 114–115
mosses, 54
moths, 118
multicellular organisms, 18, 23, 40, 42, 52
mushrooms, 42
poisonous, 43
reproduction of, 46–47
structure of, 42
mussels, 106, 111
mutations, 19, 133
myriapods, 114

**N**

nematodes, 104
newts, 130
nitrogen, 41
nitrogen-fixing bacteria, 34, 71
nonvascular plants, 52–54
notochord, 126–127
nucleus, 43, 46
nymph, 120

**O**

octopuses, 106
open circulatory system, 114
opossums, 126, 141
oral groove, 36
orders, 18
organisms
classification system for, 18–19, 22–23
in daily life, 44–45
multicellular, 18, 23, 40, 42, 52
names for, 24–25
scientific names of, 19
unicellular, 36, 40
organs, 52
organ systems, 126
ovaries, 84, 86
oysters, 106, 111

**P**

paramecium, 36
parasites, 44, 104
parenting, 148
parrots, 126
Pasteur, Louis, 34
pasteurization, 35
peacock, 148
peat as fuel, 55
peat bogs, 55
penicillin, 47
*Penicillium roqueforti*, 44
perfect flowers, 80
petals, 80, 86
phloem, 72–74
photosynthesis, 31, 33, 40–41, 52, 76–77, 88
phototropism, 92
phyla, 18
physical science, 142
pigments, 40
separating, 77
pine cones, 61
pines, 60
pinworms, 104
pioneer plants, 55
pistil, 80, 86
parts of, 84
placenta, 140–141
placental mammals, 141, 144–145
planaria, 104, 110
plankton, 40
plant cells, 52

plant divisions, 52
plant geneticists, 83
plant kingdom, 23
plants
asexual reproduction of, 90–91
characteristics of, 52
classification of, 52–53
effect on economy, 64–65
nonvascular, 52–54
physics of, 78–79
pioneer, 55
reproduction of, 69
responses to changes in environment, 92–93
seed, 85
spore, 54
transport in, 73
vascular, 52–53
plant taxonomy, 19
platyhelminthes, 104
pneumonia, 35
poison ivy, 75
poison oak, 75
poison sumac, 75
pollen, 82
pollen tube, 84
pollination, 82–83
pollution, 41
polyp, 102
pond water, life in, 38–39
pores, 100
poriferans, 100
potatoes, 64
prehistoric ferns, 57
pressure, 78
primate, 18
protists, 22, 36–41
protozoans, 36, 44
pseudopods, 36
public health scientists, 33
punishment, 147
pupa, 120–121

**Q**

quality protein maize, 83

**R**

radial symmetry, 109
radula, 106
Ray, John, 19
regeneration, 110–111
renewable resources, 55
reproduction
asexual, 46, 90–91, 110, 135
of bryophytes, 54–55
of flowering plants, 82–83
of flowers, 80–81
sexual, 46–47, 82
of viruses, 26–27
reptiles, 126–127, 134–135, 148
resources, renewable, 55
rewards, 147
rhizoids, 54–55

rhizomes, 56, 58, 92
ribonucleic acid (RNA) virus, 27
root cap, 70
root hairs, 70
roots, 52–53, 56, 70–71, 76, 78, 90
    functions of, 70
    kinds of, 70
    parts of, 70–71
root tip, 70–71
rot, 35
roundworms, 104

## S

salamanders, 126, 130, 132–133
salmon, 129
*Salmonella* poisoning, 137
sand dollars, 108
scent-marking, 148–149
scientific names, 19, 24–25
scorpions, 114
sea cucumbers, 108
sea stars, 98, 108–111
    hydraulic systems in, 109
    regeneration in, 111
sea urchins, 108, 117
seaweed, 40
sediments, 37, 57
seed coat, 88
seed plants, 62, 85
seeds, 60, 62
    dispersal of, 89
    forming, 84
    growing, 89
    parts of, 88–89
segmented worms, 104–105
self-pollination, 82
sepals, 80
sequoias, 60
setae, 104–105
sexual reproduction, 46–47, 82
sharks, 126, 143
shells, classifying, 20–21
shrimp, 114
silica, 31
silica shells, 31
silkworm, 149
simple leaf, 74
skeletons, 142–143
Skinner, B. F., 147
slime mold, 36, 41
slugs, 106
snails, 98, 106
snakes, 126, 134–135
snorkeling, 101
social behaviors, 148–149
social insects, 118–119
societies, 149
soil, 71
    formation of, 55
species, 15, 18
sphagnum moss, 55
spicules, 100
spiders, 98, 114–115

spiny lobster, 117
spiracles, 118
spirilla, 32
sponges, 98, 100–101, 110, 116
    life functions in, 101
    structure of, 100
spongin, 100
spore cases, 46, 54, 56, 58
spore plants, 54
spores, 42, 54, 56
sporulation, 46
spruces, 60
squid, 106–107
stalks, 42, 54
stamens, 80–82, 86
stems, 52–53, 70, 72–73
    functions of, 72
    kinds of, 72
    structure of, 72–73
stigma, 84
stimulus, 92
stomata, 74–76
storm water, 133
strep throat, 35
*Streptococcus thermophilus*, 44
swim bladder, 128–129
symmetry
    bilateral, 109, 126
    radial, 109

## T

tadpoles, 132–133
tapeworms, 104
taproot system, 70
taxonomists, 16, 99
taxonomy, 16
    plant, 19
tentacles, 102–103
termites, 118, 120
territory, 148
Theophrastus, 16
therapsids, 140
thigmotropism, 92–93
thorax, 118
thrust, 137
ticks, 114
tissues, 52
    transport, 53
    vascular, 53
toads, 126, 130
tortoises, 134
touch, 93
tracheophytes, 52–53, 56, 62
transport
    active, 78
    in plants, 73
transport tissue, 53
tree rings, 73
trees, 69
tropical rain forest, 51
tropisms, 92–93
trunk, 79
trypanosomes, 36–37

tuataras, 134
tube feet, 108–109
tuberculosis, 33, 35
tuna, 129
turtles, 126, 134
tympanum, 118

## U

unicellular organisms, 36, 40

## V

Vasal, Surinder K., 83
vascular plants, 52–53
vascular system, 70
vascular tissue, 53
vegetative propagation, 90, 110
veins, 74
venom, 135
Venus' flytrap, 93
vertebrae, 143
vertebrates, 98, 126–127
    skeletons of, 142–143
veterinarians, 127
Villegas, Evangelina, 83
viruses, 26–27
    classifying, 27
    modeling, 27
    reproduction in, 26–27

## W

walking stick, 98
warmblooded animals, 136
water
    molds, 41
    stimulus of, 93
water pollution, 133
water-vascular system, 108–109
West Nile virus, 115
whales, 98, 141
wheat rust, 43
White Cliffs of Dover, 37
Whittaker, Robert, 22
Wilson, Edward Osborne, 119
woody stems, 72
worms, 98, 104–105
    classification of, 104–105

## X

xanthophyll, 75
xylem, 72–74, 79

## Y

yeasts, 43, 46
yogurt, 44

# Photo Credits

**Photography Credits:** All photographs are by the Pearson Learning Group (PLG), John Serafin for PLG, and David Mager for PLG, except as noted below.

**Cover:** *bkgd.* Australian Picture Library/Corbis; *inset* © Manfred Kage/Peter Arnold, Inc.

**Table of Contents:** iv t Volker Steger/Peter Arnold, Inc.; iv b Werner Muller/Peter Arnold, Inc.

**Frontmatter:** P001 l Susan Leavines/Science Source/Photo Researchers, Inc.; P001 r William Lampas/Omni-Photo Communications; P001 t David Julian/Phototake; P002 l John Pontier/Animals Animals/Earth Scenes; P002 r Michael Bisceglie/Animals Animals/Earth Scenes; P003 Ventura Educational Systems; P003 Siede Preis/Getty Images; P005 r Siede Preis/Getty Images; P007 r Siede Preis/Getty Images; P009 bl American Museum of Natural History/Dorling Kindersley Limited; P009 br Dr. Michael Howell; P009 Phil Degginger/Color-Pic, Inc.; P009 r Siede Preis/Getty Images; P010 Jim Zipp/Photo Researchers, Inc.; P011 r Siede Preis/Getty Images; P013 r Siede Preis/Getty Images

**Chapter 1:** P15 Gary Braasch/Corbis; P16 Michael Viard/Peter Arnold, Inc.; P17 Ralph Lee Hopkins/Wilderland Images; P19 Francois Gohier/Photo Researchers, Inc.; P22 Division of Rare & Manuscript Collections/Cornell Library; P23 col. 1 Biophoto Associates/Photo Researchers, Inc.; P23 col. 2 Manfred Kage/Peter Arnold, Inc.; P23 col. 3 Robert Planck/Photo Researchers, Inc.; P23 col. 4 Jean Claude Revy/Phototake; P23 col. 5 Michael Evans/PhotoDisc, Inc.; P26 l Oliver Meckes/Photo Researchers, Inc.; P26 r Lee D. Simon/Photo Researchers, Inc.; P28 Gary Braasch/Corbis; P29 Gary Braasch/Corbis; P30 Gary Braasch/Corbis

**Chapter 2:** P31 North Carolina Biological Supply/Phototake; P32 l David M. Phillips/Visuals Unlimited, Inc.; P32 m G. Murti/Visuals Unlimited, Inc.; P32 r CNRI/Science Photo Library/Photo Researchers, Inc.; P33 R. Maisonneuve/Publiphoto/Photo Researchers, Inc.; P34 Breck P. Kent/Animals Animals/Earth Scenes; P35 Volker Steger/Peter Arnold, Inc.; P35 inset M. Abbey/Visuals Unlimited, Inc.; P36 b M. I. Walker/Photo Researchers, Inc.; P36 t Eric Grave/Phototake; P37 b Lynn McLaren/Photo Researchers, Inc.; P37 inset Manfred Kage/Peter Arnold, Inc.; P37 t John D. Cunningham/Visuals Unlimited, Inc.; P39 Science VU/Visuals Unlimited, Inc.; P40 b Jeffrey L. Rotman/Peter Arnold, Inc.; P40 t R. Kessel-G. Shih/Visuals Unlimited, Inc.; P41 b Tom and Pat Leeson/Photo Researchers, Inc.; P41 inset T. E. Adams/Visuals Unlimited, Inc.; P41 t Bill Beatty/Visuals Unlimited, Inc.; P43 Inga Spence/Visuals Unlimited, Inc.; P44 b Sparky/GettyOne; P44 b inset Biodisc/Visuals Unlimited, Inc.; P44 t inset SPL/Custom Medical Stock Photo; P44 t Steve Lupton/Corbis; P45 b Catherine Karnow/Corbis; P45 b inset Philip Sze/Visuals Unlimited, Inc.; P45 t David Young-Wolff/PhotoEdit, Inc.; P45 t inset Jerome Paulin/Visuals Unlimited, Inc.; P46 l J. Forsdyke/Gene Cox/Science Photo Library/Photo Researchers, Inc.; P46 r E. R. Degginger/Photo Researchers, Inc.; P48 North Carolina Biological Supply/Phototake; P49 North Carolina Biological Supply/Phototake; P50 North Carolina Biological Supply/Phototake

**Chapter 3:** P51 David Julian/Phototake; P53 l Inga Spence/Visuals Unlimited, Inc.; P53 r Jim Zipp/Photo Researchers, Inc.; P54 l Carolina Biological Co./Phototake; P54 m Patricia Armstrong/Visuals Unlimited, Inc.; P54 r Ed Reschke/Peter Arnold, Inc.; P55 John D. Cunningham/Visuals Unlimited, Inc.; P56 l Steve Callahan/Visuals Unlimited, Inc.; P56 r Ed Reschke/Peter Arnold, Inc.; P57 Science VU/Visuals Unlimited, Inc.; P60 l Helmut Gritscher/Peter Arnold, Inc.; P60 r Ed Reschke/Peter Arnold, Inc.; P61 Walter Hodge/Peter Arnold, Inc.; P62 Werner Muller/Peter Arnold, Inc.; P64 l Peter Menzel/Stock, Boston Inc.; P64 r Bill Bachman/Photo Researchers, Inc.; P65 r Sydney Thomson/Animals Animals/Earth Scenes; P66 David Julian/Phototake; P67 David Julian/Phototake; P68 David Julian/Phototake

**Chapter 4:** P69 Anthony Mercieca/Photo Researchers, Inc.; P70 l John D. Cunningham/Visuals Unlimited, Inc.; P70 r Michael P. Gadomski/Photo Researchers, Inc.; P71 Gary Carter/Visuals Unlimited, Inc.; P72 Grace Davies/Omni-Photo Communications; P75 Gary W. Carter/Visuals Unlimited, Inc.; P78–81 Zefa Visual Media, Germany/Index Stock Imagery, Inc.; P79 b Manfred Kage/Peter Arnold, Inc.; P79 t Dr. Jeremy Burgess/Photo Researchers, Inc.; P80 b Karl Shone/Dorling Kindersley Limited; P81 t Glenn Oliver/Visuals Unlimited, Inc.; P81 Njell Sandued/Visuals Unlimited, Inc.; P82 William Lampas/Omni-Photo Communications; P83 Barry L. Runk/Grant Heilman Photography, Inc.; P85 b H. Taylor, OSF/Animals Animals/Earth Scenes; P85 t Harry Rogers/Photo Researchers, Inc.; P88 l M. & D. Long/Visuals Unlimited, Inc.; P88 r Wally Eberhart/Visuals Unlimited, Inc.; P90 Kim Taylor/Jane Burton/Dorling Kindersley Limited; P91 John D. Cunningham/Visuals Unlimited, Inc.; P92 Runk/Schoenberger/Grant Heilman Photography, Inc.; P93 b Kim Taylor & Jane Burton/Dorling Kindersley Limited; P93 t E. R. Degginger/Color-Pic, Inc.; P94 Anthony Mercieca/Photo Researchers, Inc.; P95 Anthony Mercieca/Photo Researchers, Inc.; P96 b Karl Shone/Dorling Kindersley Limited; P96 t Anthony Mercieca/Photo Researchers, Inc.

**Chapter 5:** P97 Fred Bavendam/Minden Pictures; P98 b Alex Kerstiten/Visuals Unlimited, Inc.; P98 t Gerard Lacz/Animals Animals/Earth Scenes; P99 b Runk/Schoenberger/Grant Heilman Photography, Inc.; P99 t Joyce and Frank Burek/Animals Animals/Earth Scenes; P101 b James Watt/Animals Animals/Earth Scenes; P101 t Clay Wiseman/Animals Animals/Earth Scenes; P102 l Herb Segars/Animals Animals/Earth Scenes; P102 r Fred Bavendam/Minden Pictures; P103 R. Calentine/Visuals Unlimited, Inc.; P104 l T. E. Adams/Visuals Unlimited, Inc.; P104 r Arthur M. Siegelman/Visuals Unlimited, Inc.; P105 Breck P. Kent/Animals Animals/Earth Scenes; P106 b Fred Bavendam/Minden Pictures; P106 t Sylvan Wittwer/Visuals Unlimited, Inc.; P108 l David Wrobel/Visuals Unlimited, Inc.; P108 r Gerald & Buff Corsi/Visuals Unlimited, Inc.; P109 C. Milikins OSF/Animals Animals/Earth Scenes; P110 l Dr. Ellen K. Rudolph/Omni-Photo Communications; P110 r Tom Adams/Visuals Unlimited, Inc.; P111 Scott Johnson/Animals Animals/Earth Scenes; P114 bl Victoria McCormick/Animals Animals/Earth Scenes; P114 br James H. Robinson/Animals Animals/Earth Scenes; P114 tl Ken Lucas/Visuals Unlimited, Inc.; P114 tr Gary Meszaros/Visuals Unlimited, Inc.; P115 Fred Whitehead/Animals Animals/Earth Scenes; P116 inset Siede Preis/PhotoDisc, Inc.; P116–119 Fred Bavendam/Minden Pictures; P117 l inset Corbis; P117 r inset Andrew Wood/Photo Researchers, Inc.; P118 Maresa Pryor/Animals Animals/Earth Scenes; P119 b Michael Dick/Animals Animals/Earth Scenes; P119 t Konrad Wothe/Minden Pictures; P122 Fred Bavendam/Minden Pictures; P123 Fred Bavendam/Minden Pictures; P124 Fred Bavendam/Minden Pictures

**Chapter 6:** P125 Joe McDonald/Visuals Unlimited, Inc.; P126 bl Gerry Ellis/Minden Pictures; P126 bm Mitsuaki Iwago/Minden Pictures; P126 br Tom Walker/Visuals Unlimited, Inc.; P126 tl G. I. Bernard/Animals Animals/Earth Scenes; P126 tm Bill Kamin/Visuals Unlimited, Inc.; P126 tr Zig Leszczynski/Animals Animals/Earth Scenes; P127 Jessie Cohen/Smithsonian's National Zoo; P128 Zig Leszczynski/Animals Animals/Earth Scenes; P129 Tui De Roy/Minden Pictures; P130 l Zig Leszczynski/Animals Animals/Earth Scenes; P130 m Suzanne L. Collins & Joseph T. Collins/Photo Researchers, Inc.; P130 r George Bryce/Animals Animals/Earth Scenes; P131 b Ventura Educational Systems; P131 t Juan Manuel Renjifo/Animals Animals/Earth Scenes; P133 Mark Smith/Photo Researchers, Inc.; P134 br Victoria McCormick/Animals Animals/Earth Scenes; P134 l Michael Dick/Animals Animals/Earth Scenes; P134 tr Joe McDonald/Visuals Unlimited, Inc.; P135 l Michael Bisceglie/Animals Animals/Earth Scenes; P135 m John Pontier/Animals Animals/Earth Scenes; P135 r Joe McDonald/Visuals Unlimited, Inc.; P136 col. 1 Gerard Fuehrer/Visuals Unlimited, Inc.; P136 col. 2 David Stuckel/Visuals Unlimited, Inc.; P136 col. 3 Jeff Greenberg/Omni-Photo Communications; P136 col. 4 Shelley Rotner/Omni-Photo